Anti-Drugs Policies of the European Union

Anti-Drugs Policies of the European Union

Transnational Decision-Making and the Politics of Expertise

Martin Elvins
Department of Politics
University of Dundee, UK

First published 2003 by
PALGRAVE MACMILLAN
Houndmills, Basingstoke, Hampshire RG21 6XS and
175 Fifth Avenue, New York, N.Y. 10010
Companies and representatives throughout the world

PALGRAVE MACMILLAN is the global academic imprint of the Palgrave
Macmillan division of St. Martin's Press, LLC and of Palgrave Macmillan Ltd.
Macmillan® is a registered trademark in the United States, United Kingdom
and other countries. Palgrave is a registered trademark in the European
Union and other countries.

ISBN 0–333–98213–4

This book is printed on paper suitable for recycling and made from fully
managed and sustained forest sources.

A catalogue record for this book is available from the British Library.

Library of Congress Cataloging-in-Publication Data

Elvins, Martin, 1963–
    Anti-drugs policies of the European Union : transnational decision-
    making and the politics of expertise / Martin Elvins.
        p. cm.
    Includes bibliographical references and index.
    ISBN 0–333–98213–4
        1. Narcotics, Control of – European Union countries. 2. Transnational
crime – European Union countries. 3. Drug abuse – Government policy –
European Union countries. 4. Drug abuse – European Union countries –
Prevention. 5. European Union countries – Politics and government.   I. Title.

HV5840.E85E48 2003
363.45′094—dc21   2003042937

10   9   8   7   6   5   4   3   2   1
12 11 10 09 08 07 06 05 04 03

Printed and bound in Great Britain by
Antony Rowe Ltd, Chippenham and Eastbourne

For my parents

Dedicated to the memory of Harry Turner (1904–1997)

Contents

Figures, Table and Map

Figures

Table

Map

Acknowledgements

Without the constant support of my parents and my friends this book would not have been possible. Kay Alexander, Paul Doughty and Robin Jones were exceptionally tolerant observers and kind supporters during the period when I was writing the final manuscript. In their many different ways, Kristel Bruynseels, Simon Eversley, Phil Hadfield, Scott Jones, Robert Limb, Guy and Milly Parrott, Claudia Scott, Jan Selby, Dave Swann and Kevin Young have all helped the author remain (relatively) sane. Thank you all.

Sol Picciotto and Peter Wilkin, respectively of the Departments of Law and Politics and International Relations, Lancaster University, provided pertinent and helpful comments on earlier drafts of this work. The author is deeply grateful to them both. Many people have been directly involved at key stages of this project. Their help and support was greatly appreciated in each case. Particular thanks go to Bob McKinlay, John Benyon and Jonathan Sweet in this respect. The author would also like to thank Stephen Gill for his lasting inspiration.

Without the existence of Statewatch (http: <www.statewatch.org>) it is doubtful whether this book would exist. By providing access to primary documentation from the Council of the European Union in the area of justice and home affairs policy Statewatch open up possibilities for research that might otherwise be restricted or impossible in practice. The author wishes to record his total support for the important work carried out by the dedicated team at Statewatch in monitoring the activities of the European Union, highlighting vital issues of civil liberties and accountability. Particular thanks go to Ben Hayes for his help during the final stages of this book. Kind permission to adapt and use several figures included in this work was much appreciated.

Finally, thanks go to my patient and professional publishers. The author is deeply grateful to Heather Gibson for showing faith in the ideas behind this book and in the author personally. The author also thanks Jennifer Nelson for her helpful, patient and calming input during the production stage of the project. Lastly, sincere thanks to Linda Auld for her equally patient help and advice.

Acronyms and Abbreviations

ACP	African Caribbean, and Pacific countries
AHWGE	Ad Hoc Working Group on Europol
AHWPD	Ad Hoc Working Party on Drugs
AIC	Advanced Industrialized Country
AIDS	Acquired immune deficiency syndrome
ATS	Amphetamine-type stimulants
Benelux	Belgium, The Netherlands, and Luxembourg
BKA	Bundeskriminalamt (German national police force)
CARICOM	Countries of the Caribbean Community
CATF	Chemical Action Task Force
CCWG	Customs Cooperation Working Group
CDI	Caribbean Drugs Initiative
CEECs	Central and Eastern European countries
CELAD	European Committee to Combat Drugs (Comité Européen de Lutte Anti-Drogues)
CFSP	Common Foreign and Security Policy
CICAD	Inter-American Drug Abuse Control Commission
CIS[1]	Commonwealth of Independent States (ex-USSR)
CIS[1]	Customs Information System
CND	Commission on Narcotic Drugs
CODRO	Common Foreign and Security Policy Working Group on Drugs
Commission	European Commission (sometimes also referred to in legal or formal contexts as the Commission of the European Communities)
COREPER	Committee of Permanent Representatives
Council	Council of the European Union
DEA	(United States) Drug Enforcement Administration
DG	Directorate-General
DLOs	Drugs Liaison Officers
DOCWG	Drugs and Organized Crime Working Group (also sometimes called WPDOC)
EC	European Community

---

1 The author has attempted to avoid potential confusion between uses of these terms in the text, which should be distinguishable through the contextual use.

ECDCO	European Commission Drug Control Office
ECJ	European Court of Justice
ECSC	European Coal and Steel Community
EDU	Europol Drugs Unit
EDIU	European Drugs Intelligence Unit
EEC	European Economic Community
EIS	European Information System
ELOs	European Liaison Officers
EMCDDA	European Monitoring Centre for Drugs and Drug Addiction
EMEA	European Agency for the Evaluation of Medicinal Products
EMU	Economic and Monetary Union
EP	European Parliament
EPC	European Political Cooperation
EU	European Union
Euratom	European Atomic Energy Community
Europol	European Police Office
FATF	Financial Action Task Force
FBI	Federal Bureau of Investigation (United States)
FIU	Financial Intelligence Unit
G-7	Group of Seven industrialized countries (now G-8)
GATS	General Agreement on Trade in Services
GATT	General Agreement on Tariffs and Trade
HDG	Horizontal Drugs Group (also sometimes referred to as the Horizontal Working Party on Drugs [HWPD])
HIV	Human immunodeficiency virus
HWPD	See HDG above
ICDAIT	International Conference on Drug Abuse and Illicit Trafficking
IGC	Intergovernmental Conference
IGO	International Governmental Organization
INCB	International Narcotics Control Board
INGO	International Nongovernmental Organization
Interpol	International Criminal Police Organization
JHA	Justice and Home Affairs
K4 Committee	Committee of senior officials for JHA policy-making under the original TEU (now Article 36 Committee)
LAC	Latin America and the Caribbean
MAG	Customs Mutual Assistance Group
MAG 92	Customs Mutual Assistance Group for 1992

MDG	Multi-Disciplinary Group on Organized Crime
MDMA	3,4-methylenedioxy methamphetamine (commonly known as 'ecstasy')
MEP	Member of the European Parliament
MOU	Memorandum Of Understanding
NAFTA	North American Free Trade Agreement
NATO	North Atlantic Treaty Organization
NCIS	National Criminal Intelligence Service (United Kingdom)
NDIU	National Drugs Intelligence Unit
NGO	Nongovernmental Organization
NIS	New Independent States
OAS	Organization of American States
ODCCP	United Nations Office for Drug Control and Crime Prevention
OECD	Organization for Economic Cooperation and Development
OJ	*Official Journal of the European Communities*
PAPEG	Pre-Accession Pact Expert Group
PGE	Project Group Europol
qmv	Qualified Majority Voting
REITOX	European Information Network on Drugs and Drug Addiction
SEA	Single European Act
SEM	Single European Market
SG	Steering Group
SIC	Schengen Implementing Convention
SIRENE	Supplementary Information System of Schengen (Supplément d'Information Requis a l'Entrée Nationale)
SIS	Schengen Information System
TACIS	Programme for Technical Assistance to the Independent States of the Former Soviet Union and Mongolia
TB	tuberculosis
TCO	Transnational Criminal Organization
TEC	Treaty Establishing the European Community
TECS	The Europol Computer System
TEU	Treaty on European Union (Maastricht Treaty)
TOR	Terms of Reference
Trevi	The Trevi Group
UK	United Kingdom
UKREP	United Kingdom Permanent Representation to the European Communities
UN	United Nations

UNDCP	United Nations International Drug Control Programme
UNEP	United Nations Environment Programme
UNGASS	United Nations General Assembly Special Session
US	United States of America
WCO	World Customs Organization
WG	Working Group
WG III	Trevi Working Group III
WHO	World Health Organization
WP	Working Party
WPDOC	Working Party on Drugs and Organized Crime (also sometimes called DOCWG)
WPLAC	Ad Hoc Working Party on Latin America and the Caribbean (Drugs)

Glossary of EU and EU-related Terms

Acquis communautaire

The *acquis communautaire* (more often just *acquis* for short) is the body of 'common rights and obligations' that binds together all the member states within the European Union. It is constantly evolving and is made up of:

- the content, principles and political objectives of treaties agreed by member states
- the legislation adopted in application of the treaties and the case law of the European Court of Justice
- the declarations and resolutions adopted by the European Union
- measures relating to common foreign and security policy
- measures relating to justice and home affairs policy
- international agreements concluded by the Community and those concluded by the member states between themselves in the field of the Union's activities.

Thus the Community *acquis* comprises not only Community law in the strict sense but also all acts adopted under the second and third pillars of the European Union and, above all, the common objectives laid down in the Treaties. Candidate countries have to accept the Community *acquis* before they can join the European Union. Exemptions and derogations from the *acquis* are granted only in exceptional circumstances and are limited in scope. The EU has committed itself to maintaining the Community *acquis* in its entirety and developing it further.

Article 36 Committee (EU Treaty, Title VI)

A 'Coordinating Committee' consisting of senior officials was set up under Article 36 (former Article K.4 of the original TEU) of the post-Amsterdam consolidated EU Treaty to prepare the ground for Council deliberations on police cooperation and judicial cooperation in civil matters. In practice the committee had already been in existence since the Rhodes European Council in December 1988, first, up to 1993, as the Co-ordinators' Group – Free Movement of Persons, and then the K4 Committee, 1993–99.

COREPER

COREPER, the French acronym by which the Permanent Representatives Committee is known, consists of the member states' Permanent Representatives (Ambassadors) and is responsible, at a stage involving preliminary negotiations, for assisting the Council of the European Union in dealing with the items on its agenda (proposals and drafts of instruments put forward by the Commission). It occupies a pivotal position in the decision-making system of the European Union, in which it is both a forum for dialogue (among the Permanent Representatives and between them and their respective national capitals) and a body which exercises political control (by laying down guidelines for, and supervising, the work of expert working groups). Depending on the policy area, work is covered by either COREPER I, consisting of the Deputy Permanent representatives, or COREPER II, consisting of the Permanent Representatives themselves.

Council of the European Union

The Council of the Union (Council, sometimes also referred to as the Council of Ministers) is the European Union's main decision-making institution. In taking policy and legislative decisions Council has generally sub-divided into relevant formulations to deal with different policy areas, such as agriculture or transport. Relevant national ministers attend these formations, although the Council is none the less a single institution. The Seville European Council (21–22 June 2002) decided to reduce the number of formations from around twenty to nine, effective from August 2002 (including, as before, a Justice and Home Affairs Council).

Each country in the Union in turn holds the chair for six months. Decisions are prepared by the Committee of Permanent Representatives of the Member States (COREPER), assisted by working parties of national government officials. The Council is assisted by its General Secretariat.

European Council

The European Council is the term used to describe the regular meetings of the heads of state or government of the EU member states. It was set up by the communiqué issued at the December 1974 Paris Summit and first met in 1975 (in Dublin, 10–11 March). Before that time, from 1961 to 1974, the practice had been to hold European summit conferences. Its existence was given legal recognition by the Single European Act while official status was conferred on it by the Treaty on European Union. Since then it has generally met at least twice a year and the President of the European Commission attends as a full member. Its objectives are to give the European Union the impetus it needs in order to develop further and to define general policy guidelines.

As part of the preparations for the next phase of EU enlargement, proposing to extend membership to a total of 25 states from 2004, the Seville European Council (21–22 June 2002) decided that in principle the European Council should meet four times per year in future (two meetings per Presidency).

Justice and home affairs

Cooperation on justice and home affairs was institutionalized under Title VI of the EU Treaty (also known as the 'third pillar'). The theoretical aim of this cooperation was to give practical effect to the principle of the free movement of persons. It covered the following:

- asylum policy
- rules governing the crossing of the external borders of the member states
- immigration policy
- combating drugs
- combating international fraud
- judicial cooperation in civil and criminal matters
- customs cooperation
- police cooperation.

Pillars of the European Union

In Community parlance people often refer to the 'three pillars' of the EU Treaty. These are:

The first pillar

Incorporated most of the policy responsibilities for the EU, adopting the *acquis communautaire* of the European Communities (the EEC, ECSC and Euratom treaty base) and strengthened the treaty base in some respects, notably with regard to the EEC Treaty. The EEC was renamed the European Community (EC) by what became known as the Treaty Establishing The European Community (TEC).

The second pillar

A Common Foreign and Security Policy (CFSP); comes under Title V of the EU Treaty.

The third pillar

Cooperation in the field of Justice and Home Affairs (JHA). Defined a range of policy areas as matters of 'common interest' (including asylum policy, judicial cooperation in civil and criminal matters and customs cooperation). Comes under Title VI of the EU Treaty.

The Treaty of Amsterdam transferred some of the fields covered by the old third pillar to the first pillar (free movement of persons).

Schengen (Agreement and Convention)

Belgium, France, Germany, Luxembourg and The Netherlands signed the Schengen Agreement on 14 June 1985, agreeing that they would gradually remove their common frontier controls and introduce freedom of movement for all individuals who were nationals of the signatory member states, other member states or third countries. The Schengen Convention was signed by the same five states on 19 June 1990. It laid down the arrangements and guarantees for implementing freedom of movement. Italy (1990), Spain and Portugal (1991), Greece (1992), Austria (1995), Sweden, Finland and Denmark (1996) have since joined the list of signatories, while Iceland and Norway are also parties to the Convention.

The Agreement and the Convention, together with the declarations and decisions adopted by the Schengen Executive Committee, make up what is known as the Schengen *acquis*. When the Treaty of Amsterdam was being drafted, it was decided to incorporate this *acquis* into the European Union from 1 May 1999 onwards, since it relates to one of the main objectives of the single market, that is, the free movement of persons. For that purpose, the Council of Ministers first identified the measures which formed the real Schengen *acquis*. Subsequently, in order to give them a legal basis, it established whether they came under the new Title IV (visas, asylum, immigration and other policies related to the free movement of persons) of the Treaty establishing the European

Communities or Title VI (Provisions on police and judicial cooperation in criminal matters) of the Treaty on European Union. The legal incorporation of Schengen into the European Union was accompanied by integration of the institutions. The Council took over the Schengen Executive Committee and the Council's General Secretariat took over the Schengen Secretariat.

An agreement was signed on 18 May 1999 between the European Union and Iceland and Norway, countries outside the Community which are party to Schengen. It associates them with the implementation and development of the Schengen *acquis,* and sets out how they are to participate in the free movement area in the European Union.

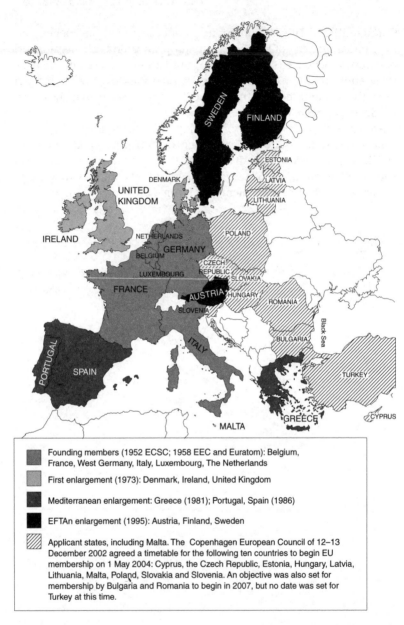

Founding members (1952 ECSC; 1958 EEC and Euratom): Belgium, France, West Germany, Italy, Luxembourg, The Netherlands

First enlargement (1973): Denmark, Ireland, United Kingdom

Mediterranean enlargement: Greece (1981); Portugal, Spain (1986)

EFTAn enlargement (1995): Austria, Finland, Sweden

Applicant states, including Malta. The Copenhagen European Council of 12–13 December 2002 agreed a timetable for the following ten countries to begin EU membership on 1 May 2004: Cyprus, the Czech Republic, Estonia, Hungary, Latvia, Lithuania, Malta, Poland, Slovakia and Slovenia. An objective was also set for membership by Bulgaria and Romania to begin in 2007, but no date was set for Turkey at this time.

Member states and applicant states of the European Union

Source: Nugent, N. (2003) *The Government and Politics of the European Union*, 5th edn (Basingstoke: Palgrave Macmillan). Reproduced with permission of Palgrave Macmillan.

1
Introduction

Drug trafficking is routinely described as an 'evil' activity. It is generally placed second only to terrorism on the international scale of threats to society, and is often portrayed as a threat to the state itself. Unlike terrorism, however, drug trafficking is inherently based on a rational economic logic. Prohibition, in place internationally since early in the twentieth century, provides that logic. Certain drugs are defined as illegal, yet demand for them exists on a worldwide scale, hence traffickers are attracted by the very high potential profits from this untaxed trading activity and are prepared to offset financial reward against the risk of prosecution and disruption of their activities. National political leaders have sought to suppress trafficking via the use of all means of law enforcement at their disposal, to the point that virtually any law enforcement measure taken against drug traffickers is now claimed to carry unquestioned political legitimacy. This is despite a systematic failure by political decision-makers either to contextualize the nature of the threat or to provide clear evidence on the efficacy of enforcement strategies. International cooperation to 'fight drugs' has become a distinctive feature of contemporary international relations.

Most us now have a strong sense that the world has become a more insecure place. This is largely as a result of a range of global problems that seem both familiar and mysterious. A significant consequence of 'globalization' has been the way that we now perceive the spatial dimension to the causes of these problems. Issues such as terrorism, global warming, or 'illegal' immigration are seen as emanating from a broad set of transnational forces beyond the control of an individual state or government. Our familiarity with these issues arises primarily from our awareness of public policy initiatives and media representation rather than direct experience. When most people think of the drugs issue, international

1

drug trafficking is generally perceived to be the most significant cause of 'drug problems' around the world. Tackling drug problems thereby tends to be seen as fundamentally a matter of law enforcement. This mono-causal interpretation is remarkably pervasive and heavily influences the extent to which anti-drugs policy is seen as a wholly legitimate area in which the state exercises its powers of authority and control, often unchallenged.

This book examines the specific case of joint policy development by member states of the European Union (and, before that, the European Community) in response to the issue of drug trafficking. The book provides a comprehensive empirical account of the evolution of policy in this field since the late 1960s. On one hand, it provides a critical survey of the course of European drug enforcement policy development, its underlying logic and rationale, and the principal events and actors that have shaped it. On the other hand, it uses this account to explore and understand wider questions concerned with the changing nature of state power and of state sovereignty. In the process, the practices of contemporary European governance are critically assessed, with particular regard to the transparency and democratic accountability of policy-making where notions of threat and security are the legitimizing principles for collective state action. A central theme here is evaluation of the extent to which policy development has become increasingly transnational and technocratic and assessment of the consequences of this situation. In other words, are enforcement-based anti-drugs policies in Europe the product of some form of transnational technocracy? If so, what does this reveal and should we be concerned by it?

Since the late 1980s there has been a clear convergence in anti-drugs trafficking policies adopted by states across the world. As a result of international negotiation (most prominently via the UN), states have collectively defined the parameters for a new set of measures that constitute a revised set of policy norms with the objective of significantly reducing levels of drug trafficking. This has had a direct impact on national criminal laws, policing and regulatory practices. By way of contrast, states have been much less able to reach agreement on what are generally termed 'harm reduction' strategies that work on the premise that people will take drugs but that net harm can be reduced (for example, needle exchange schemes for intravenous drug users to reduce the risk of spreading HIV via needle sharing). The only agreement has been that such strategies should be unequivocally a matter for national preference and implementation. This has led to a much more heterogeneous range of policies in different countries, in marked contrast to the increased similarity in anti-trafficking policies. However, the primary rationale employed by political decision-makers for all forms of drug policy is based on some notion of protection: from the impact of drugs on public health, from crime associated with drug users, and – more potently, it is usually suggested – from the use of violence and corruption by traffickers.

The idea of the state as the legitimate *protector* of its citizens is, of course, deeply rooted in the liberal tradition. Liberal democracy offers the trade-off between open democratic standards in return for placing enforcement power exclusively in the hands of the state. It is thus axiomatic that if the political commitment to prohibition remains and drug demand continues to expand, then increased levels of enforcement will follow. In fact, this might be taken as a 'standard' reading of the past two decades in the drug enforcement policy domain. However, no credible evidence has been provided to support the idea that increased enforcement has been effective in reducing the scale of drug problems either in individual states or in some collective sense. A number of critics have argued persuasively that in fact it has had quite the opposite effect. That is, the increased countermeasures have failed to prevent the 'threat to society' from growing. So, why are state decision-makers prepared to commit to the continued expansion of enforcement strategies as an effective means of tackling drug problems? We must ask if there is a deeper reasoning that is more fundamentally linked to the institution of the state and to state power. It could be suggested that greater enforcement of drug policy reflects a broader commitment to strengthen the institution of the state at a time when there has been an apparent diminution of state power across certain dimensions of what have traditionally been regarded as core areas of state activity, generally viewed as resulting from the set of changes associated with globalization. This is a highly complex matter, fraught with countervailing arguments. This book does not attempt to produce a general theory of this situation in any case (nor does the author see this as a credible exercise), but focuses on the attempt at cooperative statehood that has been the hallmark of European integration since 1957. This book examines the empirical evidence as to the practice and motives that have characterized policy-making in relation to drug trafficking in this context.

The book provides a perspective that is rooted in contemporary understanding of the state and employs theoretical and analytical tools from the discipline of International Relations to assess how governance practices have evolved in response to the implications of globalization for the institution of the state. It aims to understand how and why the member states of the European Union (and, before that, the European

Communities) have been able to reach consensus on measures aimed at combating drug trafficking. Analysis is focused on uncovering the processes that have generated a normative consensus, with particular reference to the policy-making structures and institutional competences through which policy ideas and the rationale that underpins them have been developed. The approach that is taken here focuses on the role of expert knowledge and the transnational expression of that knowledge via various forms of transnational policy-making networks and fora. This allows an important insight into how 'the state' (that is, in the guise of governmental authority) engages in policy development at intergovernmental level with regard to an issue that is explicitly propounded as being an intrinsic threat to national (state) security. The book is therefore concerned to place these observations in the context of the changing basis of state power in the era of globalization. This provides a basis on which to assess the degree to which the 'inalienable' principle of drug prohibition has provided a means through which to reorient the power of the state at a time when questions have been raised as to the viability and changing basis of state power, of state sovereignty, and about the rise of alternative sources of power in the international system.

The wider contention of this book is that the key to understanding contemporary state power in the area under discussion lies in understanding the policy-making actors whose control over knowledge is vital in providing the rationale for policy and in creating and sustaining a normative framework through which policy decisions are filtered by the political decision-makers of national states. The concept of epistemic communities, as developed through the work of Peter Haas, is introduced as a basis for understanding the key dynamics in the process of identifying state interests and in formulating policy ideas and proposals. The book assesses the extent to which a pseudo-scientific 'technical' approach has become the dominant means through which policy 'solutions' for complex transnational problems (such as drug trafficking) are mediated. The questions are posed as to whether this represents an attempt to depoliticize certain types of policy response and whether it leads to the deeper embedding of normative conditions and policies. Within the empirical ambit of this book, the creation of new institutions, most notably a European Police Office (Europol) – originally established to counter drug trafficking – is placed in wider context in relation to the collective security preferences of EU states. The book describes how policy development has emerged out of secretive and anti-democratic intergovernmental decision-making by EC–EU member states and addresses a number of important concerns raised by this situation.

The book has three parts.

Part I assesses the links between the processes of 'globalization' and notions of transnational threat (Chapter 2) and provides historical context through an account of the evolution of international drug control policy (Chapter 3). Chapter 4 assesses the emergence of new forms of transnational governance and decision-making, and links this to the specific focal point of the book: European drug enforcement. Chapter 5 outlines the concept of epistemic communities and critically examines the qualities of this concept as a heuristic device in understanding the complex changes and power relationships that the book attempts to analyse.

Part II presents a detailed empirical survey of the development of European drug enforcement policies by EC–EU states since the late 1960s, focused on the convergence apparent since the mid 1980s. By way of orientation, Chapter 6 gives a short account of the course of European integration and describes how drugs were first discussed in the context of this process. Chapters 7 and 8 focus on the period before the entry into force of the Treaty on European Union (TEU), describing the institutional architecture through which policy was developed during this period. Chapter 9 concentrates on the period after the entry into force of the TEU in 1993, describing the legislative and institutional changes that were the hallmark of this period. Chapter 10 looks at the period following the entry into force of the Treaty of Amsterdam in 1999, which marked the first formal changes to the TEU system. Chapter 11 features two case studies of policy development: first, examining EU drug policy expert missions to the Caribbean, Latin America and Central Asia and, second, the development of drug policy under the UK Presidency of the EU during the first half of 1998.

Part III draws a number of conclusions in relation to the themes set out in Part I of the book. Chapter 12 examines the question of control over knowledge as a central dimension of power in relation to European anti-drugs enforcement and looks at the role of expertise as well as the issue of technocratic policy development. An assessment is also made of the extent to which an epistemic communities hypothesis is helpful in understanding these issues. Finally, Chapter 13 looks at the politicization of anti-drugs enforcement policies in Europe and examines what this contributes to our understanding of contemporary state behaviour and of wider responses to drug issues, raising a number of concerns that are inherent to these matters.

Part I

State Sovereignty, Drug Trafficking and Global Change

2
Transnational Threat in the 'Globalized' Era

During the Cold War, international threats were universal in the sense that they were almost always viewed through the lens of East–West rivalry. With the ending of the conflict in 1989, it was widely claimed that a more favourable climate for international cooperation would be one of the main results of this event. Since then, threats have once more taken on a universal quality, only this time as part of a contention by political elites that certain forms of cooperation and behaviour are not only desirable but also unavoidable, due to the emergence of a qualitatively new set of 'challenges' that threaten 'all nations' in a more interdependent world.[1] Based on this, the period since the late 1980s has been marked by rigorous attempts to universalize the principles on which international action in these areas is founded and to build or revise international institutional arrangements.

The primary source of this normative consensus has been the governments of advanced industrialized countries (AICs), which have been instrumental in delimiting a particular set of problems that are characterized collectively by their lack of 'respect' for territorial borders. This (now familiar) list is headed by terrorism, international crime, drug trafficking, nuclear proliferation and environmental damage, and is often joined by concerns regarding flows of 'illegal' immigrants and the spread of diseases such as AIDS. Most analyses have focused on the contribution of broader global changes to the emergence and expansion of these issues, with a wider debate among prominent theorists of international relations concerning how such issues represent part of a more general challenge to national states that, it is argued, has not only limited the capacity of states to act autonomously but has also begun to impinge upon their sovereignty.[2] Others have suggested that, while sovereignty has been clearly eroded in some areas (such as economic management), state managers have made attempts to consolidate their hold over other areas where the state has traditionally tended towards monopolistic control, especially those related to security matters.[3] However, most perspectives accept, either implicitly or explicitly, that 'new' or expanded transnational problems have been important dynamic influences behind a significant growth in multilaterally constituted policy initiatives; a process which some claim has also led to a diffusion of power away from states to non-state actors.[4] Much of this work has tended to overlook the critical influence that discourses of transnational threat have exerted upon political and social ideas, providing both context and rationale for action at all levels: from global to national, down to region, city, even individual. From this perspective, the construction and legitimization of action contingent on particular forms of threat becomes a highly important factor in ensuring that particular actions are favoured over others.

Recognition within AICs of more problematic conditions for national governance has stimulated a process of professionalization of 'expert' groups with discrete areas of technical knowledge and competence. This has been based on a perceived need to give such groups a more flexible and quasi-autonomous role in the design and implementation of policy. It is also linked to the much broader and embedded belief inherent in post-industrial societies of the need to maximize the application of technology to address complex problems. The reasons for this lie in the uncertain impact of transnational forces on national structures and the need for state managers to assess both the extent of this impact and to act in ways which can be legitimized (to electorates and to political elites from other states) on the basis of this assessment.

However, the response to transnational problems since the 1980s has led directly to changes in the form and practices of the state apparatus. At the international level, a parallel trend has been apparent in the emergence of complex networks with regulatory or policy implementation functions across a wide variety of transnational issue areas (from economic and environmental through to security issues). Many of these networks have arisen as a result of closer and more extensive intergovernmental cooperation that has led to direct contact between national 'experts' from different states. As certain national actors have been assigned competence to assess and address problems whose dynamics are seen as having an 'external' aspect, they have also acquired legitimacy to exercise competence in transgovernmental policy-making fora (for example, civil servants from home affairs ministries). Groups of this type are distinguished by their possession of a successful claim to recognized competence or knowledge; they thereby become *authoritative* sources of knowledge. This is generally as a direct result of their political legitimacy or pre-existing functional location within the state apparatus rather than of intrinsic 'expertise' alone. As a result, groups of this type have an influential role in shaping and framing the ideas that underpin policy frameworks used to tackle problems seen as having grown as a result of complex transnational forces and for which outcomes are highly uncertain. State managers have a clear requirement for ways of reducing that uncertainty. Indeed, this might be portrayed as a kind of knowledge market, although it is apparent that only empirical assessment can identify the dynamics and key actors in a particular situation: generalized claims are unlikely to provide real insight.

As coping with transnational problems has become an increasingly prominent dimension of state activity, the actors assigned competence as sources of authoritative knowledge in relation to such problems have acquired a corresponding increase in their status within the policy-making process. This status is both functional and political. The primary role of such actors is, unambiguously, to establish a basis for consensus and to find policies that are acceptable to some collective of state managers. To do this, actors must have actual or presumed functional knowledge of a specialist domain based to some degree on their institutional location, practices and assumed technical competence. The views of 'knowledge brokers' are also intrinsically political in the sense that they are referenced against an existing way of doing things politically. A presumed ability to define and evaluate threat is perhaps an equally important part of the qualifying criteria for the role. This ability is thus necessarily based upon an interpretation of the cause-and-effect relationships that apply in a given situation. However, for a host of international policies this role is performed in the context of deeply rooted principles of public international law that have evolved over considerable periods of time (international drug prohibition being a prime example). These principles generally serve to define shared notions of what constitutes the dominant view of the cause-and-effect relationships considered to shape a given problem, acting as a normative convention around which policy preferences can converge. The mutual recognition of such principles is also deeply rooted in the notion and practice of state sovereignty. Hence, if transnational problems *are* – or, equally, *are construed as* – a threat to the state then it follows that they will also be a threat to the sovereign power of the state on a more fundamental (albeit abstract) level. This has the effect of reinforcing the 'principled' notion of a given response through the construction of a reciprocal basis for action, that is to say the idea that if more states agree to something then it has a greater mutual sense of received ethical meaning.

Of course, how state decision-makers conceptualize threat fundamentally depends on to whom they turn for an assessment of that threat. In the case of drug trafficking, the clandestine and criminal nature of the activities involved means that any quantitative measurement of the problem is the exclusive (and 'legitimate') domain of the policing and intelligence arms of the state apparatus. Also, in cases where an activity is criminalized then data can generally be classified as 'secret' on the grounds of protecting security agencies (either to protect individuals or to conceal strategic actions). This makes it particularly difficult to gain objective data: security agencies' conceptualization of threat is intrinsically related to their construction of threat as a criminal justice problem. Not only do they define problems (or 'solutions') within pre-defined dimensions, their rationale for doing so is 'legitimately' couched in secrecy. In these ways a normative preference for the conceptualization of a problem is created, as the main source of threat assessment has authoritative status within the decision-making framework of the state. This book attempts to explore not only how this is manifested in practice, by looking at empirical evidence in a specific case, but also raises the more fundamental question of why particular forms of authoritative knowledge shape the *range* of policy actions that are considered. To the extent that this is related to the state functions of authority and control, it raises the equally fundamental question of the extent to which policies are determined not by some pluralistic bargaining process but on the basis of a more deeply embedded pressure to both recreate and reinforce the institution of the state itself. Before these points can be considered further it is necessary to look at recent perspectives on the concept of state sovereignty.

Sovereignty under threat?

Halliday (1987: 219) makes the important point that conventional political discourse assumes that state and government are identical, and that this pairing represents society as a whole, with political outcomes being the direct product of a constant process of state–society bargaining. Advocates of holistic concepts of 'the state' that take it as the repository of all things within a delimited territory – government, people, society and nation – may well believe that their concepts are purely theoretical devices, but they have the effect of rigidly defining what a *non*-state actor 'is' by default, when in practice such distinctions are far more complex. If a state can be broadly defined as a set of bureaucratic and regulatory apparatuses headed by some form of executive personnel (which I prefer to call state managers) then it becomes possible to understand that there may be conflict between elements of the state and between state and society, both forms of which can be observed empirically.[5] The degree to which state managers can either adopt policies that are against the wishes of large parts of society or convince society of the need for certain kinds of action rests with the concept of state autonomy. To understand the meaning of this concept is to understand why sovereignty remains such an important and closely guarded attribute of national states, irrespective of differences in their internal structures.

Sovereignty is emblematic of statehood, and is widely understood to be so. The question of whether state sovereignty is itself under threat as a result of expanded transnational problems is a particularly contentious one for international relations theorists, who have been unable to reach consensus on either the theoretical or empirical aspects of this issue. This has led to a situation whereby the realist school of thought (re-formations and variations accepted) has generally taken sovereignty as being about the ability of a state to take authoritative decisions: ultimately, to declare war. In contrast, the liberal interdependence school (which first emerged in the 1970s) has tended to view sovereignty in terms of the ability of a state to control flows across and within its territorial borders. However, both schools have contributed to the notion that conceives of the state as a unitary entity, viewing it holistically. The result of this has generally been the promotion of an ideological (liberal) perspective of state–society relations wherein the state simply represents 'society', while in practice it is subject to any number of potential conflicts with the interests of society.

Thomson (1995) successfully conveys the multidimensional character of sovereignty, illustrating the difficulties inherent in even a simple measurement of the concept, let alone assessment of whether it has been eroded, consolidated or changed in some way. She suggests that, with sovereignty, recognition is everything; it is not an automatic attribute of the state but one that is conferred externally by other states or – more accurately – by a majority of political elites representing individual states. Numerous authors have suggested that sovereignty is not (and never has been) absolute but is a matter of degree, and that the functional attributes that stem from it have a direct relation to power capabilities. None the less, as Thomson suggests, sovereignty is – fundamentally – the means through which states claim and are recognized to have the authority to define 'the political'. This can be defined as that which is ultimately subject to state coercion, that is to say, not regulated via individual, social or market relations. She terms this 'meta-political authority', and suggests that it is through the institution of sovereignty that it has become pluralistic and global in character as mutual recognition has reinforced this authority as an 'inalienable' right of each state. She cites the example of tobacco and cocaine: while the former is regulated predominantly through private (individual and market) relations, the latter is subject to the full coercive power of the state and has become subject to more intensive interstate control over time.

Hence, it is possible to suggest that there is no immutable set of contents of the 'private' and 'public' spheres; an *active* decision must be made to place certain items or activities into the realm of the political, and this decision will be related to what some collectivity of states define to be their common interests (which may or may not entail restrictions on individuals). History overwhelmingly suggests that in practice this is likely to be based not on unanimity but on the preferred actions or interests of a select number of states (and, perhaps, powerful groups within those states), and to be variable over time. It is sometimes forgotten that states have *always* been formed and shaped to some extent by international interaction, particularly since the development of industrial capitalism in the nineteenth century. When the broad terms of the international trading system were agreed internationally, however, the precedent was firmly established that the actual methods that created the conditions to fulfil international requirements were fundamentally and 'rightfully' the product of national processes.

The way that states exercise meta-political authority is based upon two fundamental attributes of a state: authority and control. Authority is the claim to the exclusive right to make rules, while control is the capability of enforcing that claim and the rules made under it (a category that may broadly be termed policing). Although Weberian notions of authority distinguish between rulers and ruled, at the level of states it is more difficult to think in this way, as no one state *claims* a monopoly on the use of coercion at the global level and also for the reason that recognition is coming from rulers (some collectivity of political elites) not the ruled (societies).[6] Although it may be reasonable to think of state control as simply a function of capabilities to *enforce*, the modern state also has increasingly sophisticated means of controlling behaviour at its disposal, including surveillance and proactive monitoring methods utilizing information technology.

Within its own territory an advanced industrialized state generally enjoys a high degree of freedom from interference by other states as to the practices that it chooses to adopt to ensure that its preferred rules are complied with.[7] However, the existence of international norms and rules represents intervening variables that act as (normative) dynamic influences towards homogenization of 'acceptable' or 'desirable' state practices.[8] Thomson suggests that what is often portrayed as an erosion of sovereignty may actually be a change in the norms or rules that define the legitimate forms of functional authority and means of enforcing those rules. If transnational problems are asserted to represent threats to national territory then cooperation with other designated states is automatically legitimized. Hence, although intensified interdependence may have threatened the ability of individual states to assert and make good their authority claims it has also created a basis on which to consider some form of homogenization of authority claims and rule enforcement.[9]

The policing function (of territory and people) is often argued to be an important dimension of state sovereignty, dependent on the ability of a state to monopolize the major organized means of violence within its territory. One aspect of this ability of course is the defence of territorial boundaries, though Giddens (1990) has rightly pointed out that it is incorrect to assume that there was ever a 'golden age' when borders were impermeable. Thus territoriality can itself be challenged as ever having been a truly all-encompassing attribute of sovereignty; there have clearly always been degrees of sovereignty across issue areas and comparatively between different states. None the less, states have always sought to *assert* their sovereign authority within their given territory. Crucial to state authority is close identification between 'the state' and 'the people', creating a society or nation that identifies with 'the state' as the legitimate defender of its interests. Naturally, if a society is told – and as a result believes – that it is subject to internal or external threat then it will generally look to the state for protection. Once this logic acquires a critical mass of support, state managers may in turn employ international norms as devices to assert the legitimacy of action that they take to address problems at national level. Citizens might also expect that state leaders will act in what they perceive to be the interests of 'their country'; pragmatic, and well informed about the threats faced and the options available to address them. Such a view contains several normative aspects, however, in that it assumes:

1 a congruence between the interests of state and society
2 a direct link between political democracy and the actions of state managers, and
3 a neutral, objective basis for decision-making.

Each of these points is open to challenge, and will be addressed in the course of this work with specific reference to the issue of drug enforcement policy.

To recap, sovereignty is thus the means through which states mutually recognize meta-political authority. Issues that have a direct bearing on the ability of the state to demonstrate its powers of authority and control provide the most meaningful basis on which to assess any changes in the norms and rules that define the legitimate forms of functional authority and means of enforcing those rules – in other words, a way of observing whether state sovereignty has been eroded or changed in some way. If transnational problems have been a critical factor in any change then it is important to understand why particular problems have generated consensus rather than others. Let us turn then to the question of the 'new threat' posed by drug trafficking since the 1980s.

Transnational drug trafficking: something old, something new?

Chapter 3 provides an account of how the norm of international drug prohibition has evolved over what is now more than a century. However, there has been a significant broadening and deepening of the 'core' set of drug enforcement policies since the late 1980s along with pressure for wider international compliance. So, while the problem of illegal drugs crossing borders (that is to say, violating territorial integrity) is not new, it is reasonable to presume that the convergence in anti-drug trafficking policies apparent since then reflects a state-level belief that the threat posed by trafficking organizations became significantly greater around that point in time.

Under prohibition, drug trafficking is by definition a clandestine and entrepreneurial activity intent on circumventing enforcement countermeasures put in place by the state and enforced by its agencies. Traffickers both create and respond to market forces, seeking to facilitate (and, wherever possible, expand) drug markets across and within state borders. By the 1980s, the governments of most AICs were already accustomed to investing significant resources to try and enforce drug prohibition. The new, globalized era was soon seen as opening up new opportunities for drug trafficking and thereby bringing an increased level of threat. But how did state decision-makers arrive at the conclusion that more enforcement resources would be the best way to tackle this threat? It certainly appears that they made their decisions on the basis of a simple cause-and-effect belief: that if trafficking was increasing then this would be a greater threat and require more enforcement resources to counter it. More specifically, how was this situation understood and rationalized by decision-makers?

The authoritative source of information for state decision-makers about drug trafficking tends to come from national policing and customs agencies, based on their knowledge of conditions 'on the ground'. Threat assessment carried out by such agencies is, by definition, a measure of the extent to which prohibition itself is being challenged by criminality. Substantive questions about the actual effectiveness of enforcement and interdiction strategies are not part of this process, it would seem. Of course, the use of enforcement has two dimensions: first, it is a declaration of state power and, second, it is a device to manage the scale of activity by criminals (who are criminalized on the basis of prohibition). The actual effectiveness of enforcement is not simply a matter of objective measurement, however. Political decision-makers have to decide whether or not they think increased enforcement is something that can be both justified and rationalized to a public audience. Embodied in this decision-making is a value-based commitment to the possibility of forcibly restricting the supply of drugs. This decision is fundamentally linked to the projection of threat, but not necessarily to an objective measure of that threat. European (EC–EU) governments have tended to portray the threat from drug trafficking in the broadest of terms, focusing largely on the removal of internal border controls as a factor likely to raise trafficking levels (and hence deemed to increase the supply of drugs and levels of associated violence and money laundering).

During the 1980s, official discourse began to support the idea that drug trafficking organizations were operating in ways that made them akin to clandestine corporations (often working together in 'cartels'). This attribution of sophistication not only made notions of threat seem to carry more weight but also contributed to the popular notion that drug markets are pyramidal, with a 'Mr Big' figure heading operations. However, European governments failed to provide any contextual assessment of the threat posed by drug trafficking organizations to their respective countries, relying on vague concepts based primarily on images of 'outsiders' bringing violence and corruption. This is not to say that no evidence of this kind of activity was or is available; in fact plenty of evidence can be found to establish that trafficking organizations are both powerful and dangerous, in contrast to a lack of evidence that more enforcement action would significantly reduce or constrain the threat posed by these organizations. Academic work on the nature of drug distribution and drug markets has generally refuted the archetype used in official discourse (that is, cohesive organizations operating in unison), suggesting that a much more fragmented situation applies. Ruggiero and South (1995) carried out ethnographic research on drug markets in the United Kingdom and Italy, finding that not only was drug distribution carried out by diverse and changing groups but also that the characterization of drug markets as definitively involving 'crime in organization' was itself misleading. The work of Ruggiero and South fundamentally questions the 'standard' (that is, official) account of drug markets and distribution. European governments have thus failed properly to contextualize the threat from drug trafficking, relying on more general fears about 'the drugs problem' to legitimize their policy actions. Let us turn now to the question of how globalizing discourse may be linked to broader notions of insecurity at state level.

Globalizing discourse and insecurity

Transnational problems are fundamentally about uncertainty, linked to some notion of large-scale risk.[10] Risk associated with transnational problems is directly related to territorial integrity, to 'invasion' of borders; national governments have thus tended to assume a defensive stance, promulgating the idea that such problems have externally derived causes in the process. This has an important psychological impact in that it supports the notion that it is the territorial integrity of the state that is ultimately 'under attack'. The simple corollary of this proposition is that without some form of defensive action individual states will be at risk of losing their sovereign power (based on the received meaning of this term). The implication that transnational problems have a range of causal factors in common is part of a globalizing discourse that not only has influenced the way we conceptualize the world spatially and temporally but also has brought a more nebulous sense of insecurity. Let us now consider the impact of the globalized era in more ontological terms and how this may be linked to policy-making.

A widespread notion has been apparent since the late 1980s projecting the idea that there is a simple cumulative dimension to global threats, that is, implying that the more types of threat there are, the more states become insecure. However, such a view ignores the multifaceted and discrete cause-and-effect relationships that underpin particular transnational problems. Equally, there is no objective basis for measurement of the comparative threats posed by, say, drug trafficking and environmental damage. There is an important difference between them in political terms, however. This is identified by Williams (1994), who points out that where transnational criminal organizations (TCOs) are involved this is generally considered to be 'an implicit challenge to state authority and sovereignty. The threat is insidious rather than direct: it is not a threat to the military strength of the state, but is a challenge to the prerogatives of statehood' (p. 111). The observation is a pertinent one. When compared with, say, environmental damage (with its imprecise long-term impact) drug trafficking TCOs are a source of 'risk' and insecurity that can more easily be articulated, not least because they involve individuals who can be demonized. TCOs have frequently been associated with a specific ethnic group or individual (the best examples being the heads of Colombian and Mexican drug trafficking organizations such as Pablo Escobar or the Arellano-Felix brothers), fitting more easily into established notions of territorial threat from 'outsiders'. This has also reinforced the aforementioned idea that drug trafficking is a hierarchical activity invariably headed by a 'Mr Big' figure. If an all-embracing causal phenomenon (that is, 'globalization') is cited, then this means that other causal explanations associated with *specific* issue areas or problems tend to become marginalized. The central questions here are thus how, in the broadest sense, have both the concept and practical experience of global change been instrumental in shaping the decision-making preferences of the state managers of AICs?; what exactly do they perceive to be under threat?; which information sources do they rely on to base this perception?; how, and to whom, do they perceive that their actions need to be justified? Let us now consider the concept of globalization in more detail.

In the mid 1990s one author detected a 'fashionable consensus' favouring the idea that globalization, allied to the information revolution, had invariably brought earth-shattering change in its wake.[11] The author was sceptical that such rhetorical language matched reality, arguing for developments to be seen in a context of evolution, not revolution. Indeed, many commentators have for some time portrayed 'globalization' as the product of a process with its origins in the earliest stage of the formation of the modern state and economy. Based on this viewpoint, the longstanding nature of certain international rules and norms of behaviour imbues them with a double-edged character: they have a constitutive quality as a dimension of internationally agreed behaviour, but they are also interactive variables in that they can also determine and shape other variables.[12] International agreements are constitutive (and demonstrative) elements of statehood, hence they typically show strong inertia as features of the international system. The long-standing, state-generated norms and rules of drug prohibition are clearly both constitutive of *and* influenced by the processes of global change. Nevertheless the notion that we are living through some kind of transformative era – what James Rosenau (1990: 5) has termed a 'historical breakpoint' – still runs deeply through contemporary life. The term 'globalization' is still widely used in media, business, financial and academic discourses, yet conceptual work on the logic and dynamics of globalization has served largely to highlight an inherent, and intense, set of ambiguities and complexities. Undergraduate students are generally taught to regard globalization as a broad range of contending perspectives.[13] The vast scale and range of literature that now exists on the subject of globalization makes it impossible to provide a summary here.[14]

A distinctive feature of the globalized era is the way that state managers have increasingly come to measure each other's probity by their democratic credentials and formal commitment to public international laws (such as UN conventions, for example). Global change has provided the pretext to broadly reconstruct the international system based around these normative principles. In broad terms this has been attempted along neo-liberal lines, with restatement of the principle of national sovereignty uppermost in this process. The constraints of the process are that it has also brought change at national and sub-national levels, putting pressure on state managers to adapt existing political structures and systems of control to this new situation. However, this has also been a clear source of utility for certain parts of the state apparatus in AICs. The end of the Cold War left a question mark against the role of specialist national security agencies, for example, which was soon filled by their co-option into the fight against TCOs.[15] Although pressure to coordinate international action has grown significantly, this has been confined solely to actions that allow sovereign control to be retained (at least formally) by AICs. Despite this, the boundaries of what actually constitutes 'internal' politics are harder than ever to draw. In a context of ever-denser interconnections and forces, and processes of regional and global integration, Held (1995a: 99) defines the salient characteristic of this situation when he points out that 'national communities by no means make and determine decisions and policies exclusively for themselves, and governments by no means determine what is right exclusively for their own citizens'. Although there has been little real challenge to the legitimacy of the *entitlement* of states to rule over particular territories, state activities are now more constrained in a world where social relations have been stretched across space and time.[16] The effects of this process have varied widely across different states and issue areas, but it is important to focus on the powerful uncertainties engendered by these wider processes.

Giddens (1990: 53) has suggested that there are three essential aspects to the dynamism inherent in modernity: time–space distanciation (see note 16), the reflexive appropriation of knowledge, and the development of 'disembedding mechanisms' that ' "lift out" social activity from localized contexts, reorganizing social relations across large time–space distances'.[17] He argues that each of these features is interrelated, though it is disembedding mechanisms that provide one way of understanding how subject populations are prepared to accept that their political representatives can represent the 'reality' of events and processes to them. A key component of disembedding mechanisms (made up of what Giddens terms 'symbolic tokens' and 'expert systems') is the involvement of trust, a concept linked to the idea of risk. Although it is not possible to provide a full account of this analysis here, it does provide a basis on which to explain any link between risk and ontological security as related to state actions. What Giddens (1990) terms 'lay trust' in expert systems, and how this may be linked to feelings of ontological security, necessitates consideration of 'The *inevitability* of living with dangers which are *remote* from the control not only of individuals, but also of large organizations, including states; and which are of *high intensity* and *life threatening* for millions of human beings' (p. 131). Globalization, and the rhetorical discourse that it has generated, thus supports a normative faith or trust in state managers to manage uncertainty. It also places the power of quantifying that uncertainty and related 'dangers' in the hands of state managers or those whom they consider to be authoritative sources of knowledge and understanding about transnational problems.

One impact of globalizing discourse has been to cause a rethink of the traditional idea that organized crime was 'rightfully' and naturally a matter of domestic law and order. Since the 1970s, organized crime has begun to show increasingly transnational characteristics, accompanied by a trend towards increased sophistication on the part of TCOs. In recognition of this, the policy discourse about organized crime has itself been internationalized over time. This has led to greater emphasis on 'defending' borders and, as a result, those seen as 'defenders'. This has important implications for the cognitive authority given to those national level groups who are associated with this aspect of the role of the state and to whom state managers turn for their perception of threat and for policy 'solutions'. The parallel expansion in the intensity of international networks (particularly those based around intergovernmental decision-making) has important consequences – and has created opportunities – for the consolidation of certain dimensions of state power based on normative policy preferences. Analysis of changes in European policing by den Boer (1994) places the emphasis on the discourse-based aspects of policy-making, highlighting the need for analysis that examines the interaction between the ideological horizons of participants in the policy-making process and the outcomes of that process. In other words, common ideas of validity (that is, tacit agreement on the 'right' ways of addressing a problem) may be crucial in framing and shaping normative policy preferences.

Propositions of the book

The preceding analysis provides the basis on which to put forward some propositions about the issues that are addressed by this book. The main propositions are as follows.

1   Transnational drug trafficking has significant negative consequences, including the use of 'illegitimate' violence (that is, in opposition to the claimed monopoly of the organized means of violence by the state), the corruption of public officials and the laundering of money that was gained illegally and its investment in 'legitimate' enterprise. Trafficking is of course the delivery system for a range of drugs that are classified as illegal, hence on the basis that the rule of prohibition applies it is definitively an illegal activity. The scale of these activities is almost impossible to assess reliably due to the clandestine nature of the activities involved.

2   In global terms, the threat posed by transnational drug trafficking is unquestionably significant (albeit extremely difficult to quantify) and has become a great deal more so since the 1980s in both scale and character. This is generally considered to be related to the freer transnational environment linked to the processes of globalization. The relative, contextual nature of this threat is rarely addressed, however, nor are the highly differentiated effects on specific groups and countries. If the threat is primarily related to crossing borders then it can also be seen as a threat to the territorial prerogatives of statehood (which some argue have become something of a chimera under globalization). The failure to contextualize the threat leads to a series of questions about the basis on which a significant extension in the enforcement regime that is nominally in place to 'make prohibition work' has been legitimized. This book works on the proposition that more extensive enforcement has failed to reduce the overall supply of drugs in any advanced industrialized country since the 1980s (in fact, significant increases have been the norm over this period).

3   Drug prohibition is different from most other internationally agreed rules because it is so overtly connected to the validation of meta-political authority: the right of each state to define the political. This is directly linked to state sovereignty, hence the renewed international affirmation of prohibition (and the authority and control functions

of the state that it embodies) has come at a time when the institution of the state and the nature of statehood have been subject to well-documented challenge.

4   In normative terms, drug trafficking is considered a problem that can only be addressed via an 'enforcement solution' (generally equated with a proportionality principle whereby if trafficking increases additional enforcement resources are claimed as the appropriate response). This creates a further normative preference such that the enforcement arms of the state apparatus are the only legitimate and authoritative sources of knowledge on the drug trafficking problem and the causal dynamics that relate to the problem. It is proposed that this relationship has become more deeply embedded in the international system as the increased level of drug trafficking has created new levels of uncertainty (and demands for ways of managing this) as well as a growth in inter-governmental decision-making fora that have given a more influential role to experts in developing policy ideas.

5   Finally, the empirical material on the EC–EU outlined in this book aims to test the proposition that drug threat and the enforcement rationalized on the basis of that threat have provided a basis on which to legitimize a broader set of cooperative security measures among EU member states while marginalizing alternative analyses and policies on drugs. It is also proposed that drug threat has provided a basis on which to legitimize a secretive and anti-democratic style of policy-making over a considerable period of time and that this may reflect a modification of the norms of sovereignty for EU member states and also show how state power has been consolidated in the areas of rule making and policing.

This book aims to provide a basis on which to assess any relationship between the attempt to strengthen the state functions of authority and control with regard to the issue of drug trafficking and the broader challenge to the institution of the state posed by global change. In the process it looks at how this uncertainty may have influenced normative preferences in decision-making. In analysing the development of European policy on drug enforcement it seeks to examine which groups have authoritative knowledge, why this may be so, and the consequences of this situation. The analysis also seeks to understand the institutionalization of normative knowledge and how this may present a powerful barrier to alternative causal analysis and policy development. Empirical evidence spanning some thirty years of what has been a formative period in the development of a European 'community' of states is examined. First, the next chapter provides an essential contextual overview of the evolution of international drug prohibition.

3
The Evolution of International Drug Control Policy

Throughout recorded history, human beings have shown a desire to alter their state of consciousness using whatever psychoactive substances their particular era has made available to them: from coffee to opium, and from alcohol to 'ecstasy'. Equally, public authorities have tried to regulate the use of such substances at particular junctures – often in draconian fashion – while at other times no controls whatsoever have been applied to the very same substances. Not until the twentieth century, however, was an attempt made to universalize the norms and legal sanctions regarding the use of and trade in certain categories of psychoactive substances. Today, virtually all states consider themselves members of what Nadelmann (1990) has termed the 'global drug prohibition regime'.

Progressively and inexorably, the principle of prohibition has become internationalized, adopted by societies in all parts of the world, spanning the widest possible cultural spectrum. The principle is formalized through the treaties and conventions of public international law and the criminal laws of nation-states, but is also reflected in deeply seated social, cultural and moral understandings that define the boundaries between 'licit' and 'illicit' drugs (each of which have the capacity to produce changes in behaviour and cause ill-effects of varying degrees). In the latter case, outside of tightly regulated medical and scientific use, legal (generally criminal) sanctions of some form apply in virtually all states to the production, distribution, sale, possession, and – in most cases – consumption of cannabis, cocaine, most opiates, hallucinogens, barbiturates, amphetamines and tranquillisers.[18] A penal or 'enforcement' model has long been the predominant means of attempting to ensure compliance, the natural corollary of which has been a prominent role for national law enforcement agencies. This role has long been preoccupied with attempts to counter distribution and production of illicit drugs, primarily at national level, but also abroad given the transnational dimension inherent to the trafficking of most (though by no means all) illicit drugs.[19] In parallel with this, other psychoactive drugs such as alcohol and tobacco have, in general, been socially regulated, as the problems related to these substances have been deemed to be predominantly matters for public health rather than law and order. This represents a considerable paradox to many observers. This chapter looks at the factors that lie behind the rigorously enforced precept of international drug prohibition and describes its evolution.

The emergence of what has now become a global market for illicit drugs has been directly influenced by the existence of prohibition but also by a complex amalgam of social, political and economic forces that have determined its shape and character.[20] Demand has unquestionably been generated, at least in part, by the forbidden status of (particular) drugs that is enshrined in the very fact of their prohibition. With a massive proliferation in the range of drugs available and rising demand in almost all countries, potential profits from the sale of illicit drugs remain exceptionally high (hence offsetting the manifest risks involved for potential drug producers and distributors). Illicit drugs are among the most profitable traded commodities in the world economy (licit or illicit) although estimates of the scale of this most clandestine of markets is inevitably vague. None the less, estimates of total revenue accruing to the drug industry have still generally placed it at around 8 per cent of world trade, making it greater than the international trade in iron and steel and about the same as that in textiles (UNDCP, 1997a: 124).

It is generally acknowledged that the worldwide problems related to drug trafficking and drug use have escalated massively since the 1960s (as cannabis use boomed), and especially since the 1980s (when widespread abuse of cocaine in industrialized countries fuelled a massive increase in production and distribution of the drug). Prohibition, backed by an almost unparalleled set of international legal and enforcement resources, has neither broken the cycle of criminal involvement nor discouraged the use of drugs. Despite this failure there appears to be little sign of a break in the normative consensus that has sustained prohibition internationally at the governmental decision-making level. The response has been to build on the existing foundations, to broaden and deepen the provisions of the international drug prohibition regime, backed by globalizing pressures and language: prohibition has become one of the inalienable principles that shapes international affairs, as seemingly unshakeable as the precepts of national sovereignty. 'Fighting the drugs problem' has become a uniquely powerful rallying call for the mobilization of resources across a wide range of institutional and organizational domains at national, regional, international and even quasi-global levels. Let us now consider the origins and foundations of international drug prohibition in order to begin an assessment of what might be the longer-term basis for this enduring strength.

Drugs and morality

International drug prohibition emerged out of a series of events that took place shortly before and after the turn of the nineteenth century. Analysis of these formative events reveals the close association between moral notions and drug control. Drugs have always meant, and continue to mean, different things to different cultures; they are not merely substances that affect behaviour, they also have symbolic value and culturally based meanings. Nadelmann (1990) suggests that the processes by which the *global* drug prohibition regime has evolved: 'must be understood as a confluence of the perceptions, interests, and moral notions among dominant sectors of the more powerful states along with the exceptional influence of American protagonists in shaping the regime according to their preferred norms' (p. 503).

The predominance of American and European influence is shown in the global regime that is now so widely adopted: consider the various meanings associated with, say, alcohol in Muslim states, cannabis or khat in some African states; or coca in certain Latin American states.[21] Virtually all states are now formally committed to the prohibition of substances that in some cases have deep traditions and cultural or religious associations in their societies, however. Berridge and Edwards (1981: 259–61), although making a point about the specific circumstances of England, illustrate the wider point that this is a reflection of a lack of faith in traditional informal controls that served societies for many years.[22] For example, the introduction of formal controls on opium in England may be seen to reflect a profound mistrust of the strength and quality of culture in English society, a factor perhaps better explained in this case by class-based notions held by political elites fearful of the consequences of an opium-addled working class. Fears of the potential effects of drug use have been a consistent *leitmotif* associated with prohibition. The association of drugs with 'outsiders' or minority groups has consistently been mobilized to support prohibition, though this merely illustrates the impossibility of treating 'the drugs problem' as a phenomenon that is in any sense independent of prevailing social and political forces and interests.[23]

Bruun et al. (1975: 28) make the important point that international drug control was initiated in response to 'a specific problem in a specific area of the world – opium in China'. Until well into the nineteenth century, Britain was the dominant force in the trade of exporting opium to China from British India (it fought two 'Opium Wars' with China to defend its interests: in 1839–42 and 1856–58). Opium use in nineteenth-century England was confined to a relatively well-defined social group, though opium itself formed the active ingredient of a wide range of palliative treatments that were self-administered and also widely given to children: opium use was, in other words, deeply embedded in cultural practices. Berridge and Edwards (1981: 250) suggest that, in England, images of drug addiction were first mobilized to justify bringing opium under the control of the medical profession in the nineteenth century. By the last quarter of the century a relative decline in British involvement in the Indian opium trade was becoming apparent. The demise of British involvement was hastened, however, by the ministrations of what Nadelmann (1990) has termed 'moral entrepreneurs' whose success in winning official commitment to phase out British participation in the trade was 'almost entirely a reflection of the triumph of moral (religious and humanitarian) impulses over political and economic interests' (p. 504).[24] The opposition to British involvement in the opium trade did not extend to calls for a global campaign to ban the drug, however; the impetus for this was to come from American nationals. Nadelmann has chronicled the emergence of a broad cross-section of moral entrepreneurs within the United States who were instrumental in stimulating both state and federal drug prohibition legislation.[25]

Moral and emotional factors tied in some way to religious beliefs, humanitarian sentiments, faith in universalism, compassion, conscience, paternalism, fear, prejudice and the compulsion to proselytize form a heady brew of forces that found – and arguably continue to find – an outlet for expression in relation to drugs.[26] A series of developments during the nineteenth century cumulatively raised levels of concern and fostered legislation regarding the potentially harmful effects of drug use on public health. The isolation of morphine from opium (1805), the synthesis of heroin from morphine (after 1874), of cocaine from the coca plant (1855) and the advent of hypodermic injection (1843) all provided evidence of the increased potency of drugs. The decision to bring drugs under the control of the medical profession was wholly supported by the emergent professional bodies, of doctors and of pharmacists, whose motives lay – at least in part – in securing their own financial and professional status. Nadelmann contends that moral entrepreneurs played a critical role in the US through lobbying for federal and state legislation against an array of substances and activities considered to be vices: from opiates and cocaine through to alcohol and prostitution. Several accounts identify the US acquisition of the Philippines in 1898 as a catalytic event in internationalizing the idea of prohibition, as it focused attention on the effects of opium smoking on the citizens of the newly acquired territory. The influential role played by Bishop Charles H. Brent in persuading President Roosevelt that it was in US interests to control the opium trade on humanitarian grounds as well as in strategic terms is cited in several accounts.[27]

The impact of what the bishop saw

Most accounts suggest that a report prepared by Bishop Brent was significant in persuading the US government of a need for international action as it was becoming clear that domestic legislation alone (for example in China) had done little to reduce the effects of the opium problem. To this end, the US mobilized diplomatic channels in order to convene an international opium conference, which took place in Shanghai, China in January 1909, attended by China, the United States, Britain and ten additional countries. As Bruun et al. record (1975: 11), the conference was marked by an underlying conflict of interests between the 'Big Three', but even though the outcome was far from unanimous a resolution was passed stating that 'most' parties were agreed on the principle that the use of opium for other than medical purposes should be a matter for prohibition or at least careful regulation. This is the point at which the first seeds of international prohibition were clearly sown.

Three years later, a further international opium conference took place in The Hague, in The Netherlands, resulting in the first international legal instrument to enshrine the prohibition principle: the International Opium Convention of 1912. Bayer and Ghodse (1999: 3) note that in the following two years diplomatic channels were used to obtain the signatures of all except five of the, at this time, 46 nominally sovereign states in the world. Although it was decided at this point that the Convention would enter force at the end of 1914, the outbreak of the First World War meant that universal ratification of the Convention did not occur until 1920. Interestingly, this was tied to the treaties of Versailles, as 'every peace treaty (in 1919 with Germany, Austria and

Bulgaria; and, in 1920 with Hungary and Turkey) contained provisions about the obligations of the High Contracting Parties to ratify and apply the 1912 Convention' (Bayer and Ghodse, 1999: 3). The formal inter-nationalization of drug control was thus assured to a large extent by a mechanism that was principally based on the coercive power held by the states that were victorious in the First World War. Bruun et al. (1975) suggest that the 1912 Convention marked the beginning of a shift away from a Sino-centric focus to a more fully developed international one. The conference itself was attended by the same powers as had been pres-ent at Shanghai, and the resulting Convention left the interpretation and administration of controls to national governments alone; no interna-tional enforcement or monitoring machinery was provided for. Although this was partially corrected with the establishment of The League of Nations and the setting up (in 1920) of an Advisory Committee on Traffic in Opium and Other Dangerous Drugs, US failure to join the League restricted its potentially influential involvement in the Committee to an advisory capacity.

In summary, then, the first international conferences, at Shanghai and The Hague, though influential in establishing the principle of prohibition of opium and beginning discussions on morphine and cannabis, did little to create international enforcement machinery. Between 1924 and 1931, under the auspices of Advisory Committee, further drug treaties focused on the regulation of drug distribution and on limiting opiate production to meet the amounts needed for scientific and medical purposes.[28] The International Opium Convention of 1925 established the principle that the suppression of opium smoking could not be achieved without international monitoring, establishing the Permanent Central Board (at first termed the Permanent Opium Board and later the Permanent Central Narcotics Board).[29] The Convention also contained provisions relating to the control of coca leaf exports as well as the first provisions associated with cannabis, restricting export of cannabis resin to countries that prohibited its use. The 1925 treaty was successful in limiting the amount of narcotic drugs that leaked from legal to illegal marketplaces, but illicit drug trafficking did not cease by any means, as clandestine laboratories soon 'took up the slack'. This practice prompted a convention in 1936 calling for harsher measures to be adopted in the penal systems of contracting parties against illicit drug traffickers (a measure, claim Bruun et al., prompted at the direct initiative of the forerunner organization to Interpol). In the meantime, a further convention had been drafted in 1931, notable for establishing a require-ment on governments to supply annual estimates of the amount of narcotic drugs needed for medical and scientific purposes. After the Second World War was over a new international system took shape, and so did a new system of international drug control.

The UN as catalyst

With the formation of the United Nations in 1945 several important changes occurred to the system of international drug control. The League of Nations machinery was transferred almost in its entirety and incorporated into new institutions formed within the UN system. The Commission on Narcotic Drugs (CND) was founded in 1946, taking on the functions of the aforementioned Advisory Committee.[30] In a move of great significance, the World Health Organization (WHO) was given responsibility to evaluate new drugs in order to determine whether or not they should be controlled. Three drug-related UN Protocols (1946, 1948 and 1953) sought to close what at the time were seen as loopholes in the regulatory system, particularly with regard to the increasing number of synthetic drugs.[31] The Protocols, notably the latter of the three, paved the way for what was to be a much more significant international instrument: the 1961 UN Single Convention on Narcotic Drugs (henceforth 'The Single Convention').

The Single Convention (which entered force in December 1964) unified and consolidated all existing international drug control treaties, with the exception of the 1936 convention against trafficking. It also marked the first instance of the prohibition of cannabis herb (rather than resin alone), a step widely acknowledged to be the result of unilateral pressure from the United States government.[32] The Convention also provided for a restructuring of UN drug control institutions: the Permanent Control Board and the Drug Supervisory Body were merged into a single UN agency, the International Narcotics Control Board (INCB). The INCB was given broader responsibilities as the system of estimates was extended to cover *all* narcotic drugs. Although the provisions of the Convention were primarily aimed at preventing the diversion of drugs from licit to illicit channels, this was not accompanied by measures aimed at preventing traffic in clandestinely produced or manufactured drugs. Bruun et al. note that at the time of drafting the Single Convention a number of new drugs (such as barbiturates and tranquillisers) were not included in its provisions, despite concerns from the WHO. Such drugs were the lauded symbols of a burgeoning post-war pharmaceutical industry, buoyed by post-war optimism on the potential role of drugs in the treatment of psychiatric illness.

Not until 1971 and the UN Convention on Psychotropic Substances of that year were moves made to place amphetamines under international control, prompted by pressure from Sweden; even then the Convention did not enter force until August 1976.[33] The strong implication here is that commercial interests prevailed until rising examples of misuse – in effect, obvious signs of failure to keep commercial production within 'legitimate' channels – made international action imperative. In this regard, the WHO might well be argued to have been given an unrealistic post-war role: it must first weigh potential public health benefits from new drugs before judging any additional risks of 'non-medical' use, while being simultaneously aware of the commercial impact of any decisions it takes. This process is time consuming, creating considerable time lags before a decision to ban a particular substance can be implemented internationally. Even after 1971, Bruun et al. (1975: 18) claim, the international community's 'long-standing preoccupation with opiates' remained in place, suggesting that, while the illicit market expanded, regulators were extremely slow to react. In 1972, a further UN conference took place – again chiefly at the behest of the US – to update the provisions of the 1961 Convention with regard to traffic in opiates. This resulted in the 1972 Protocol Amending the 1961 Single Convention in this regard. Bayer and Ghodse (1999: 12) suggest that the 1972 Protocol (which entered into force in August 1975) can be considered 'the first response to the increased illicit cultivation of the opium poppy and the cannabis plant, the increased illicit production of cannabis, cannabis resin and opium, the increased illicit manufacture of heroin, and the increased illicit traffic in all of those drugs'.

In other words, a new era had dawned, although few at the time would have anticipated the subsequent developments in drug trafficking and use. International efforts thus remained heavily focused on measures designed to control supply at this time, despite the emergence of a new language emphasising 'drug abuse control'. A new phrase entered the lexicon of international politics around this time too: President Nixon of the US announced a 'total war on drugs', aimed squarely at the source countries for the main botanically derived drugs.[34] Once again the US took a lead in calling for tougher enforcement of international prohibition. Nadelmann (1993) argues that the attractiveness of such a strategy lay in its appeal as a 'rare' area of criminal justice activity in which the US federal government could prevail over state and local agencies and in the process avert discussion of the domestic factors contributing to the drugs problem.[35]

Despite the flurry of early 1970s activity aimed at making the international drug prohibition regime more watertight, Stares (1996: 28) argues, 'from 1974 to 1988 there was an explosive worldwide growth in the production and trafficking of virtually all types of illicit drugs'. During the 1970s as a whole, Western European countries saw what Bayer and Ghodse (1999: 12) term 'a propagation of the modern (that is to say non-traditional, non-medical, non-ceremonial) use of cannabis smoking'. This led to the creation of large markets and traffic in cannabis and cannabis resin in the region. The wider story of this period is of a series of complex political and economic changes culminating in the 1980s and contributing to the mobilization of key groups, most notably Colombian cocaine traffickers and Peruvian and Bolivian cultivators of coca, each with powerful domestic reasons of their own to seek the attractive revenues available through the drug trade.[36] The purported sophistication of the trafficking 'cartels' became almost legendary, with their leaders portrayed in the mass media as latter-day Al Capone figures, which had the effect – as cocaine use soared in the US – of heavily focusing US drug control policy on the Andean region.[37] At the same time, political changes in Southeast and Southwest Asia – the so-called 'Golden Triangle' and 'Golden Crescent' countries respectively – led to a significant expansion in the production of opium and its refining into heroin. Whilst accurate analysis of the precise chain of events is impossible to verify there is also some evidence that both heroin and cocaine traffickers saw Western Europe as their key growth market around this time.[38]

Amid mounting international concern, the UN took the lead in starting discussions on how the existing multilateral drug control system might be expanded to meet what was now seen as a massively increased threat. Part of this process included the realization that the precepts of territorial sovereignty were a barrier to effective action against increasingly adept transnational criminals, for whom the procedural niceties and technicalities of cross-border judicial and police cooperation were of no concern.[39] The UN International Conference on Drug Abuse and Illicit Trafficking (ICDAIT) was convened in 1987 in Vienna, Austria, two years after the UN General Assembly agreed on the need for such a conference. A notable outcome was the fact that the conference declaration (United Nations, 1988) formally advocated equal status for measures aimed at drug prevention and treatment alongside enforcement-led supply measures in what is generally termed a multidisciplinary approach. However, the subsequent 1988 Convention Against Illicit Traffic in Narcotic Drugs and Psychotropic Substances which rapidly came into force in November 1990 focused heavily on supply-side measures aimed at disabling what were perceived to be ever more powerful drug trafficking organizations. The 1988 Convention (widely referred to as the 'Vienna Convention') obliged signatories to: criminalize money laundering; seize drug-related assets; and regulate the market for key precursor and essential chemicals used to produce illicit drugs.[40] Bayer and Ghodse (1999) point out that it is incorrect to say (as some accounts have) that the Vienna Convention introduced control of precursors for the first time, as 'In reality precursors of opiates (including thebaine) have been under international control since 1931, and ecgonine and all of its derivatives (e.g. all of the cocaine precursors) were put under international control in 1925' (p. 4). This point highlights how inefficient controls of this kind have generally been, weakened by the requirement to avoid placing undue restrictions on legitimate trade. The Vienna Convention was the first international drug law machinery of the globalized era. It was both a powerful restatement of the normative foundations of the existing legal framework for prohibition as well as a basis for the creation of new and closer methods of international cooperation (including controlled deliveries of drugs: so-called 'sting' operations). Implementation of the provisions of the 1961 and 1971 Conventions was made a treaty obligation of all parties to the Vienna Convention, thereby giving a renewed impetus and mark of legitimacy to the existing body of public international drug laws (several decades old by this time). By December 1996, 138 states were party to the Convention; by October 2002 this had risen to 166 – an extraordinarily rapid take-up.[41] In December 1990 the UN also took the decision to merge what had become a fragmented set of drug control organizations within the UN system into a single executive agency, the UN International Drug Control Programme (UNDCP), though the role of the WHO was largely unaffected by this.[42]

Altered states: drug markets and sanctions since 1988

Since 1999, the research section of the UNDCP has produced an annual document entitled *Global Illicit Drug Trends*, providing the most comprehensive published source of estimates and statistics about supply and demand for illicit drugs worldwide.[43] In the preface to the 2002 annual report (covering the years 2000 and 2001) it was stated that 'Reliable and systematic data to assess the drug problem, and to monitor progress in achieving the goals set by the General Assembly, however, is not readily available' (UNDCP, 2002: 1).[44] This comment makes reference to the 1998 Special Session of the UN General Assembly (UNGASS) on international drug control at which member states agreed 'to make significant progress towards the control of supply and demand for illicit drugs by the year 2008' (ibid.). The Political Declaration adopted at UNGASS did not contain any 'hard' criteria on which to measure this progress, however.[45] The manifest difficulties in acquiring data from direct observation of drug cultivation, manufacture, trafficking, consumption or the investment of proceeds from drug crime means that only indirect measures are available in practice. Data on the quantities of drugs seized by enforcement authorities is one of the most popular official indicators, for example. Seizure figures provide a seriously flawed basis on which to make general assessments, however. The efficiency of interdiction is dependent on so many factors: each state has different border conditions and enforcement capabilities; recording practices vary; and demand for different drugs differs widely across different countries and regions, even those in close proximity. The UNDCP (1997a) itself has acknowledged that 'A rise in volume and numbers of seizures could be a sign of increased trafficking, but it could also be the result of increased enforcement activity, or else of a single outsize seizure which distorts a national trend. In either case, an assertion of trends is hard to make without knowledge of prices and purity' (p. 12).

Despite these quite serious reservations, trend data in UNDCP publications is drawn almost exclusively from seizure data (derived from governments, the UNDCP itself and other specialized agencies and institutions). For example, the 2002 UNDCP report provides figures on global illicit drug trafficking trends for the 11 years from 1990–2000. Over this period, seizures increased an average of 8 per cent *per year* for heroin, 6 per cent for cannabis herb, 5 per cent for cannabis resin and 1.5 per cent for cocaine. The most spectacular rise in this period was an annual average increase of 28 per cent in seizures of amphetamine-type stimulants (ATS), notably MDMA (3,4-methylenedioxy methamphetamine, commonly known as 'ecstasy') and its analogues.[46] These are remarkable figures, particularly as drug use was widely considered in official accounts to have reached 'epidemic' proportions by 1988. Despite the caveats, single-year annual rises shown as a percentage still have the capacity to astonish: worldwide heroin seizures increased by 44 per cent in 2000, for example.[47] By looking at the latest evidence of patterns in consumption it appears that drug use is increasing in some areas and falling in others. Patterns in the use of specific drugs vary quite considerably across the world, but Western Europe seems to have fairly stable levels of opiate use, increasing levels of cocaine use (though less rapidly than before), increasing cannabis use, signs of stabilization in amphetamine use (after years of increase) and a more inconsistent pattern of ecstasy use (UNDCP, 2002).

This book cannot provide a fully nuanced interpretation of the changes in drug markets since 1988, but the UNDCP figures outlined above provide strong evidence to suggest that the new anti-drug regime fostered by the Vienna Convention has not been successful in reducing either of the two dimensions of the drug problem at which it was directed: production and trafficking. The main impetus of the Convention was to focus enforcement countermeasures on controlling large-scale, transnational drug trafficking networks. Since the Convention entered force one of the most significant developments has been the emergence of substances that can be easily produced near to their intended market (that is, synthetic drugs), thereby shortening trafficking routes considerably. Unlike the illicit manufacture of heroin or cocaine, which is essentially an extraction process and one in which all the substances involved are controlled, 'A heterogeneous group of chemicals can act as precursors to produce a range of amphetamine-type stimulants' (EMCDDA, 1997c: 59). This raises serious questions about the potential effectiveness of interdiction against ATS and the feasibility of precursor control when ATS can be produced using commonly available chemicals.

By 1996, the UNDCP was portraying stimulants as the main drug threat of the twenty-first century.[48] Significantly, the rise in production of synthetic drugs during the 1990s was accompanied by a shift in cultural attitudes towards illicit drugs more generally.[49] The 'modern' image of amphetamine-type stimulants made them attractive to a generally younger generation of drug user in AICs for whom they were 'socially acceptable' in the same way as alcohol or tobacco. The link of ATS to mass 'recreational' usage has also broken a long-established image of the drug user as confined to the margins of society or to supposedly deviant groups. 'Hard drugs', such as cocaine and heroin, show contemporary use patterns suggesting that heavy users form a relatively low proportion of the total volume of the drugs consumed and that it is this group which generates most of the problems caused by the need to sustain an expensive 'drug habit'.[50] A clear trend towards formal acceptance of multidisciplinary drug control (that is, highlighting a need for 'balance' between measures that control demand for drugs as well as supply) has been apparent in the national drugs strategies of AICs over the past decade. Only on the supply side have national policies been driven by a clear set of international obligations and clearly defined policy directions (as specified in the Vienna Convention), however.[51] The effect has been a strengthened and broadened framework of measures related to what Stares (1996) terms 'negative sanctions'. Negative control measures apply across the three key dimensions of production, trafficking and consumption (see Table 3.1 for a summary), although since 1989 initiatives have focused on strengthening interdiction and on 'disabling' tactics, principally the control of money laundering, and precursor and essential chemicals. This process as been led by AICs, notably through the forum of the G-7.[52]

Under G-7 auspices, the Financial Action Task Force (FATF) was set up in 1989, followed in 1990 by the Chemical Action Task Force (CATF). The main rationale for both bodies was to generate 'model legislation' and to promote practices to support this. The aim was to develop 'global' standards and norms designed to counter money laundering (via the FATF) and to prevent the diversion of essential and precursor chemicals to make illicit drugs (via the CATF). Of the two organizations, the FATF has proved the most enduring, with the CATF meeting only until 1992.[53] Both organizations were based on the principle that international 'experts' should be responsible for problem definition, for recommending policy responses and for monitoring performance, with a specialist intergovernmental organization providing a basis for these functions to cohere. The operations of the FATF have exemplified this bureaucratic–technocratic organizational model, bringing together financial, legal and law enforcement expertise coordinated via a small Paris-based secretariat. A little over a year after it was formed the FATF produced a report containing 'Forty Recommendations on Money Laundering' (subsequently updated in 1996, and under review again since 2000).

Table 3.1 Negative and positive drug control measures

	Production	Trafficking	Consumption

Negative control measures	Forcible eradication
	Chemical controls
	Destruction of
	  processing centers
		Interdiction
		Disabling
		  trafficking
		  networks
			Laws and legal sanctions
			Policing
			Mandatory drug
			  testing

Positive control measures	Crop substitution
	Alternative
	  development
		Legal amnesty
		  and clemency
		Alternative
		  employment
		Trade and
		  industry
		  cooperation
			Drug prevention
			  education
			Mass media
			  campaigns
			Drug treatment
			  programs
			Drug-free zones
			Harm-reduction
			  techniques

Source: Stares (1996: 64)
Reprinted with permission of the Brookings Institution Press.

The Forty Recommendations are one of the best examples of international 'soft law' whereby the regulatory framework that exists to enforce drug prohibition internationally has been broadened and in the process many new powers have been added to regulatory and enforcement agencies via new criminal laws and norms backed by the most powerful states in the international system. FATF membership was initially only 16 states, but by 1992 this was soon broadened to include all OECD countries (then 28), all of which have subsequently signed bilateral and multilateral agreements based on the principles espoused in the Forty Recommendations. The FATF now has 29 member states (plus the European Commission and Gulf Cooperation Council) and is also responsible for coordinating a process of multilateral monitoring and peer review for and by its member states with regard to anti money laundering measures. During the 1990s, AICs took the lead in developing 'financial intelligence units' (FIUs), specialized government agencies for addressing the money laundering issue. In 1995, the work of the FATF was complemented by the formation of the Egmont Group, an informal – and unaccountable – network. The aims of this Group were to make the exchange of financial intelligence among FIUs more systematic, to improve the expertise and capabilities of the personnel of such organizations, and to foster better communication through the application of new technologies.[54]

The FATF is little known outside governmental circles, the Egmont Group even less so. Although money laundering is not exclusively a drug-related matter, the Vienna Convention was a catalyst for the creation of international institutions that exemplify the principle that the problem of drug trafficking can be effectively tackled through the application of enforcement expertise. The post-1988 era also saw the formation of an influential IGO on international drugs control, the Dublin Group. The Group met for the first time in June 1990, bringing together EU member states with the US, Australia, Canada, Japan, Norway and Sweden. The Group continues to meet twice per year, focusing exclusively on the production and trafficking aspects of international drug control. Membership now also includes the UNDCP and (since 1999) Russia, although Norway no longer participates. The Group meets in Brussels, with the secretariat of the Council of the EU providing administrative support, illustrating the close links between the EU and a small group of the world's most powerful states on drug enforcement policy development. The Dublin Group is thus essentially a diplomatic forum, without formal status and with an entirely secret agenda: details of meetings are not released into the public domain.

A significant number of so-called 'mini-Dublin Groups' have also been established on a regional basis across the world, coordinated by Dublin Group members, adding considerably to the network and its capacity to promulgate policies favoured by leading states.

By way of contrast, and in spite of recent UN efforts, there is no international consensus on the appropriate form, mix or efficacy of 'positive control' measures (see Table 3.1) – particularly those aimed at reducing consumption, from education to harm-reduction techniques such as needle exchange programmes – hence the right of initiative is left primarily in the hands of national (and to a large extent regional and local) authorities. In general, positive control alternatives for tackling the reasons behind production and trafficking have been massively underfunded in comparison with negative control strategies, lacking a single unifying justification in the way that the 'iron law' of prohibition has come to provide for negative control measures. The possibility of causal links between prohibition and the drug trade are generally ignored in official publications and pronouncements, as is particularly shown by the low priority given to alternative development programmes in drug-producing areas compared with negative control measures.[55]

The period since 1988 is remarkable for how quickly the Vienna Convention provided a basis for international norms and practices to coalesce, leading to a 'toughened' international drug enforcement framework. Alongside this, levels of illicit drug trafficking (and drug production and consumption) have continued to rise significantly. Intergovernmental decision-making inspired by Vienna provisions has been characterized by a preference for the use of expert knowledge to formulate norms and rules before political sanction by the most powerful states in the international system. The Vienna Convention has thus provided a normative base around which individual states have structured and rationalized their individual responses since 1988. The European responses outlined in Part II of the book must therefore be set against this background.

Summary

The die of international drug prohibition was cast in the first decade of the twentieth century. Policy-makers drew upon the social and economic conditions of the time in forming their judgements, the sheer newness of drugs like heroin magnifying the uncertainty that surrounded them. Morality filled the breech of uncertainty at this time, and the state took responsibility for 'protecting' its citizens from a proscribed set of substances. At this time, threat was seen as principally related to opium which, for nearly all states, was (and still is) an imported substance. Once these conditions were established, the portrayal of drugs versus authority as an *adversarial* relationship has become ever more deeply embedded in national politics and international relations, and the range of proscribed substances has progressively and massively expanded.

As the ideas and practices of international drug control began to take shape they did so in a form preferred by leading states (remember that there were less than fifty sovereign states at this time). Economic factors also influenced the blueprint for drug control as newly professionalized work sectors were given jurisdiction to control emergent pharmacological technologies. This was replicated in the post Second World War international drug control machinery, with the WHO given the task of effectively defining the boundary between legal and illegal drug 'worlds'. This approach, rooted in a desire to protect commercial interests, introduced a significant time lag into the international decision-making process where new drugs are concerned.[56] Furthermore, the globalized era, in a world of almost two hundred sovereign states, has fostered an environment conducive to a massive expansion in transnational trafficking (that is, driven by the liberalization of international trade). Equally, innovation has been a key feature of the illicit drugs trade since the 1980s. The introduction of 'crack' cocaine in the mid 1980s in the US and the diversification of Colombian traffickers into heroin in the 1990s clearly show this, but it is drug consumers that have consolidated the pattern of change. The changing demographic profile of the drug user in advanced industrialized societies (in general, familiarity with drug use now occurs at an earlier age, for instance) and the broader cultural assimilation of drugs such as ecstasy, cannabis and cocaine have ensured that demand has remained buoyant in illegal drug markets.

With regard to the language of prohibition itself, Arnao (1990) points out the non-scientific basis for terms that are often used as if they have the weight of scientific consensus behind them. In the process, he highlights the legal-bureaucratic meanings implicit in the supposedly objective language of prohibition. He also traces the subjective basis in successive UN definitions of drug 'abuse' as the product of a discrimination between medical and non-medical use, such that 'The semantic system of the UN authorities, when examined critically evinces a tautology … Some substances are illegal because they are "abused"/"abuse" equals "non-medical use"/"non-medical use" is any use of illegal substances' (p. 33).

Arnao illustrates the often-contradictory character of prohibition: once it is abstracted from any moral or legal dimension then it is revealed as an edifice without logical support. This is not in any way to downplay the seriousness of drug use in terms of public health and crime, but drug users – demonized for so long – become, in a significant sense, a product of prohibition in that their criminality derives from their participation in an illegal activity rather than being an issue of individual morality or a personal health and social issue. Equally, the innovation that is so characteristic of the illicit drug marketplace may be seen more as a response to the rigid enforcement of prohibition as much as to any social or cultural stimulus emerging from user (that is, citizen) demand.

Research by Stimson et al. (1996) into the spread of drug injecting in developing countries makes depressing reading but raises the important point that the (global) diffusion of drug use practices must be placed in a wider context that considers such factors as trade and cultural links, urbanization, social dislocation and income inequalities among nations. The illegal drugs issue is thus one of the most complex international problems, which requires careful contextual analysis. This book does not set out to assess the relative merits of arguments for and against legalization or decriminalization of drugs (a massive and often divisive subject in itself) or to debate the 'need' for enforcement *per se*.[57] However, it does work on the premise that anti-trafficking policies are an embodiment of state power as well as – nominally – a means of protecting citizens from particular forms of threat. The efficacy of anti-trafficking measures as a device to control or reduce drug trafficking in anything other than a marginal sense is open to serious doubt, however, based on the empirical fact that the availability of illegal drugs has risen significantly despite the extensive anti-trafficking 'countermeasures' introduced since the late 1980s. This book focuses on the enduring appeal of drug prohibition to the state and how this is related to normative aspects of contemporary state practices and preferences (of advanced industrialized states, that is). The bulk of this work traces how this has been manifested in the cooperative intergovernmental interactions and policy decisions taken by member states of what is now the European Union. The next chapter looks at the relationship between contemporary changes in international governance and the strengthened edifice of international drug prohibition.

4
Networks, Expertise and International Governance

For some time now, many authors have linked the more fluid and – it is generally argued – *more uncertain* international environment associated with globalization with a corresponding shift in the modes and methods of international governance. This is also seen as having led to a rapid increase in transnational policy interactions and to the emergence of transnational and transgovernmental policy-making networks. The analysis so far has identified that drug enforcement policy-making has been largely determined through intergovernmental negotiation. It is therefore particularly important to examine accounts that seek to identify any changes in the nature of contemporary policy-making between governments and the actors who are most prominent in this process. A particularly important dimension of this debate concerns the role and power of 'knowledge-based' policy actors who frame and shape the ideas that inform decision-making. Advocates of the epistemic communities model, outlined in Chapter 5, claim that it enables empirical study of the role of ideas in policy-making and in generating international cooperation. Before examining these claims, let us first consider a range of viewpoints on the changing nature of international governance and the role of networks and expertise in this process.

A body of literature began to emerge in the late 1990s concerned with the state and 'global civil society', serving to focus attention on the idea of power sharing in the international system.[58] The core of this debate centred upon the now familiar viewpoint that the power of national governments has been dissolved to the extent that governments increasingly share power with business corporations, with international organizations and with burgeoning numbers of NGOs. Mathews (1997: 50) suggests that this sharing of power includes 'political, social, and security roles at the core of sovereignty'. The debate is an important one because it is directly related to the fundamental questions raised at the beginning of this work: if power *is* in some way more diffused throughout the international system, how does this affect attempts to resolve some of the most intractable of international problems? To answer this question it is first necessary to establish some broad dimensions regarding the nature and extent of this diffusion. This perspective is an important orientation device for detailed empirical work in relation to specific problems or issue areas. Implicit in such a process is a search to uncover the extent to which state power – or, in a more direct empirically observable sense, governmental power – has been modified, constrained or, alternatively, concentrated. Let us now consider some perspectives.

A new transgovernmental order?

Slaughter (1997) offers a broad summary of the debate about the changing nature of 'state power' by breaking it down into liberal internationalists who see a need for international rules and institutions to solve states' problems and 'new medievalists' who proclaim the end of the nation-state. She contends that neither vision accurately reflects the contemporary world, putting forward her own argument, centred on the contention that 'The state is not disappearing, it is disaggregating into its separate, functionally distinct parts. These parts – courts, regulatory agencies, executives, even legislatures – are networking with their counterparts abroad, creating a dense web of relations that constitutes a new, transgovernmental order' (p. 184). This view positions networks as the central dynamic element in this 'new transgovernmental order'. However, unlike earlier work by Jacobson (1984), which saw international organizations as the main catalyst for networks to develop, Slaughter posits a central and resurgent role for the state – or at least some of its component elements – in fostering and providing structure to the relationships and conditions around which networks are formed. Picciotto (1996: 1036) observes that the phenomenon of networking is 'somewhat inherent' in the system of liberal internationalism. He also notes (1996: 1036) that as evidence grows of international institutions and governance arrangements cutting across states in a wide variety of issue areas, and the involvement of 'all kinds of private and public actors: social activists, scientific experts, professionals, academics, business managers, and various public officials' in this process, those from a neo-liberal perspective have begun to argue that 'these groupings and interactions begin to create a global policy arena in which issues are increasingly resolved free from the refraction of the state and national interest prism' (p. 1036).

However, Picciotto is rightly sceptical of the accuracy of this characterization, viewing it as a far more conflictual and problematic process in practice. What is not in dispute, however, is that a significant growth in the amount of transnational interaction has occurred in the globalized era. This raises two points: (1) by what method(s) can such a process be critically appraised? and (2) what are the dynamics that drive it?

Slaughter cites 'today's international problems' as both the creative and sustaining force behind the rash of new transnational interactions.[59] She recognizes, however, that it was as long ago as the 1970s when Robert Keohane and Joseph Nye first traced the emergence of transgovernmentalism but argues that in the late 1990s this had 'rapidly become the most widespread and effective mode of international governance' (Slaughter, 1997: 185). Slaughter provides a highly normative perspective, reflecting an implicit faith in governmental accountability and in the ability of the state to act as 'protector' of the interests of its citizens, typified by her generalized claim that judges are building a 'global community of law' independent of political influence. Even more problematic, however, is her analysis of interaction between national regulators; what she terms the 'densest area of transgovernmental activity'. She characterizes this interaction as: 'Bureaucrats charged with the administration of antitrust policy, securities regulation, environmental policy, criminal law enforcement, banking and insurance supervision – in short, all the agents of the modern regulatory state – regularly collaborate with their foreign counterparts' (p. 189). While this general statement can be supported empirically, cooperation takes a variety of different forms. Cooperation may be *ad hoc* or informal in nature (compare the FATF and Dublin Group for example) or of a formal nature, leading directly to the creation of bilateral or multilateral agreements. Agreements may vary from the most formal (such as mutual legal assistance treaties) to looser forms of cooperation, such as the memorandum of understanding (MOU), termed 'the preferred instrument of cooperation' by Slaughter. She notes that MOUs are not treaties, and do not as a rule involve the executive or legislature in negotiation, deliberation, or signature, but 'Rather, they are good-faith agreements, affirming ties between regulatory agencies based on their like-minded commitment to getting results' (p. 190). This analysis contains a normative construction of the linkage between the state, its agents and the agents of other states. Slaughter goes on to say, 'Transgovernmental networks often promulgate their own rules, but the purpose of those rules is to enhance the enforcement of national law' (p. 191). It is also claimed that transgovernmental regulation 'produces rules concerning issues that each nation already regulates within its borders: crime, securities fraud, pollution, [and] tax evasion' (p. 191). This seems to ignore the facts that in many cases the main principles underpinning these rules have been established through *international* interaction and that the pressure to enforce (and reinforce) them has been legitimized and strengthened through such a process over time. Slaughter suggests that national regulators form networks internationally, cooperating on the operational aspects of policy where required, which is – presumably – how they are able to promulgate what Slaughter terms 'their own' rules. The notion of ownership is a strange one here, especially when we are told that regulators also work on the creation of new or revised legislative measures and site their activities predominantly within and around existing institutions. However, since the principle that underpins the activities of regulators may have been developed and legitimized over time by international action, regulators thus operate within a constrained set of normative decision-making parameters. What of the accountability of transgovernmental regulation? This is a particularly important matter if the issue that is being discussed on a transgovernmental basis involves rules that have a direct impact at a national level with implications, say, for civil liberties. The wider impact on 'locking-in' a normative way of addressing a given problem is more difficult to assess, and not even considered by analyses that view bureaucratic action as essentially a functional–technocratic process rather than a politicized process (varying across issue areas).

Meetings between political leaders (that is, heads of state and government ministers) increasingly define international 'problem agendas' when they meet at international summits or under the auspices of international organizations. This frequently creates the basis for new regulatory measures backed by regulatory functions relating to implementation, monitoring and evaluation. In practice, this has fostered a demand for increased specialization and expertise on the part of those charged with 'getting results' (civil servants, practitioners and anyone who is drawn into the process on the basis that they are considered to have authoritative knowledge). This can be observed across a very broad range of activities where the state has traditionally exercised control at national level. However, there is an important distinction between issues directly associated with state security – generally involving law enforcement agencies of one form or another – and those that relate to, say, trade or the environment. Matters involving state security have a long tradition of secretive policy-making at national level, legitimizing a more limited form of scrutiny when the same problems are discussed at intergovernmental level: once a problem is labelled 'security' it is extremely difficult to re-cast it in any other sense.[60] A strong bureaucratic dynamic is thereby created in which participants are involved in such a complex process that they are unable to see the end result of their involvement, focusing only on their own link in the 'chain'. The globalized era has unquestionably increased the opportunities to reinforce this dynamic both within and across national boundaries. 'Getting results' may well mean more to those involved in relation to their own bureaucratic position than any sense of enhancing national laws.

Slaughter's notion that regulators are 'like-minded' raises a series of questions as to what might be the basis for such cognitive agreement. In a patently hierarchical world system, the idea that regulators from, say, Bolivia, would view the kind of issues that Slaughter lists as the key contemporary problems in the same way as their counterparts from the United States seems both fanciful and misrepresentative of contemporary structural power relations. Of course, if we think only of AICs then it is more reasonable to surmise that regulators from different national jurisdictions may have 'common ground'. Perhaps certain issues may invoke more 'like-mindedness' than others? This raises some important questions about why regulators might be 'like-minded' in certain cases and not in others. This naturally leads toward enquiry about the actual 'practitioners'; those whose work places them at the forefront of making, negotiating, implementing and monitoring policy. Mathews (1997) characterizes these actors in the following all-encompassing statement:

> Behind each new agreement are scientists and lawyers who worked on it, diplomats who negotiated it, and NGOs that back it, most of them committed for the long haul. The new constituency also includes a burgeoning, influential class of international civil servants responsible for implementing, monitoring and enforcing this enormous new body of law. (p. 59)

Relatively few international issues are predominantly scientific in character, hence we may think of this reference as hinting at the way that international regulation is often portrayed as an essentially technocratic process led by experts.[61] Almost certainly unintentionally, the 'new constituency' image presented here by Mathews strongly evokes the contemporary European Union. Chapter 6 outlines the institutional machinery and legal instruments that relate to EU drug enforcement policy, providing a basis on which 15 states are prepared to enact and abide by collectively agreed regulation.

To understand policy-making on transnational problems, two things must be assessed: first, the mechanisms through which new rules and laws are established and, second, the basis of participant agendas. Only then can it be asked why might transgovernmental networks cohere and generate consensus around certain issues and not others? Most vital of all: what is the degree and nature of 'independence' possessed by participant actors? There is thus a need for:

1 a systematic method through which to direct empirical work
2 a methodology focused on uncovering normative processes.

Despite the largely uncritical stance of the descriptive accounts assessed above they do serve to shed light on the contemporary dynamics that are shaping international policy and focus attention on the issue of governance. The globalized era has also seen the emergence of some new types of international agreement. Let us now consider these tools of governance and consider how this is related to state authority.

International soft law

Since the 1970s, the whole concept and perception of international problem-solving has been transformed, although the primary means of expressing agreement – the international treaty – has remained the most potent symbol of consensus. However, alongside this has come a proliferation in so-called international 'soft law'. Soft law takes a wide variety of forms: from guidelines, recommended practices, and non-binding resolutions through to memorandums of understanding. Soft law has become one of the most important methods of securing practical cooperation between governments and international institutions. One of the main attractions of soft law is the speed with which agreement can generally be reached when compared with international treaties, largely because formal ratification machinery is not normally required. In other words, the time-consuming process of formal approval and oversight by national legislatures is avoided.[62] This is partly a reflection of the speed of change associated with the globalized era and how this has created political pressures to demonstrate that 'countermeasures' are put in place as quickly as possible so as not to be redundant by the time they come into effect. This point was raised in Chapter 3 with regard to international drug control, where international conventions have consistently lagged behind market trends and behaviour.

The growth of soft law also returns us to the fact that in certain issue areas there is already a comprehensive set of international legislation defining the broad parameters of action (that is, international norms). International drug prohibition is perhaps the foremost example of this situation. In effect, international soft law adds to the layers of conformity that exist around an issue. It also provides the basis for a more autonomous role for particular organs of the state in certain policy or issue areas. Consider the case of memorandums of understanding. An MOU is an agreement that may be intergovernmental, may exist between governments and agencies (such as customs and police, for example) or may be signed between governments or agencies and commercial organizations (airlines or haulage companies, for example). An MOU normally relates to a commitment to collaborate in a specific field but may cover a very broad range of activities. In the case of cooperation involving anti-drug trafficking measures, an MOU may have the effect of legitimizing the principle of transnational exchange of the kind of information that has traditionally been regarded as under the strict control of national states and the supposed national safeguards that are associated with this (that is, a clear chain of democratic accountability). On a more symbolic level, MOUs reinforce the machinery of problem solving in ways that have the effect of building bureaucratic power and inertia around a normative 'solution framework'. By binding specific national agencies – and the individuals who work in them – with their equivalents in other countries (police and customs officials, for example) in a shared problem-solving approach, an incentive is also created for the development of mutual reinforcement of mission, both at an individual and organizational level. In short, delegating responsibility for cooperation to specific agencies adds to the incentive to maintain the status quo as it links their ongoing role and status more closely with a specific policy approach.

Transgovernmental *regulation*, in Slaughter's view, results simply in the nationalization of international law. However, by suggesting that outcomes are determined by what are termed the 'makers and enforcers of rules' (simply 'national leaders' in her analysis) she indicates a normative faith in expert systems to provide neutral, objective advice: the classic image of knowledge speaking truth to power. Slaughter (1997) characterizes the liberal internationalist response to the perception that the power of national regulators to implement national regulations within national boundaries has declined simply as pressure for building a larger international apparatus. She states that 'Globalization leads to internationalization, or the transfer of regulatory authority from the national level to an international institution' (p. 192). This rather simplistic analysis fails to recognize the fragmented nature of the response – by powerful AICs – to relative loss of sovereign control in certain domains. She goes on to suggest that 'Transgovernmental initiatives are a compromise that could command bipartisan support. Regulatory loopholes caused by global forces require a coordinated response beyond the reach of any one country' (p. 193). She believes that this need not come from building more international institutions, but 'can be achieved through transgovernmental cooperation involving the same officials who make and implement policy at the national level' (p. 193). This is a curious concept, striking for the fact that it again fails to recognize the politicized nature of governmental decision-making. The idea that this 'technocratization' is a neutral process in which national officials simply translate national strategies into international agreements is both deeply normative and a fundamental misreading of the modern liberal democratic state. Transgovernmentalism is clearly a formal expression of state power, but it does none the less reveal a looser notion of the idea that the state, and agents of the state act within rigidly defined and proscribed boundaries. It also directs attention toward the role of 'knowledge brokers' who carry out functions relating to definition, implementation and monitoring of transnational policy.

International soft law is an illustration of how networking between national regulators has now – in certain policy domains – become transgovernmental in character on a routine basis. This marks a shift away from the diplomatic model of interaction that has characterized intergovernmental relations within international organizations: interaction increasingly involves direct contact between functional experts and civil servants with defined areas of competence (generally a narrow field within a set of fields covered by a ministry for example). While experts may have 'technical' competence, this is inevitably applied in the context of a socially constructed policy environment. This means that where a process of technocratization has been facilitated (and legitimized), political decision-makers have in effect empowered particular forms of socially constructed knowledge. This clearly has the effect of 'narrowing' a policy domain and will favour a dominant cognitive interpretation of a given problem. If this is so, and can be assessed empirically, we need to find a way of understanding the implications of this development, and what it reveals about the modern state and about knowledge and power in this context.

Slaughter (1997: 193) cites an initiative by the US State Department launched in 1991 and reinvigorated in 1995 as a practical example of transgovernmentalism: the New Transatlantic Agenda. The initiative is an agreement that structures the relationship between the US and the EU, 'fostering cooperation in areas ranging from opening markets to fighting terrorism, drug trafficking and infectious disease'. For Slaughter, this example demonstrates the 'bipartisan appeal' of transgovernmentalism, but – viewed critically – the very broadness of the initiative implies a normative valuation that the issues concerned are non-contentious at the national level. One aspect of the Transatlantic Agenda entails a linkage between the FBI (a US federal agency) and Europol (an executive agency of the 15 EU member states) on the sharing of intelligence data.[63] Putting aside questions relating to the accountability of Europol (developed later in this work) the agreement appears – in a carefully selective fashion – to facilitate a significant degree of autonomy to law enforcement agencies in setting and implementing policy. Such a development thus relies heavily on the quality of systems of political accountability, but Slaughter fails to recognize an obvious deficiency with the Transatlantic Agenda in this respect. This dimension is crucial to understanding the real significance of transgovernmental relations: a depoliticization of 'problem' areas and their projection as a technocratic exercise, utilizing 'experts' to carry out neutral, value-free actions. In this way, states are able to imply that politicized issues are now 'solvable' *only* by increased use of authority and control measures.

Why a different theoretical perspective is needed

A large part of this chapter has indicated that transgovernmental policy-making networks are a growing feature of international cooperation, especially between AICs. This is generally presented as a pragmatic response to transnational problems, but such a view fails to identify the normative links to the modern state and the ability of the state to exercise authority and control. To explore this oversight, a theoretical lens is required in order to illuminate empirical work on where power lies and how that power is exercised.

It has been suggested that the 'knowledge brokers' to whom governments turn for policy advice (including the perceived need to reduce uncertainty) play a pivotal role in framing and shaping policy development and outcomes. If a relatively discrete group or network of actors can be shown to exert significant influence over public policy at a multilateral level then this raises a series of questions about the role and power of such a group. More specifically, in the context of this book, the challenge is to evaluate the issue of drug enforcement policy between EU member states in order to assess the technocratization of transnational policy development in this area, and to explore the question of how this may be related to the challenge to state sovereignty embodied in more extensive transnational forces (including transnational problems). Finally, what are the political implications of this process? In order to explore these questions, a methodological approach is required that allows both the structural and cognitive dimensions of power to be examined. The complexity of intensified regional and 'global' interconnection poses a particularly acute theoretical challenge. International relations theory has generally focused on macro-level changes rather than the micro-level where the role of particular types of policy actor or the role of knowledge in this process can be considered. This book examines the epistemic communities hypothesis, which works on the premise that control over knowledge and information is an important dimension of power. The hypothesis focuses on the role of networks of 'professionals' with recognized expertise and competence to provide policy-relevant advice to political decision-makers and stresses the role of a shared normative framework in binding such groups together, allowing exploration of the issues identified in the previous section. The next chapter provides a critical account of the epistemic communities hypothesis.

5
Epistemic Communities

In order to try and explain the policy process that is associated with the development of drug enforcement policies in Europe we must be able to identify the main actors and the political mechanisms that have shaped this policy process. We may need to do this over a considerable time period, examining what appear to be 'formative' phases in more detail. Richardson (2001: 5) suggests that a dominant 'model' for analysing the policy process in Western Europe has emerged: the 'so-called policy community/policy network model'. He points out that the primary feature of this approach is that it is 'actor-based', and tends toward an interest-based analysis of the policy process. Closely related concepts from public policy analysis (notably the work of Sabatier on advocacy coalitions, and Kingdon on 'policy streams') also take an actor-based approach but attempt to integrate this with analysis of the role of ideas as well as interests.[64] In noting the increasing permeability of the EU's policy agenda to extra-territorial influences – from other AICs, IGOs and via EU participation in global regulatory agencies – Richardson (2001) points out that

> The EU is not only a form of 'supranational' system of policy-making in its own right; it is also part of a higher level of supranational policy-making beyond the regional level. Such complex policy-making arrangements privilege the role of experts and technocrats who are increasingly transnational in their focus and activities. (p. 5)

The most important characteristic of experts and technocrats is their possession of specialized knowledge in relation to a particular domain. Richardson highlights the importance of understanding the role of actors whose attributes are principally knowledge based, particularly during what he terms the agenda-setting phase of policy development. In his examination of the concept of technocracy with regard to the EU, Radaelli (1999: 47) stresses the role of technocratic theory in outlining 'certain areas of policy-making where experts stabilize the policy-making process by providing assumptions, rules and models'. He goes on to say that 'if an issue becomes politicized yet remains uncertain ... one should expect a different political role of experts' (ibid: 47). As a result of these views both Radaelli and Richardson give consideration to a concept that examines the role of 'networks' of experts: the epistemic communities model.

The epistemic communities model has been most closely associated with the work of Peter Haas, who has developed and applied the concept to the study of international policy coordination.[65] His empirically grounded work *Saving The Mediterranean* (1990) examined the influence of knowledge held by expert actors operating in networks with regard to efforts to coordinate marine pollution control practices by Mediterranean countries. Haas subsequently edited a Special Edition of the journal *International Organization* (Haas, 1992c) in which a more developed conceptual framework was outlined. This chapter provides a critical exposition of the concept so that it can be used to examine the influence of knowledge-based actors in relation to the empirical material considered in Part II of this book. One of the primary aims of this chapter is to correct an omission apparent in many applications of the epistemic communities concept, that is, a failure to examine the mode of social science enquiry fostered by the model.

Most applications of the model have focused on areas where pluralistic bargaining is, nominally at least, the characteristic mode of policy development. Radaelli claims that the utility of the epistemic communities model is highest in cases where a policy process shows high uncertainty and high political saliency. His own empirical examples cover EU policy-making on European Monetary Union (EMU), taxation policy, and policy on ownership of media organizations. He concluded that epistemic communities had been influential in the design of the EMU and in some aspects of tax policy. Similarly, McGowan (2001) has applied the concept to European competition policy, concluding that an 'epistemic community' of economists and lawyers played an influential role in policy development.

Radaelli (1999) is entirely correct in describing the European Commission as 'the main initiator of policy in the EU' (p. 44). Equally, most accounts tend to depict EU policy-making as a process in which a series of coalitions vie for power. Whilst both of these descriptions capture the essential features of the policy environment they do not apply in all of the policy-making areas with which the EU is concerned. Chapter 6 contains an overview of EU institutional structures and powers relating to the policy field addressed in this book, highlighting that member states – not the European Commission – closely control the right to initiate policy in this area.

The epistemic communities approach has been applied in a wide range of empirical settings, from a number of environmental policy arenas through to nuclear arms control and trade in services as well as the EU examples noted above. In each case, authors have been primarily concerned with why *particular* policies emerge at *particular* times. Richardson (2001: 18) contends that understanding the stage of the policy process that relates to the emergence of problems, issues and policy proposals is problematic for most available models of the EU policy process. However, he finds that the epistemic communities concept offers real potential insight for analysis of this stage. Let us now consider the epistemic communities concept in more depth.

Definition of an epistemic community

The concept of epistemic communities is concerned with the role played by networks of what Haas (1992b) terms 'knowledge-based experts': 'In articulating the cause-and-effect relationships of complex problems, helping states identify their interests, framing the issues for collective debate, proposing specific policies, and identifying salient points for negotiation' (p. 2).

The concept is primarily concerned with the coordination of international policy and the understanding and representation of complex problems that have transnational dimensions. Haas defines an epistemic community as follows:

A network of professionals with recognized expertise and competence in a particular domain and an authoritative claim to policy-relevant knowledge within that domain or issue-area. Although an epistemic community may consist of professionals from a variety of disciplines and backgrounds, they have (1) a shared set of normative and principled beliefs, which provide a value-based rationale for the social action of community members; (2) shared causal beliefs, which are derived from their analysis of practices leading or contributing to a central set of problems in their domain and which then serve as the basis for elucidating the multiple linkages between possible policy actions and desired outcomes; (3) shared notions of validity – that is, intersubjective, internally defined criteria for weighing and validating knowledge in the domain of their expertise; and (4) a common policy enterprise – that is, a set of common practices associated with a set of problems to which their professional competence is directed, presumably out of the conviction that human welfare will be enhanced as a consequence. (p. 3)

The definition is founded on the premise that control over knowledge and information is an important dimension of power, and that the diffusion of new ideas and information can generate 'new' patterns of behaviour and thereby determine the course of international policy coordination. The suggestion here is that an epistemic community is capable of developing some form of 'vision' concerning a particular issue *before* introducing it into the political policy arena. Haas leaves no ambiguity about who is doing the influencing and who is being influenced here: 'Members of transnational epistemic communities can influence state interests either by directly identifying them for decision-makers or by illuminating the salient dimensions of an issue from which the decision-makers may then deduce their interests' (p. 4).

Let us move now to questions of how and why an epistemic community may emerge.

Why epistemic communities emerge

A dramatic expansion of the tasks associated with governance has brought a concomitant rise in bureaucratic regulation and demands for specialist expertise.[66] Haas (1992b) argues that 'the expansion and professionalization of bureaucracies and the growing technical nature of problems have fostered an increase in the deference paid to technical expertise and, in particular, to that of scientists' (p. 11). This reflects a move to a more instrumentalist view of politics in which incremental, piecemeal changes stem – and are pivotal upon – the actions of various expert groups in society.[67] These developments do not automatically generate a situation whereby more consensus in policy-making is likely, however; they may conceivably support the opposite in fact. Simply because 'experts' operate within the bureaucracy does not necessarily give them any degree of power over and above more overtly political decisions of an allocative nature resting with decision-makers: in short, decision-makers can choose to override or simply ignore technical advice where it conflicts with other interests or values. Haas concedes this, but argues that the increasing uncertainties of modern international governance 'have led policymakers to turn to new and different channels of advice, often with the result that international policy coordination is enhanced' (p. 12). This statement contains a number of implicit assumptions; that:

1 epistemic communities offer policy-makers an 'alternative' and objective/neutral source of advice and knowledge; that is, in some sense external to state structures and interests
2 international policy coordination is based primarily on consensual rather than coercive relations
3 the outcomes are often qualitatively 'better' than they otherwise would have been.

If specialist advice proffers an *opinion* that suggests an impending shock (an environmental disaster for example) – particularly if a public audience simultaneously takes up that opinion – then a state of uncertainty is generated, creating potential doubt in the minds of political decision-makers. The politicized nature of such advice is thus assured: decision-makers must ultimately assess the political consequences of advice (or, more pertinently, the consequences of *not* acting on particular advice). Uncertainty on the part of decision-makers is argued to be the main 'germination' factor behind the emergence of epistemic communities. They emerge to fill an 'ideas vacuum' in issue areas where existing cause-and-effect relationships may either be unknown, unclear or (claimed to be) incorrect. Epistemic community members offer explanations to decision-makers about the *implications* of different courses of action. A decision has to be made whether to accept, or to ignore 'advice'. A number of important points are raised here in relation to the notion of causation employed by Haas, worthy of more in-depth analysis.

Questions of causation

In the definition of an epistemic community (Haas, 1992b) it is stated that community members share causal beliefs derived from their analysis of practices leading or contributing to a central set of problems in their domain. This analysis then informs their understanding of the possible links between policy actions and desired outcomes. However, this statement does not reveal the underlying concept of causation that underpins the epistemic communities concept and which plays an

important role in determining how the model represents social phenomena and the actions of members of an epistemic community.

Haas avoids simplistic notions of scientific objectivity but seems to
imply that the shared causal understandings of epistemic communities
stem from some form of independent epistemological position held in
common by members.[68] Keat and Urry (1982: 27) help us to understand
the implications of this point in their assessment of the main difficulty
for positivist accounts of scientific explanation. They suggest this arises
from 'the existence of logical arguments which, though satisfying
the specified conditions, enable us only to predict, and not to explain, the
occurrence of particular events'.[69] Furthermore, they argue that this
approach may lead to situations where providing grounds for expecting
an event to occur is confused with giving a causal explanation. The positivist analysis of scientific explanation is based upon Hume's view of
causation as a kind of 'regularity theory'; an innately forward-looking
model that presupposes the recurrence of an event. If such a concept of
causation is applied in a social context, then a deeply conservative
notion is introduced, that is, because an event happens repeatedly then
it is taken as providing *evidence of causation*.

Of course, an 'epistemic community' is entirely free to suggest any
'causal' ideas that it wishes. However, at some point, its members must
be cognizant of *pre-existing* social and political conditions in framing
those ideas. This is particularly true for policy areas that do not involve
what we might call 'pure' science but draw upon technical experts from
specific professions. In evaluating the epistemic communities model
and its depiction of causation, it is important to consider the effects of
cognitive processes that essentially treat social phenomena as if they
were natural objects; that is to say, that they are broadly unchanging
both in terms of a causal chain of events and the relationship between
causal factors. If the influence of an epistemic community is based upon
its effective association of a set of causal beliefs then it is important that
the underlying basis of those beliefs is questioned. Why are the beliefs
held? An epistemic community *could* be successful precisely because its
causal analysis does not challenge certain social or political values; that
is, its success is based not upon the radical 'newness' of its 'causal' ideas
but on their conservatism (in taking social relations as emerging out
of an established and 'given' pattern of causal factors). This contrasts
with the image of an epistemic community working from some kind of
'neutral' epistemological position.

The work of Keat and Urry stimulates discussion of the nexus between
'science' and social processes and is particularly relevant to the issue of

how epistemic community members acquire their cognitive authority and the related question of whether this arises primarily through social processes or not. We thus need to focus on the differences between 'professional' authorities or experts in specific issue areas, and to ask how this contributes to the effectiveness (that is, ultimately, political influence) of an epistemic community. What is it about the causal beliefs of an epistemic community that make them salient to political decision-makers? Are these beliefs premised upon challenge to existing social and political processes or do they regard those processes as a 'fixed' set of causal criteria that will generate a 'fixed' set of possible outcomes (implicitly generating a conservative approach)? In terms of causation, the attribution of technical status to phenomena not traditionally conceived of as 'scientific' regularizes the relationships involved to the extent that they become more predictable. Hence, as professional groups increasingly acquire a more 'technical' role, this favours a *de facto* prioritization of prediction over explanation. The deep and enduring influence of positivism appears far stronger, viewed from this perspective.[70] Keat and Urry (1982: 227) advocate social theory that involves both interpretive and explanatory understanding but unifies them 'in the analysis of structural relations, and in the way in which these affect, and are affected by, the subjective meanings of human agents'. This offers a basis through which these deeper questions can be illuminated and through which the epistemic communities approach may also be judged.

What is unique about an epistemic community?

Why do decision-makers turn to an epistemic community for advice rather than other sources of knowledge? Haas (1992b: 15) suggests that there are cases where decision-makers will seek advice to gain information that will justify or legitimate policy that they wish to pursue for political ends. He does not explicitly acknowledge the possibility that epistemic community members may offer and tailor advice in ways that make it congruent with the preferences of decision-makers. This could only be assessed on a case-by-case basis, naturally, but it is important at least to recognize the possibility. Such a view runs counter to the idea that community members are pure 'ideas brokers', suggesting that they are both constrained by, and reflexively aware of political and social conditions.

In 'political ends' cases, Haas suggests that the role of the epistemic community may be confined to detailed submissions on policy detail, setting out potential conflicts of interest and then 'building coalitions in support of the policy' (Haas, 1992b: 15). This does seem to acknowledge that politicization is a *strategic* element of the process, actively employed by advice-providers as well as advice-seekers. Haas in fact acknowledges that 'epistemic communities called in for political reasons may succeed in imposing their views and moving toward goals other than those initially envisioned by the decision-makers' (Haas, 1992b: 16). In what he vaguely terms 'less political' instances, Haas envisages a broader role for epistemic communities, extending to introducing policy alternatives, selecting them and building national and international coalitions in support of them. The power here lies in the capacity of an epistemic community to limit the range of alternatives addressed, which for Haas stems from their *causal* understanding of the problems to be addressed. This boundary-drawing effect clearly has important implications for policy-making. The key question here is *why* are some cases 'less political'? Haas fails to address the significant potential obstacles to the implementation of ideas. Policy-related ideas are considered within a prevailing social and political context, thus forcing evaluation of their impact on existing institutions, interests and prevailing power structures. Why is it that certain groups are more likely than others to gain credence for their viewpoint at a certain point in time (that is, credence for their analysis of cause-and-effect relationships)?

In terms of membership, Haas (1992b) suggest that epistemic communities

> need not be made up of natural scientists; they can consist of social scientists or individuals from any discipline or profession who have a sufficiently strong claim to a body of knowledge that is valued by society. Nor need an epistemic community's causal beliefs and notions of validity be based on the methodology employed in the natural sciences; they can originate from shared knowledge about the nature of social or other processes, based on analytic methods or techniques deemed appropriate to the disciplines or professions they pursue. (p. 16)

It is suggested that professional training, prestige, and reputation for expertise in an 'area highly valued by society or elite decision-makers' affords members of an epistemic community 'access to the political system and legitimize[s] or authorize[s] their activities' (Haas, 1992b: 17). The notion of an area highly valued by society is itself a normative concept, of course. The whole idea of a body of knowledge 'valued by society' is a curious one, for it appears to assume that this qualifies as something that states and citizens identify with, when in practice there are often manifest conflicts between things valued by society and actions taken 'on behalf of society' by state officials. Equally, expertise highly valued by elite decision-makers may favour outcomes that conflict with the interests of society, or certain parts of society. Policing agencies are a good example. While their primary function is to maintain order, can we say that society as a whole values this? The interests of society are clearly served by being protected, but not if agencies are (politically) allowed to use practices that infringe on individual rights.

For Haas, the 'primary social power resource' of an epistemic community stems from its claim to knowledge supported by tests of validity, which, in conjunction with 'professional pedigree', sets community members apart from other social groups. This is the crucial point in distinguishing an epistemic community: there are significant barriers to entry to the community that may also diminish the relative status of other actors or groups in given policy debates. The more fundamental distinguishing features stem from 'the combination of having a shared set of causal and principled (analytic and normative) beliefs, a consensual knowledge base, and a common policy enterprise (common interests)' (Haas, 1992b: 18). As for 'professions and disciplines', Haas suggests that 'although members of a given profession may share a set of causal approaches or orientations and have a consensual knowledge base, they lack the shared normative commitments of an epistemic community' (Haas, 1992b: 19).[71]

It is the set of principled values – and the attachment to them – that marks out epistemic community members from, say, bureaucrats, Haas argues. While community members are pragmatically concerned with administrative empowerment they are differentiated according to Haas because 'bureaucratic bodies operate largely to preserve their missions and budgets, whereas epistemic communities apply their causal knowledge to a policy enterprise subject to their normative objectives' (Haas, 1992b: 19).

Uncertainty, interpretation and institutionalization

Haas suggests that whether decision-makers turn to an epistemic community depends on the level of uncertainty about an issue area: 'Failed policies, crises, and unanticipated events that call into question their understanding of an issue-area are likely to precipitate searches for new information, as are the increasing complexity and technical nature of problems' (Haas, 1992b: 29). Haas would probably argue that he accounts for the demand for epistemic advice, but the key point here is that there is generally a pre-existing articulation of reality in respect of a given issue area and established practitioners (or knowledge brokers) associated with this. An epistemic community could equally draw strength from pre-existing associations and positions within, say, a bureaucratic organization. Epistemic consensus may be as much about accepting certain fundamental issues as effectively given, and working towards finding new ways of achieving the same goals, albeit based on applying new or modified causal beliefs to (changed) contemporary circumstances.

Decision-making at the national level is characterized by a tendency for discussion, agenda setting and policy formulation to take place in small groups outside of formal bureaucratic channels: interest groups, advocacy coalitions, issue networks or policy networks. The ability to exercise 'leverage' over policy choices may arise from participation in think tanks, regulatory agencies or governmental policy research bodies. What the epistemic communities literature fails to explain is the process by which decision-makers take up and act upon specialist advice. What is clear, however, is that this process takes place in the context of existing social, political and economic structures.

It is now widely recognized that transgovernmental and transnational channels afford significant opportunities for 'political alliances' to be built and information regarding technical issues to be 'transmitted between government officials, international secretariats, nongovernmental bodies, and nongovernmental actors, including bodies of professional scientists' (Haas, 1992b: 32). However, Haas sees this approach as saying little about the outcomes that are likely to be generated other than producing short-term alliances. He is right to say that assertions of 'functional' independence reveals nothing about the origin of the interests of those involved in, say, transgovernmental alliances. He asks, 'Do their interests stem from their common bureaucratic roles within their own governments, or are they based on pre-existing beliefs and interests which they brought to their jobs and which are likely to be pursued even after they leave their current posts?' (Haas, 1992b: 32). He argues that it is *shared causal beliefs* that introduce the missing ingredient capable of transcending and joining together disparate elements. Again, empirical analysis is the only way to assess such beliefs on a case-by-case basis.

Applying the epistemic communities model

Haas argues that the epistemic communities approach offers a way of specifying the factors that lead knowledge-based groups to cohere and the mechanisms by which they gain and retain influence in the policy-making process. Haas claims that the research techniques to identify an epistemic community are 'straightforward but painstaking', and involve:

> identifying community membership, determining the community members' principled and causal beliefs, tracing their activities and demonstrating their influence on decision-makers at various points in time, identifying alternative credible outcomes that were foreclosed as a result of their influence, and exploring alternative explanations for the actions of decision-makers. (Haas, 1992b: 34)

These techniques may be straightforward but they raise some practical problems: identification and isolation of principled (normative) and causal beliefs is not a process that can be easily measured. The methodological criteria provided by Haas represent an essentially sound guide for empirical research, but they lack guidance on how to ascertain at what point conditions of uncertainty generate demands for advice over and above 'normal' levels of uncertainty present in any complex interaction? The idea of shock thus becomes a relative term: a shock only has the power to transform if decision-makers can be persuaded of the implications of an event. If an epistemic community advocates a 'new' or revised set of causal and principled beliefs, then why are those beliefs necessarily challenging deeper pre-existing beliefs? Conceivably they could reinforce or reinterpret them. This is something that must be taken into consideration when applying the model.

Haas asserts that uncertainty, interpretation and institutionalization are the main dynamics underpinning the emergence of epistemic communities. Allied to this is the proposition that epistemic communities develop and cohere around shared causal understandings, yet Haas fails to substantiate and differentiate basic questions concerning causation. In practice transnational links are also far more contingent and institutionally grounded than the model implies (once again, detailed empirical research is the only method of assessing the factors that affect this). In failing to question the nature of different types of causation the theory risks reinforcing normative ideas about political action itself. In positing a scenario through which expert knowledge offers a rational, objective source of influence over political decision-making, two possibilities must be considered; that:

1 this reinforces the idea of a model of social life that hinges upon processes of verification or falsification; processes that rest in the hands of 'experts' whose principal task is to make the management of international problems more predictable

2   critical processes based upon explanation are marginalized and de-legitimized through increased emphasis on rational, 'scientific' or 'professional' logic.

This has important implications for the nature of politics that results: on one hand it suggests an increasing shift of power towards elite, technocratic groups whose power stems from knowledge in a given domain; and on the other a displacement away from participatory, democratically grounded forms of (national) political life to transnational networking. The participants in this networking can only be identified on a case-by-case basis regarding specific international issues, but Haas is adamant that an epistemic community is distinguishable from, say, a coalition of bureaucrats or an interest group due to its association with causal and principled (analytic and normative) beliefs. The question here is about structure and agency. Loyalties independent of existing institutions are ascribed to one group (epistemic communities) while 'institutional' loyalties are assumed to shape the actions of another (bureaucrats, regulators and so on). The latter depiction fits the largely faceless conception of the modern state projected in much international relations literature. However, increased amounts of transnational networking by state officials and their participation in fora through which expert groups engage with policy-making structures (as described in Chapter 4) strongly suggest a more fragmented form of interaction. This raises the following questions:

1   Does the process of interaction through which – Haas implies – epistemic communities interact with state officials intrinsically generate or involve processes of mutual legitimization?
2   Do international networks reflect supra- or sub-state mechanisms within which cognitive authority and a basis for agreement arise primarily out of socially based processes?

Haas suggests that epistemic communities are not part of a transgovernmental and international bureaucratic elite (in which states retain formal decision-making power); they are somehow autonomous from these structures. The credibility of this position is open to question largely as a result of what is a misrepresentation of 'science' as an institutionally grounded form capable of operating outside of social processes. Once again, the pivotal issue remains the relationship to 'the state'. Haas's statement that an epistemic community can consist of 'social scientists or individuals from any discipline or profession who have a sufficiently strong claim to a body of knowledge that is valued by society' renders this question more problematic. First, it amplifies the problematic use of conceptions of 'science' and, second, it reinforces the suspicion that Haas is seriously downplaying the role of politicization and its link to social processes (such as professional training and culture). Despite these reservations, the epistemic communities perspective stimulates empirical assessment of the mechanics and dynamics of decision-making around international issues. It also focuses on the participants in this process, drawing attention to the role of knowledge in affecting outcomes within the complexities of transnational interaction. The heuristic value of the model will be explored in the remainder of this book. We now move to Part II of the book, which begins with a general introduction to European integration and the issue of drugs.

Part II

The Convergence of European Drug Enforcement Policies

6
Europe and Drugs: An Introduction

This book examines how, and why, the European Union has provided a basis for the coordination and convergence of enforcement based anti-drugs policies in Europe. It is therefore important to have an understanding of the broader institutional framework that has been the fulcrum for policy development over time.[72] In providing an overview of that framework, this chapter follows a conventional path by making an analytical distinction between the pre- and post-Maastricht treaty period, that is, the period before and after 1993 when the Treaty on European Union (TEU) brought the EU into existence. The chapter outlines the contemporary division of the EU into the so-called 'three pillars' of policy-making, highlighting that drug enforcement policy-making is firmly located in the third of these: the field of Justice and Home Affairs (JHA).

The first section traces the origins and course of European integration, describing the broad context out of which policies relating to the drugs issue have emerged. A more specific assessment of the emergence of illegal drugs as a European issue is provided, placed in the context of a general expansion in the EU's policy portfolio evident since the mid 1980s. The final section sketches the basis of the current EU policy environment based on the provisions of the Maastricht and Amsterdam treaties. This chapter thus provides an orientation for the detailed empirical analysis that follows in the subsequent chapters of Part II.

Origins of European integration

What is now the European Union owes its existence to the development of a plan to place the entire French and German coal and steel industry under supranational control, with the aim – in the immediate aftermath of the Second World War – of minimizing the risk of conflict between France and Germany by direct integration of their economies. Based on proposals by Robert Schuman and the ideas of Jean Monnet, the European Coal and Steel Community (ECSC) was formed in 1951 under the Treaty of Paris. The Benelux countries (Belgium, the Netherlands and Luxembourg) and Italy also signed the treaty alongside the two founder members, and it was this same group of six countries that in 1957 signed the Treaty of Rome to form the European Economic Community (EEC). At the same meeting they also signed a treaty establishing a European Atomic Energy Community (or Euratom).[73] At this point there were thus three 'European communities'.

The Paris and Rome treaties were particularly important in laying foundations for member states of the new organizations to integrate specific and core areas of their economic activities as well as agreeing to a certain amount of supranationalism in the decision-making powers of the new communities. In 1967, ten years after the signing of the Treaty of Rome, what is generally termed the Merger Treaty entered force. This treaty, signed in 1965, established a single Council of Ministers and merged the High Authority of the ECSC, the Commission of Euratom and the EEC Commission into one Commission (the 'European Commission'). In practice, this refocusing of institutional arrangements had little impact on the real powers of the Commission, as Nugent (1999) observes: 'from the earliest days of the ECSC, political realities have dictated that the High Authority/Commission must be sensitive to governmental opinions and policies' (p. 38).

On a more general theme, Radaelli suggests that 'the founding fathers of European integration envisioned governance by technocratic consensus' (Radaelli, 1999: 38). From the outset of European integration it is thus possible to discern a 'special position' (as Radaelli puts it) for experts in the making of supranational public policy; the High Authority of the ECSC was made up of 'selected experts' for example. In a perceptive analysis, Radaelli (1999) notes that, 'The Monnet method of integration prefigured a system of *engrenage* whereby networks of interest groups, organized labour and firms affected by European public policy would be gradually involved in the making of public policy' (p. 31).[74]

The Treaty of Paris established four institutions in relation to the ECSC: the High Authority, the Council of Ministers, the Common Assembly, and the Court of Justice. The powers of the High Authority were in fact stronger than those that were subsequently given to its equivalent, the Commission, under the Treaty of Rome (Nugent, 1999). In fact, the Council of Ministers was set up largely to act as a counterweight to the powers of the ECSC High Authority (as a result – according to Nugent – of concern expressed by the Benelux countries that there was no forum for states to counteract possible Franco-German domination of decision-making). Membership of the Council comprised one minister from each member state. The Common Assembly was intended to provide democratic input and oversight of ECSC decision-making, though it was a relatively weak body in its original form. The Court of Justice was established to resolve disputed matters arising between states, between the organs of the Community, and between the states and the organs. Both the Assembly and Court assumed responsibility for all three communities after 1957 (unlike the High Authority and Council of Ministers, which remained separate until the Merger Treaty ten years later). The Assembly renamed itself the European Parliament in 1962. The institutional model outlined here has remained essentially intact and is closely replicated in the structure of the modern EU, albeit in a very different international context and range of activities.

The Treaty of Rome must be understood in a much broader political context, marking a formal commitment to further economic integration in Western Europe against the backdrop of Cold War tensions. The EEC treaty envisaged the creation of a common market that would be a free trade area, but it also made a commitment to ensure not only the free movement of goods between the member states but also the free movement of persons, services and capital. The Treaty established that an appointed Commission would be the principal initiator of policy, having some decision-making powers of its own but with less power than the High Authority had to impose those decisions on member states. The Council of Ministers was specified as the principal decision-making organ. The treaty set out various circumstances in which the Council must take its decisions unanimously and others in which majority and qualified majority voting would be allowed. Looking at the integration process overall, the treaties were highly significant in redefining post-war inter-state relations in Europe 'by laying the foundations for signatory states to integrate specific and core areas of their economic activities and by embodying a degree of supranationalism in the decision-making' (Nugent, 1999: 47).

Illegal drugs as a European issue

The issue of illegal drugs did not have any bearing on either the negotiations or substance of European integration during the principal formative period described above. Speaking from his experience as a senior

French diplomat, Raymond Césaire (1995) records how the issue of drugs first came to be raised in a collective European context: 'Drugs were not mentioned in the Treaty of Rome. They were mentioned for the first time in 1969 in a letter by President Pompidou [of France] to his five EC colleagues of the time. He was concerned particularly with the health and social aspects of the problem' (p. 353). Perceptions among political elites about the drugs problem at the time of the Pompidou letter – 12 years after the Treaty of Rome – must be considered. Despite the emergence of new kinds of drugs and growing evidence of an evolving mass market in North America and Western Europe from the 1960s, national governments clearly believed that domestic-level enforcement measures – focused on interdiction at national borders – were both sufficient and appropriate trafficking control mechanisms (with perhaps occasional recourse to Interpol). The notion that the EEC would be an important vehicle for cooperation on matters affecting 'domestic' security would have been considered anathema to the prerogatives of statehood at this point in time.

It was not until the mid 1980s that a distinctively European structural rationale for cooperation on drugs matters was to emerge. However, this did not arise out of concern with the health and social aspects of the drugs problem that had been highlighted by Pompidou.[75] The Single European Act (SEA) revising the Treaty of Rome was negotiated in 1985, signed in February 1986 and came into force in mid 1987, setting a timetable for the abolition of internal border controls within the EEC on 1 January 1993. By the time the SEA entered force membership of the European Communities had grown to a total of 12 states. A first phase of enlargement had seen Denmark, Ireland and the United Kingdom join in 1973, followed by Greece in 1981, and Portugal and Spain in 1986. The most important aim of the SEA lay in establishing a timetable for the completion of an internal market – the Single European Market (SEM) – but it also served to strengthen the institutional system of the Community. In particular, a significant increase in the treaty base for majority voting allowed for the Council to take decisions by qualified majority vote. The text of the SEA, like the Treaty of Rome, contained no reference to drugs (either legal or illegal). However, a political declaration was attached to the Act in which member states made a commitment to cooperate in the combating of terrorism, crime, the traffic in drugs, and illicit trading in works of art and antiques (Commission, 1988). The SEA also granted legal status to meetings between the heads of government that had taken place since the 1970s, although they were not incorporated into the treaty. 'European Council' meetings have subsequently become the main vehicle for collective public policy announcements by EU leaders.

Amid a plethora of measures relating to the economic implications of the SEM, den Boer (1996) notes that a parallel argument was beginning to emerge at this time: 'Politicians, senior police officers, and civil servants argued that the removal of border controls would have negative repercussions for the internal security situation of the member states, and hence that international crime would rise without compensatory measures' (p. 393). Behind this rhetorical discourse lay a carefully considered decision, constructed specifically to avoid measures designed to harmonize drugs laws at this time. Estievenart (1995) notes that the European Commission put forward a White Paper on the completion of the Single Market (June 1985), proposing a strategy that relied 'above all on the implementation of compensatory measures at the Community's external borders' (p. 57). Designed essentially to strengthen control over the movement of people and goods at the external frontiers, these measures included such steps as the redeployment of police and customs officers formerly tied up with internal frontier duties and increased surveillance at sensitive points of entry. Intensified cooperation was also advocated at this time, particularly in relation to regulatory and enforcement matters.[76] Estievenart (1995: 57) accounts for the emphasis of the White Paper by explaining that besides the legal and political considerations and sensitivities of member states on the inviolability of what were seen as unequivocally sovereign anti-drugs laws, the option of non-harmonization was based on the strategic fact that most drug hauls and arrests of traffickers had long taken place at the external frontiers.[77] Estievenart then succinctly accounts for the significance of the SEA in relation to drugs policy-making when he notes: 'Through its foreseeable consequences on drug trafficking the Single Act ... thus set off a process of intensified cooperation and exchange between Member States, without involving any Community legal measure affecting national policies and laws on drugs' (p. 58).

On the one hand, avoiding legal harmonization through a process of what is sometimes termed 'communitarization' seems to reflect a fairly classical defence of state sovereignty, fuelled by the popular and parliamentary distrust of common action that has long characterized the process of European integration. The outcome was a wholly intergovernmental form of cooperation in which national polities nominally retained full oversight. Yet, on the other hand, the cooperative process initiated as a result did not fit this model in important respects. As den Boer (1996: 389) notes, the policy-making channels into which the drug issue was introduced had been first created around a decade earlier under the aegis of European Political Cooperation (EPC) to exchange strategic information (aimed at countering the threat of terrorism). EPC had begun in 1970 in the form of a semi-informal intergovernmental network between the foreign ministries of the six EEC states at that time. In many ways it perfectly symbolized the tension between national sovereignty and common European policy, at the root of which lay strong preferences on the part of national governments to maintain national control over matters of security. The initial aims of EPC were fairly modest, seeking to build diplomatic cooperation loosely around an Atlantic security framework. None the less, this yielded a significant shift in working diplomatic relations, promoting a normative framework through which 'common' issues and problems could be more easily identified and discussed.[78]

Trevi and Schengen

In what has proved to be a highly significant event, the Trevi Group was created under EPC in 1975. This established both the principle and practice of direct, semi-informal cooperation among the security services and law enforcement agencies of member states, initially in an effort to coordinate anti-terrorist efforts. Trevi was a network of officials from the justice and interior ministries of member states, which delegated specialist assessment to a series of working groups, sometimes including senior law enforcement practitioners. Trevi engagement with the drugs issue is described in depth in Chapter 7.

The concept of European 'justice and home affairs' policies began to emerge as a shared objective around which a loose form of institutionalized cooperation was built, with the Trevi policy network a crucial factor in the development and dissemination of ideas. In accounting for the growth of such cooperation among EEC member governments in the 1970s and 1980s, den Boer and Wallace (2000) suggest that this was

> largely responsive in character, reacting to perceived threats and to public anxieties through limited initiatives. The underlying rationale for building intergovernmental cooperation follows from the cross-border character of crime, the international mobility of criminals, the permeability of national boundaries among open economies and democratic societies, and the fragmentation of jurisdictions. (p. 495)

The principal claim was that the overall threat to state security would be greater once border controls were removed, even though, as den Boer (1996) points out, 'few of these arguments were based on reliable statistics on the effectiveness of border controls for law-enforcement purposes' (p. 393). Chapter 7 considers the 1970s and 1980s in more detail, with particular reference to how this period established both the style and 'ground rules' for policy-making that subsequently became institutionalized as part of the post-TEU structures. The events of this period have been surprisingly under-analysed, in particular with regard to their impact in terms of the pre-eminence given to particular kinds of expertise in designing and shaping policy parameters where law enforcement issues are involved. This book focuses on the normative culture that emerged in this period in relation to the drugs issue.

The Schengen Agreement of 14 June 1985, signed between France, Germany and the Benelux countries, arose out of frustration on the part of this group of states at the slowness of progress on opening up borders, as well as formally affirming the need for 'compensatory measures' set out in the White Paper.[79] The Schengen Implementing Convention (SIC) was hugely significant, for the fact that it established the principle of *formal* cooperation between member states aimed at (among other things) combating drug trafficking for the first time. It also provided for various forms of cross-border police collaboration and covert police activities, particularly in relation to drug trafficking. A significant aspect of the Schengen system was the creation of a computerized data storage and analysis system for the shared use of the domestic law enforcement agencies of Schengen member states. The system was made up of two registration and surveillance databases: the Schengen Information System (SIS) and SIRENE (Supplément d'Information Requis a l'Entrée Nationale).[80] Reviewing the subsequent course of events, Mathiesen (1999: 9) notes how, despite the avowed intention of Schengen to be at the forefront of fighting cross-border organized crime, much of its work (and the information held in data files) has related to issues of immigration and more vaguely defined threats to public order and state security. Both SIS (which contained around 9 million records by 1998) and SIRENE have subsequently become an integral part of a much broader plan for a European Information System (EIS), intrinsically linked to the development of Europol.[81]

Both Schengen and Trevi focused solely on law enforcement matters; hence any discussion of drugs took place solely in that circumscribed context. Discussion of drug enforcement thus took place outside of the supranational framework and the terms of reference for EC institutions. However, in 1985 the European Parliament set up the Stewart-Clark Committee to investigate the problems caused by drugs in EC member states. In preparing a final report the Committee was dogged by disagreement between those who favoured strengthened prohibition and those who sought an approach based on 'harm reduction'. The report, submitted in 1986, did advocate a more liberal approach to policies on cannabis (following the Dutch model) but Council adopted a resolution based on the report merely 'reaffirming the illegality of all drugs listed in the relevant UN Conventions' (Boekhout van Solinge, 2002: 23). The resolution on the Stewart-Clark report passed by the European Parliament made pointed reference to the fact that the Parliament was 'appalled by Member States' reluctance to acknowledge the extent of the problem' (OJ C 283, 10 November 1986: 79). At this time, no EC-level institutional framework existed through which to address the drugs issue from a multi-disciplinary perspective. This was partially addressed with the formation of CELAD (a French acronym for European Committee to Combat Drugs) in 1989. However, CELAD (described in more detail in Chapter 7) was not an EC-level institutional framework as such as it operated as an *ad hoc* committee outside of the Community treaties. A clear demarcation of policy sub-fields in relation to drugs meant that CELAD had no right of initiative in relation to enforcement policies (again, see Chapter 7 for elaboration on the significance of this point). Nevertheless, the first European Action Plan to Combat Drugs was generated under the auspices of CELAD in 1990.

Trevi, unlike CELAD, was able to claim a clear rationalizing principle for its drug-related activities since 1985: namely, the so-called compensatory measures associated with the development of the SEM. By the time CELAD was formed the drugs issue was already clearly demarcated as predominantly an 'enforcement matter' through dint of the predominant 'causal' characterization emerging from Trevi. The Single Act was thus crucial in facilitating and legitimizing the introduction of drug trafficking issues into a style of policy-making based around a transnational network of senior national law enforcement officials (and in some circumstances practitioners). The nominally informal Trevi network, operating outside the framework of the Community treaties, became an influential model for the institutional architecture of the next, enormously significant, phase of European integration. Before considering the specific changes initiated through the Treaty on European Union it is important to understand how the emergence of EU drugs policy-making described above was part of a much broader growth in EU-level policies.

Drug policies in wider context

A general expansion in the policy portfolio of the EEC–EU has been clearly evident since the mid 1980s. A broadening of the range and weight of EU policy responsibilities has reached a point where 'there are now initiatives and developments in virtually every sphere of public policy' (Nugent, 1999: 58). By the mid 1980s a general trend for liberal democratic states across Europe to withdraw from parts of the economy, retract from the provision of certain public goods and reduce the powers of government was readily apparent (Wallace, 2000a: 47). Wallace goes on to suggest that EU-level policy regimes provided an alternative way of recouping a kind of control over public policy, albeit on a selective basis.

The creation and momentum of the SEM via the '1992' programme and the SEA itself gave the EU a huge increase in the range and extent of its regulatory responsibility for ensuring that the market functions most efficiently. The EU thus developed many policies with direct implications for the operation of the market. Examples range from the establishment of essential conditions for product standards and for their testing and certification to controlling the circumstances in which governments can or cannot subsidize domestic industries (Nugent, 1999: 55). Several policy areas in the social sphere that have market implications have also become increasingly subject to EU regulatory control, such as policies on the environment, consumer protection and working conditions. Nugent suggests that the SEM momentum also boosted many EU sectoral policies, notably transport, telecommunications and energy. Most important of all, the SEM stimulated movement towards Economic and Monetary Union (EMU). From the late 1980s, most member states came to the view that harmonized macro-economic and financial policies and a single currency were necessary if the SEM was to realize its full potential. The TEU paved the way for a single currency which, after some delay, was launched on 1 January 1999 with 11 of the 15 member states participating.

A 'striking feature' of the EU's policy portfolio has always been its limited involvement with those policy areas which account for the bulk of public expenditure – such as social welfare, education, health and defense (Nugent, 1999: 57). Beyond economic and economic-related policies, the EU has steadily moved into other policy areas, however, particularly so in the 1990s. Insecurity in Europe arising from the end of the Cold War, the outbreak of war in the Balkans, and growing concerns about immigration and various types of international crime (with drugs still the focal point for policy activity) led to consensus on the need to give EPC a formal treaty basis. Hence, moves towards highly sensitive areas far removed from the original EEC policy focus on the construction of a common market, such as foreign policy and justice and home affairs, must be seen in the context of the broader changes affecting European states. Treaty recognition for these roles emerged: foreign policy was given a legal base by the SEA and, along with justice and home affairs policy, was included in – and strengthened by – the Maastricht and Amsterdam treaties. Drug policies have emerged as a significant component of justice and home affairs and must thus be seen in a wider policy context as part of a new EU security nexus and a more complex overall policy-making environment and range of policy commitments. The policy base of European integration has thus been considerably deepened as well as widened (the EU now includes almost all of Western Europe and is set to include at least some of the countries of Central and Eastern Europe). Let us now turn to the Maastricht and Amsterdam treaties.

A new institutional framework: the European Union

The Maastricht Treaty

Amid a general sense that the 1986 Single Act had not achieved all that had been expected of it in terms of the integration process, and with the background of the break-up of the communist bloc and the Soviet Union, a series of European Council meetings between 1988 and 1990 agreed to the formation of two Intergovernmental Conferences (IGCs) to assess the basis and form of future European integration.[82] IGCs on political union and economic and monetary union (EMU) were formed, meeting throughout 1991, culminating in a submission of reports to the Maastricht European Council meeting in December 1991. The Commission and the European Parliament – the two principal non-governmental Community institutions – were effectively excluded from substantive negotiations, particularly so in the case of the Parliament (the Commission was at least able to submit opinion papers). Nevertheless, member states were able to agree the outline of a new treaty in Maastricht: the Treaty on European Union (TEU). The TEU – more commonly referred to as the Maastricht Treaty – was signed in February 1992 and entered force in November 1993 after a difficult and drawn-out ratification process (see Nugent, 1999: 65–6). The TEU was a major step in furthering the process of European integration, creating the new organization of the European Union based around three policy 'pillars'.

- *The first pillar* incorporated most of the policy responsibilities for the EU, adopting the *acquis communautaire* of the European Communities (the EEC, ECSC and Euratom treaty base) and strengthened the treaty base in some respects, notably with regard to the EEC Treaty. The EEC was renamed the European Community (EC) by what became known as the Treaty Establishing The European Community (TEC).

- *The second pillar* was a Common Foreign and Security Policy (CFSP).
- *The third pillar* was cooperation in the field of Justice and Home Affairs (JHA) and defined a range of policy areas as matters of 'common interest' (including asylum policy; judicial cooperation in civil and criminal matters and customs cooperation).

The third pillar formalized and directly incorporated all measures taken under the *ad hoc* Trevi process; hence it included all matters relating to drug enforcement, including police cooperation. Also included under the third pillar was the area of combating drug addiction. Chapter 8 gives a detailed account of the TEU institutional framework as it related to drugs. The intergovernmental third pillar was organized on the basis that unanimity was required in Council before a decision could be taken. In the broadest sense, the TEU thus 'furthered policy and institutional deepening' (Nugent, 1999: 51), in particular with regard to laying down a procedure and timetable for EMU via the single currency. It also extended provision for qualified majority voting in the Council and created a new legislative procedure (co-decision) that gave the European Parliament the power of veto over some legislative proposals. In 1995, a new phase of enlargement saw Austria, Finland and Sweden join the EU, extending the total membership to 15 states.

Chapters 8, 9 and 10 describe the evolution of third pillar policy-making and the manner in which ideas emerge from the various policy development mechanisms. The formal hierarchy of the EU dictates that all decisions are sanctioned by the Council of Ministers. Since the 1967 Merger Treaty there has legally been only one Council of Ministers but in practice the modern EU divides along functional lines, with specialist Councils for various policy themes. Until recently there were around twenty policy areas, but in order to simplify the functions of Council in the run up to the next phase of enlargement the Seville European Council (21–22 June 2002) agreed to reduce the number of specialist Councils to nine, effective from 1 August 2002. Matters relating to enforcement aspects of drug policies are discussed primarily in the Justice and Home Affairs Council. The reasons for this are explained in the course of the remaining chapters of Part II, along with analysis of the more specific roles of the Committee of Permanent Representatives (COREPER) and the specialist network of committees and working groups that relate to drug policy.

The Amsterdam Treaty

The TEU specified that another IGC should be convened in 1996 in order to review the operation of the treaty. The IGC met during 1996 and 1997, culminating in a final submission to the Amsterdam European Council meeting in June 1997. As Nugent (1999: 81) points out, the resultant Treaty of Amsterdam had a somewhat more modest impact than either the SEA or TEU, at least partly because it lacked a coordinating principle in the way that the SEM rationalized the SEA, and EMU was seen as the primary purpose behind the TEU. A significant project was in hand by 1997 – preparation for the accession of Central and Eastern European countries (CEECs) to EU membership. However, as Nugent (1999: 81) points out, this process was not placed at the centre of the Amsterdam Treaty largely because a number of the important internal EU changes needed to accommodate CEECs do not require treaty reform (for example, reform of the Common Agricultural Policy).

The Amsterdam Treaty entered force on 1 May 1999 after delays resulting from the slowness of national ratification procedures (notably in France, the last state to ratify, in March 1999). The Treaty brought about modest changes in the first and second pillars with regard to the use of qualified majority voting (qmv), but for the purposes of this work it is the third pillar that is of primary concern. Great attention was focused on measures related to 'freedom, security and justice', directly related to JHA policies, covered in Section I of the Treaty. A new Title IV: Visas, Asylum, Immigration and Other Policies Related to Free Movement of Persons, transferred policy-making in these areas to the first pillar (EC) competence, although decisions still require unanimity in Council. A highly significant decision was taken – although it barely registered in the public consciousness – to integrate the entire Schengen *acquis* into the EU framework via the Treaty (that is, incorporate the full array of Schengen rules, procedures and legal precedents, along with the database system – including historical data – described earlier in this chapter).[83] This was a particularly important step forward in the potential development of Europol and an associated European criminal 'intelligence' database. The Amsterdam Treaty maintained the principle that drug enforcement policy should be developed solely within the intergovernmental third pillar. However, Chapter 10 examines this phase in more detail and looks at how the institutions and policy actors have been affected by the transition to a reconstituted third pillar with a narrower remit, focused on 'Provisions on Police and Judicial Cooperation in Criminal Matters'.

The TEU created three legal instruments for taking action in the JHA sphere: joint action, joint position and convention. Council was also able to issue resolutions and recommendations in order to promote adherence to the relatively 'soft' joint action and joint position measures. The joint action was replaced in 1999 with the entry into force of the Amsterdam Treaty, but from 1993 to 1999 it was frequently used to promote and bolster coordinated action among member states. 'Decisions' and 'framework decisions' have now replaced joint actions. The latter are used to generate alignment in the laws and regulations of member states and are adopted only by unanimous decision. Although they are binding on member states with regard to the result to be achieved, they leave the choice of form and methods to national authorities (a classic affirmation of the primacy of state sovereignty). Decisions are used for any purpose other than approximating laws and regulations (and are adopted by qualified majority). Joint positions are a legal instrument enabling the Council of the European Union to define the EU approach on any given issue.

Summary

The idea that there *should* be joint European drug enforcement policies is no longer challenged on any political level. However, the practice of policy development and implementation reveals a complex tension between collective enforcement of drug prohibition and the preservation of sovereign control over the means of enforcement. The notion of increased threat from drugs has been a highly significant legitimizing principle for a broad range of security-related policy and institutional changes within the EC–EU. The means by which this has become a reflexive dimension of EC–EU policy over time are revealed not simply by the institutional arrangements, but in the interactions between policy actors and the ideas that are translated into policy (which subsequently become institutionalized). There is also a complex diffusion of a dominant, enforcement-based and intergovernmentally agreed set of (normative) policies that cohere around the EU as a political institution.

Dorn (1996b) provides a typology of the external policies of the EU that shape its drug policies *vis-à-vis* other trading blocs and countries. In terms of global external policies, this relates to those areas where the European Community has competence (based on the main treaty provisions) and has ratified relevant international conventions (for example, measures on the control of precursor chemicals and money laundering: see Chapters 8 and 9). Policies in these areas tend to reflect the 'international consensus' (that is, broadly, the regime described in Chapter 3) which the EU attempts in turn to apply in all of its external relations, thus helping to further reinforce that view. However, part of this 'consensus' is derived (or is at least reinforced) through work initiated in EU-specific fora, particularly within the third pillar. Additionally, the EU has what Dorn (1996b) terms 'sectorial' external policies 'in the fields of enlargement of the Union, security policy, development policy and external trade' (p. 243). This has the effect of providing a 'variety of contexts for the articulation of the Union's external policies on drugs matters' (p. 243). Dorn shows that the intergovernmental character of policy-making on drug enforcement is further embedded as a component of broader EU policies.

Anti-trafficking measures are often an integral and conditional element of policies where the European Commission has competence to act for all member states, particularly in relation to bargained outcomes on trade. For instance, in the case of relations with countries which are in major drug producing or key transit areas, Estievenart (1995: 81) points out that there are close links between 'political instruments (dialogue), financial instruments (more development aid) and commercial instruments (access to the European market for legal agricultural products in an international context characterized by saturated and depressed markets, for example coffee, cocoa, bananas, etc.). The sectorial external policies of the EU embody both the international policy 'consensus' on drugs and internally mediated policy priorities and emphases, as well as being linked in with broader policy discourse (trade and development). In this way, policies against drug trafficking are diffused within a broader framework that further shapes and institutionalizes their form and impact. The primary aim of the analysis contained in Chapters 7–11 is to investigate the role and significance of actors with authoritative expert knowledge in the process of policy development. Attention is focused on how specific forms of expert knowledge may contribute to the framing of drugs issues in particular ways. In this respect, the analysis takes account of the methodological issues raised in connection with the epistemic communities model outlined in Chapter 5.

The development of policy coordination in relation to drugs must thus be considered in the context of a broader background of evolving European integration and the expanded influence of the European Union internationally. This chapter has provided an overview of how drug policy has developed in the context of this evolution, which was given a significant impetus first in the mid 1980s by preparations for implementing the Single European Act, and subsequently by the Treaty on European Union itself. Dorn (1996b) neatly summarizes the most salient feature of this period when he suggests that, 'In relation to European laws, policing practices and cooperation against *drug trafficking*, there has been a convergence in policies as a result of close intergovernmental cooperation' (p. 155).

Chapters 7–11 provide an empirical assessment of this viewpoint. Readers who are less familiar with EU institutions, procedures and unavoidable jargon may find the glossary of EU terms provided at the front of this book helpful when reading these chapters.

7
MAG, Trevi, CELAD and the Pre-EU Blueprint for Policy-Making on Drugs

In the previous chapter it was noted that in 1969 President Pompidou became the first European leader to suggest a need for some form of coordinated, collective European action against drugs. However, two years before this, a little-known legal instrument established a basis for two principles that have proved to be highly influential in shaping the course of European drug policy development. The principles established at this time were that:

1 there was a need to coordinate the strategic and operational activities of law enforcement bodies across and between member states (of the then six-member EEC)
2 policy design of this form should be delegated *in the first instance* to functional-technical actors to establish both strategic rationale and parameters for policy actions.

On the face of it, the 1967 'Naples Convention' does not seem a likely candidate to be attributed with such significance.[84] The Convention came about as a result of a belief that cooperation between customs administrations would help to ensure accuracy in the collection of customs duties and other import and export charges and improve the effectiveness of preventing, investigating and prosecuting contraventions of customs laws. A basis for joint anti-drug activities between national customs authorities was thereby established, although – reflecting the level of concern at the time – this was essentially an administrative-level action and did not constitute a high-profile political-level initiative. Drugs were not the focus of the Naples Convention at all. The real significance of the Convention lay in its provision of a rationale for establishing the Customs Mutual Assistance Group (MAG). The MAG, formed in 1972, facilitated direct transnational dialogue between expert groups with an authoritative claim to policy-relevant knowledge (that is, customs officials). This 'model' for policy-making has proved to be an enduring one. However, the directly drug-related work of MAG was not to emerge until the mid 1980s. Nevertheless, it was the 1967 Naples Convention – a legal instrument that barely merits a footnote in most accounts of European integration – that had created a blueprint for a particular style of policy development.

The previous chapter noted the 1969 initiative of French President Georges Pompidou, and the establishment of what was to become known as the Pompidou Group. On 6 August 1971, Pompidou suggested that the member states of the (then) EEC should combine their efforts to counter drug problems, which he termed a danger of 'incalculable consequences'.[85] Charles Elsen, a participant in the meetings that established the Group, believes that the initiative of Pompidou marked the birth of European cooperation in the 'fight against drugs'. Elsen (1995) notes that 'the countries concerned responded very positively to this offer, and a first meeting was held soon after in Paris, at which a working programme leading to a first interministerial meeting in Rome was adopted' (p. 360). According to Elsen, the French initiative proposed a four-part study covering health, education and information (what today would be called 'prevention'), repression and, finally, the harmonization of legislation. The initial participants were the six EEC member states plus the United Kingdom, with whom accession negotiations were well advanced (and whose participation was effectively a form of *acquis*).

Elsen also records how a series of questions preoccupied Pompidou Group participants from the outset. Should the Commission be associated with it, and if so how? Should the forum be open to a wider range of states, or should this be restricted to candidate EC members? Answers proved ambiguous to all of these questions, resulting in a somewhat *ad hoc* evolution of the Group, involving two main phases. Initially, it simply became augmented by the new countries joining the EC and, 'curiously, almost from the outset by Sweden', giving the Group 'a life of its own' in which successive presidencies also took on the responsibility of forming a secretariat (Elsen, 1995: 360). Second – though not until 1980 – a partial agreement was signed with the Council of Europe, immediately broadening the membership base to include states from outside of the EC. By 1989, UK Government documents suggested that the Pompidou Group was 'the primary forum for developing further cooperation on drugs matters within Europe' (House of Commons, 1989a: 3). What makes this statement interesting is that it omits to mention that a more secretive and narrowly focused attempt to build law enforcement cooperation on drugs matters had begun to emerge after 1985 within the EC, rather than the 'multidisciplinary' approach to drugs issues evident within the Pompidou Group. It was in 1985 that a political decision was taken to bring drugs within the remit of what was known as the Trevi Group. This event was to prove highly significant in shaping European drug policy, particularly in terms of the dominant ideas and institutional responses to drug problems that have subsequently emerged.

The Trevi Group had been formally established in 1976 after a decision taken by the Rome European Council in December 1975, taken under the auspices of EPC (see Chapter 6) after an initiative by the UK Government. Trevi has been described as an intergovernmental 'satellite' operating in effect independently of the EC (European Commission, 1994: 41).[86] Its principal aim was to improve working levels of police cooperation between EC member states in order to assess and counter mutual problems more effectively, with an initial remit confined to building cooperation against terrorism.[87] The operating method of the Group lay in facilitating contact on an intergovernmental basis between senior EC government ministers, civil servants and police officers who, 'through their association on working groups and at intergovernmental summit meetings' aimed to 'exchange information and develop cooperative practices for policing in the EC' (Woodward, 1993: 9). The character of Trevi is captured by Benyon et al. (1993: 152) who suggest that it was probably best described as a forum rather than an organization, highlighting that Trevi functioned essentially as a policy-making network.

Trevi, the '1992' programme and Schengen

It was generally accepted that achieving consensus on moves towards the promotion of the free movement of persons within the EC would be a difficult and slow process despite an agreed completion target of 31 December 1992 for implementation of the provisions of the SEA. This was the spur for five member states (Belgium, France, Germany, Luxembourg and the Netherlands) to sign the Schengen Agreement on 14 June 1985.[88] On one level Schengen aimed to be a prototype for a wider border-free Europe under the SEA framework, while offering a pragmatic interim solution for anticipated delays to this programme. According to Anderson et al. (1995), one of the main justifications behind the way Schengen was seen as 'prefiguring' the larger SEA process stemmed from the political declaration made by the member states when the SEA itself was adopted. They note that the 1986 declaration stated that

> the introduction of the free movement of persons should be accompanied by cooperation between the member states with regard to the entry, movement and residence of nationals of third countries, and with measures to combat terrorism, crime, the traffic in drugs and illicit trading in works of art and antiques. (p. 59)[89]

At this point, drug trafficking became an intrinsic part of a broader normative policy framework, with both Trevi and Schengen designated as competent fora through which to generate cooperation in this area. However, a precedent for separate, intergovernmental discussion of drug law enforcement matters had already been set and institutionalized well before this. It might have been expected that the Pompidou Group (given Pompidou's own initial stress on the health and social aspects of drugs problems) provided a basis to bring together and integrate discussion on tackling the drugs problem in a more holistic sense. However, as Elsen records, the Pompidou Group concerned itself from its inception with matters that would today be classed as 'third pillar' activities of the EU, setting up dedicated working groups on 'repressive action' and on 'harmonization' of legislation. Elsen argues that the notion that abolishing frontiers for goods would bring with it increased drug traffic was evident even in the earliest stages of Pompidou Group discussions. This notion was presumably based on Article 8a of the Treaty of Rome (the original legal foundation for an area without internal frontiers), yet member states held off taking concerted action in this area as no specific legal basis existed under the Treaty.[90] This decision clearly reflected a lack of 'political will' on the need to overcome sovereign sensitivities over the law enforcement and judicial aspects of drugs issues at this time.

In effect a die was cast at this point, crucial in establishing an independent logic and momentum for policy discussions concerning joint European drug enforcement. Drug enforcement was clearly demarcated as a 'field' in its own right, with its own quasi-independent set of cognitive understandings about what drives drug markets, rather than as one element within an integrated multidisciplinary policy framework. This is not to suggest that a decision was taken to preclude discussions on such a basis but does indicate that it had an impact on the framing of drug policy as primarily an enforcement issue for decision-makers in EC governments from around this time. Furthermore, it rationalized and legitimized placing strategic transnational policy decisions in the hands of national law enforcement experts, adding weight to their already well established dominance on terms of cognitive authority on 'drugs matters'.[91]

Introducing drugs into the Trevi framework from 1985 (in response to an initiative by the Italian interior minister of the time) may appear to have fostered a consensus-based culture regarding drug policy that, until then, had been noticeably absent. However, consensus was based solely on the principle that enforcement matters were definitively a matter for intergovernmental decision-making. Let us now examine how Trevi functioned in more detail, along with an assessment of how this has had a significant impact on the subsequent evolution of European drug policies and the mode of policy-making.

Trevi and drugs from 1985

In June 1985 Trevi members decided to form a new working group, WG III, which was assigned the role of examining ways of improving cooperation against organized crime, principally drug trafficking.[92] WG III was incorporated into the existing Trevi structure, itself analogous to the EC Council of Ministers, with the EC Presidency country (then, as now, rotated every six months) also holding the right to chair Trevi. Trevi never had permanent staff, as up to 1989 a so-called 'troika' of the immediate past, current, and next Presidency states formed an unofficial secretariat. It was decided in May 1989 that the two states either side of the troika sequence should also provide staff, building an even more complex institutional structure.

In overall terms, Trevi was organized on a tripartite basis, with ministers forming the top decision-making tier (see Benyon et al., 1993: 153). Ministerial participation was at equivalent home secretary or attorney general level, with meetings held every June and December. Second in the hierarchical structure were meetings of a group of 'senior officials' who met every May and December, while much of the work of Trevi took place at the third level, that of working groups, which also tended to meet twice a year. The third tier – working group level – was made up of specialist officials and senior law enforcement officers.[93] In the UK, this form of representation led to questions about the democratic accountability of Trevi, expressed in a 1990 House of Commons (1990a) report. It was noted (p. xxiii) that certain 'anomalies' were created in the sense that 'These senior police officers have no direct responsibility to the Home Office as, for example, French police officers do to their Interior Ministry'. The European Parliament also made a criticism of the wider lack of accountability inherent to the Trevi structure, and was sharply critical of its own lack of purview in relation to Trevi activities. Despite this, the standard defence of the secretive and unpublished work of Trevi was always that Trevi ministers were all ultimately responsible to their national parliaments.[94]

In practice, many of the same experts were attending both Schengen and broader EC-level fora, leading to quite a high degree of overlap. The institutional structure of Schengen mirrored Trevi in terms of bringing together 'experts' at working group level (see Benyon et al., 1993: 134–7 for details). Although Trevi is generally portrayed as a closely knit EC intergovernmental forum, it also allowed 'friendly' *non-EC* states into some of its discussions, via parallel meetings with the Presidency or troika. The quaintly named 'Friends of Trevi' attended meetings of Trevi as observers, and comprised Austria and Sweden (both of whom later joined the EU in 1995), as well as Canada, Morocco, Norway, Switzerland and the United States.[95] Little is known of the outcomes of such observer status, though it is reasonable to infer that it may have built a further layer of transnational consensus around Trevi policy ideas and broadened the network of operational policing contacts. The 1985–89 period was thus one in which EC initiatives were both responding to and reinforcing the international 'consensus' on fighting the drugs problem.

Trevi marked a significant consolidation and broadening of the principle first established by the customs MAG through its promotion of a working culture based around both formal and informal transnational contacts between law enforcement specialists. The most significant tier in this respect was the working group level, for it was here that a cooperative culture was fostered between the interlocutors in the course of exchanging views on 'common' law enforcement experiences. While strategic agreement between law enforcement specialists did not guarantee political level acceptability, the degree of autonomy and positive encouragement given to ongoing 'working' contacts clearly showed a high degree of legitimacy (at ministerial level) with regard to the cognitive authority of groups with (national) law enforcement competence. However, WG III was only one element feeding into a much wider process in which Trevi was tasked with identifying the universe of so-called compensatory measures in response to the implementation of the Single Act. An important development in this regard was the establishment in

December 1988 (by the Rhodes European Council) of a group of senior officials known as the Coordinators' Group – Free Movement of Persons. The Group was responsible for producing the influential 'Palma Document' of June 1989.[96]

This report catalogued a series of measures that the Group considered to be relevant to the free movement of persons, covering matters including terrorism, visa and asylum policy, along with recommendations on action in connection with 'combating drug trafficking'. One measure listed as 'essential' with regard to the latter entailed the granting of competence for drawing up a report 'setting out the off-setting measures necessary in anticipation of the creation of the space without internal frontiers' to the Trevi 92 group, itself established only two months earlier in April 1989.[97] Trevi 92 was a working group tasked to look at the interrelationship between measures suggested by individual Trevi working groups and included in the proposed plan of action. Curiously, drug crime was part of the Trevi 92 remit 'without any specific work being devoted to the drug problem' (Elsen, 1995: 361). In all, eight measures for combating drug trafficking were listed in the 1989 Palma Document (three 'essential' and five 'desirable') with the 'competent fora' listed as: the Working Party on Drug Addiction (also set up in 1989), EPC, Trevi, the Pompidou Group, the UN and MAG. Shortly after this a new customs Mutual Assistance Group 1992 (MAG 92) was also set up, working in close liaison with Trevi 92.[98] No definition of what constitutes 'competent fora' or the system of democratic accountability associated with each body was provided in the Palma Document.   .

Official European accounts record that by the end of the 1980s the Trevi Group 'was giving priority to combating drug trafficking, organized crime and money laundering' (European Commission, 1994: 41). Measures targeted against these matters were contained in the Trevi Minister's Declaration of 15 November 1989 and the Dublin Action Programme adopted in June 1990. The June 1990 Programme of Action validated the recommendations of all of the Trevi working groups at the highest political level, affirming that 'the competent Ministers of the member states are convinced of the need for revised cooperation arrangements following the inauguration of the Single European Act' (original report quoted in Bunyan, 1997: 37). Hence the specific drugs initiatives listed above were an adjunct to the broader argument for reinforcement of police cooperation and of the endeavours to combat terrorism or other forms of organized crime. However, as Hebenton and Thomas (1992) have pointed out, drug crime was perhaps the most significant element in the argument for the creation of a European police office. At a meeting in Luxembourg in June 1992, Trevi established a new working group: the Ad Hoc Working Group on Europol (AHWGE). By this time Working Group III had already done much of the ground-work, however, paving the way with discussions considering the setting up of Europol and what was initially termed the European Drugs Unit (EDU). Bunyan (1993a: 17) notes that the setting up of the AHWGE followed the agreement of a report entitled 'The Development of Europol' at the Maastricht summit in December 1991.

This extension of the work of Trevi was soon to become directly incorporated into the institutional mechanisms of the new EU via Title VI of the TEU (see Chapter 8), hence it is important to view this process as part of a continuum within which action against drug trafficking acquired what was effectively an independent strategic 'logic' in relation to drug policy in general. This can be traced right through from the way that the structure and composition of WG III effectively precluded any alternative analysis of the range of causal factors that affected the dynamics of drug markets and the impact of law enforcement on this process, shifting attention to more generic ideas about borders and how this would affect the supply of drugs. This mode of thinking became deeply embedded in the broader discourse of European drug policy when the work of the Trevi Group was directly 'incorporated into the two European Plans to Combat Drugs' [1990, 1992] (European Commission, 1994: 41).

By 1994, the Commission, reviewing what it saw as the importance and achievements of the Trevi Group, listed the following lines of action as a 'direct result' of its work on drugs (Commission, 1994: 42):

- establishment of national drug information units
- ministerial agreement on the creation of the EUROPOL Drug Unit (Copenhagen, 2 June 1993)
- appointment of drug liaison officers to countries outside the EEC
- cooperation in the field of training
- a common policy on controlled deliveries of drugs
- a common policy on money laundering
- creation of a network of permanent correspondents on policing techniques, to assist producer and transit countries
- institution of coordinated assistance to the countries of eastern Europe to help them rebuild their police service.

It is important then to consider the institutional context out of which these measures came to be developed as well as the cognitive basis and influence of the arguments that were generated via the Trevi framework.

Drugs and frontiers: Trevi as a normative framework

A number of accounts are available of the relationship between wider arguments surrounding the relationship between the removal of border controls and changes in the field of European policing and police cooperation (namely, Anderson and den Boer, 1994; Anderson et al., 1995; Hebenton and Thomas, 1995). As Hebenton and Thomas (1995: 153) point out, the dominant discourse regarding European police cooperation has centred on the 'challenge posed' to law enforcement based on predicted expansion of crime. The views of politicians and senior police officials were instrumental in forming the dominant account of a border-free Europe (see Hebenton and Thomas, 1995: 160–1 for examples) in which crime and drug trafficking would increase. den Boer (1994: 184–92) has highlighted the rhetorical appeal of these arguments as an integral part of a process of negotiation, persuasion and consensus building. Dorn (1993) argues that Trevi played an influential role in establishing a 'working culture' of senior police officers favourably disposed to 'the task of securing within EC countries a political environment supportive of action against [drugs]' (p. 34). This culture, allied to a broad process of professionalization of police at the national level (thereby giving more independence to senior police figures to voice their opinions domestically), was typified by the prominent police calls for action against a predicted 'tide' of crack cocaine that emerged around 1989.[99] Hebenton and Thomas (1995) question the theoretical foundations that underpinned the dominant account when they argue that 'the insistence of the UK government, customs officials and police that the power to intercept transhipments of goods and movements of persons at borders is a really significant factor in controlling the international drug trade is problematic' (p. 161). Supporting evidence for this viewpoint comes largely from analysis of drug markets conducted by, among others, van Duyne (1993) and Dorn et al. (1992). Benyon et al. (1993: 25–31) also examined the evidence, concurring that the premise that 'the abolition of strong border controls will enhance the opportunities for drugs traffickers' is fundamentally flawed (p. 30). Ruggiero and South (1995) also questioned the rationale for targeting resources at 'big crime' (that is, large-scale trafficking organizations), highlighting the extent to which trafficking is carried out by highly localized operators.

As noted in the previous chapter, Estievenart has pointed out that the initial Commission White Paper on the completion of the Single Market was concerned chiefly with measures designed to strengthen *external* borders to prevent the flow of drugs. The subsequent emphasis on the impact of the removal of internal controls resulted directly from the expert deliberations that took place under Trevi auspices. So why did the argument about the scale of the drugs threat resulting from the removal of internal borders become legitimized at the political level? One explanation is to view Trevi simply as an institutional expression of an interest group – European national police agencies – whose influence and authority was enhanced via linkage to 'sensitive' political issues. Such an analysis is a superficial one, though not entirely without substance. Trevi can be said to have made a significant contribution to the framing of the drugs problem as predominantly one of law enforcement (intrinsically linked to the domain-specific experiences of the expert participants) – as opposed to one with a more complex causal structure in which demand is the crucial factor – influencing both cognitive understanding by political decision-makers and institutional momentum at a crucial juncture. However, a broader range of international developments were also reinforcing and deepening the pre-eminence of an enforcement-led approach at this time.

Origins of a new 'political will' to fight drugs in Europe

Other parallel (and to some extent overlapping) developments in the 1985–89 period that were to exert a strong influence on both individual states and collective European approaches to drug policy arose primarily as a result of the impetus generated by United Nations activities. In 1985, the UN Secretary-General proposed that an international conference be held to consider what additional measures could be taken to improve international cooperation on the drugs problem. In June 1987, 105 countries attended the International Conference on Drug Abuse and Illicit Trafficking (ICDAIT) held in Vienna. By then the Council, acting on a proposal from the Commission, had taken an initial decision paving the way for the Community to establish a common approach to drugs in terms of its cooperative external relations with producer or transit third countries. The Council decision of 26 January 1987 was significant in that it provided for the integration of certain drug related matters into policies such as alternative development as pursued at a Community level, including special preferential trade arrangements (for example, with certain Andean and Central American countries).

On a broader European canvas, the Community participated in the first Pan-European Ministerial Conference organized by the Pompidou Group in Oslo in 1991. A second conference was held in Strasbourg in 1994. Based on the 1987 decision, the EC (and now EU) have progressively introduced clauses on drugs and money laundering into its association agreements with the countries of Central and Eastern Europe (CEECs), many of which are now set to become full EU members. In November 1992, the Community approved a pilot regional drugs programme covering five CEECs, extended to a total of 11 in December 1993. The Lomé IV Convention (1990–2000), providing a framework for cooperation between the EC and the ACP (African, Caribbean and Pacific) countries, has also generated institutional and financial resources to assist in measures against trafficking and drug abuse.[100] These activities are indicative of the new political will to 'fight' the drugs problem that emerged in the late 1980s.

The Community participated in ICDAIT, and in 1988 a further mandate was given to the Commission that allowed the Community to take part in the final phase of negotiations that ultimately created the 1988 UN Vienna Convention. The basis on which Community competence was established lay in the need to regulate the (legitimate) market for precursor chemicals used to produce and refine drugs. This important step not only marked the formalizing of Community competence but also cemented the broadening of the international regulatory regime that the negotiations on the 1988 Convention were to lead to. The Community became party to the Convention on 22 October 1990, following its adoption in Vienna on 19 December 1988. The Convention, as has previously been noted, focused on implementing more stringent enforcement controls, despite the emphasis on a multidisciplinary approach to drug policy advocated during the ICDAIT. Within the EC, the Trevi-led emphasis on 'supply-side' measures took clear precedence in shaping the nascent Community approach.

CELAD and the European drug action plans after 1989

On 3 October 1989 President François Mitterrand of France sent a letter calling for more coordination between the then twelve EC members to counter the growing evidence of an 'escalation' in the drugs problem. The letter was the catalyst for a significant period of political mobilization against the backdrop of an ever more imminent Single Market and more intense international anti-drug actions by developed countries generally in the post-Vienna Convention phase (notably the so-called US 'War on Drugs'). The letter stressed the 'impunity' with which traffickers were able to operate, expressing particular concern at the situation in Latin America (Mitterrand letter quoted in Estievenart, 1995: 60). While believing that 'useful work' had already been completed,

Mitterrand felt that intensified cooperation was needed within an EC context. Echoing the words of his eminent predecessor Pompidou, Mitterrand advocated a 'multidisciplinary' approach (joining health and social aspects, law enforcement – including money laundering – and international cooperation) coupled with the key innovation of a mechanism for political coordination between the then 12 member states and the Commission. The seven recommendations contained in the letter included the setting up of national interministerial coordination points for drug policy and the establishment of a 'monitoring centre' to measure the drug phenomenon.[101]

The Strasbourg European Council of 8–9 December 1989 formally agreed to the proposals and to the setting up of a European Committee to Combat Drugs, better known as CELAD.[102] Elsen (1995) describes the original remit given to CELAD – complete with rhetorical language: 'To ensure the essential coordination of Member States' action in the main areas of the fight against this plague, namely prevention, health and social policy towards addicts, repression of narcotics traffic and action at international level' (p. 362). Estievenart (1995: 59) notes how the composition of CELAD illustrated the diversity of drug policies and priorities among the 12 member states: 'Certain countries were to designate "politicians" (as in the case of France with the appointment of Madame Dufoix, a former minister); while others – in fact the majority – were to prefer a high-ranking official'. This reflected diversity in the types of ministries given the lead on drugs matters across the member states at this time, ranging from ministries of health, social affairs, through to justice or foreign affairs. CELAD was, technically, an *ad hoc* intergovernmental group working outside EC institutions, yet – in clear contrast with Trevi – Commission involvement was positively encouraged. The Commission's first representative on CELAD was its then Vice-President, Martin Bangemann, who had also been the sole Commission member of the Coordinators' Group.[96] With one of the architects of the Palma Document present in CELAD it can thus be reasoned that support for the 'logic' of compensatory measures was well represented, and that the specific Palma recommendations on drug trafficking were likely to be taken as given. Subsequent developments, described later in this chapter, appear to support this view.

The fact that CELAD was set up as an *ad hoc* forum inevitably meant that it lacked any real decision-making power, even drawing a kind of institutional chauvinism. Estievenart (1995: 60) suggests that what he terms 'the traditional Council forums (health group, external relations group or the political cooperation drugs group)' sometimes viewed

CELAD as 'a cumbersome rival rather than a useful partner'. Figure 7.1 illustrates the overall policy-making structure in relation to drugs around this time, highlighting the three-part framework: Community, political cooperation and intergovernmental. While such a structure *appears* horizontal it should be read with the remainder of this chapter in mind. Despite certain institutional shortcomings, CELAD did generate several tangible outputs, the most notable being the two European plans to combat drugs of 1990 and 1992. Almost immediately after it was set up CELAD commenced work on drafting what was to become the first European Plan to Combat Drugs, approved by the Rome European Council of 13–14 December 1990. The most significant characteristic of this plan was its advocacy of an integrated approach focusing on five areas (European Commission, 1994: 35):

1   coordination at member state level
2   a European observatory to monitor the drugs phenomenon
3   action to reduce drug demand
4   action to combat illicit trafficking
5   action at international level.

In drafting the 1990 Plan it is clear from documents relating to the Dublin European Council of 25–26 June 1990 that CELAD simply incorporated the recommendations of Trevi and the MAG on a wholesale basis without any debate as such.[103] This is clearly apparent under the section regarding suppression of trafficking, which restated the need for compensatory measures as well as setting out the 'relevant bodies' across work areas related to the programme recommended. Liaison with the Coordinators' Group – which CELAD was mandated to do under its remit – ensured this process. At this point, an early sign of recognition that ways to strengthen national judicial and legal systems were now at least a feasible drug policy option was shown by the decision to place this matter within the remit of the Judicial Cooperation working group under EPC. After the reluctance to harmonize laws so apparent in 1985 this marked a significant shift in political acceptance of a more homogenous – as well as tougher and broader – anti-drug legislative environment. The 1988 UN Vienna Convention, for which CELAD urged rapid ratification by all EEC member states, was clearly seen as a significant 'template' here, allied to the broader UN international drug action programme. The Dublin document also records that the 'chairmen' of Trevi 92, MAG 92, the Ad Hoc Working Party on Drug Abuse and the EPC Working Group on Drugs presented outlines of their work to CELAD meetings

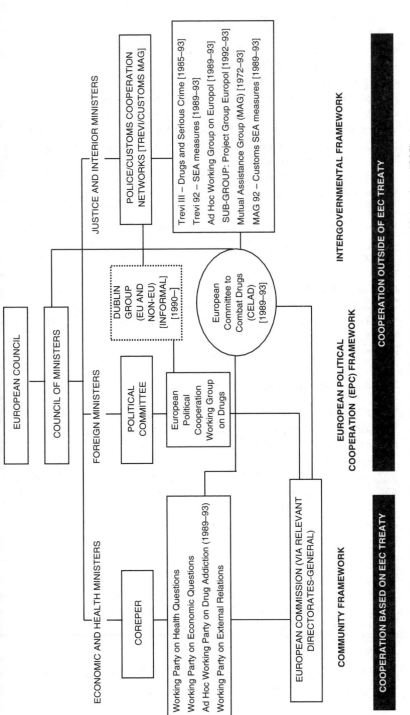

Figure 7.1 Drug policy-making institutional structure prior to European Union (pre-1993)

EUROPEAN COUNCIL

COUNCIL OF MINISTERS

JUSTICE AND INTERIOR MINISTERS

POLICE/CUSTOMS COOPERATION NETWORKS [TREVI/CUSTOMS MAG]

Trevi III – Drugs and Serious Crime [1985–93]
Trevi 92 – SEA measures [1989–93]
Ad Hoc Working Group on Europol [1989–93]
SUB-GROUP: Project Group Europol [1992–93]
Mutual Assistance Group (MAG) [1972–93]
MAG 92 – Customs SEA measures [1989–93]

INTERGOVERNMENTAL FRAMEWORK

COOPERATION OUTSIDE OF EEC TREATY

DUBLIN GROUP (EU AND NON-EU) [INFORMAL] [1990–]

European Committee to Combat Drugs (CELAD) [1989–93]

FOREIGN MINISTERS

POLITICAL COMMITTEE

European Political Cooperation Working Group on Drugs

EUROPEAN POLITICAL COOPERATION (EPC) FRAMEWORK

ECONOMIC AND HEALTH MINISTERS

COREPER

Working Party on Health Questions
Working Party on Economic Questions
Ad Hoc Working Party on Drug Addiction (1989–93)
Working Party on External Relations

EUROPEAN COMMISSION (VIA RELEVANT DIRECTORATES-GENERAL)

COMMUNITY FRAMEWORK

COOPERATION BASED ON EEC TREATY

(Commission, 1993: 48). Again this reaffirms the primacy afforded to the cognitive influence of such groups in setting important parameters of drug policy. At the same time, the consensus on the need to coordinate international action regarding the world's main producer and transit countries and regions bore fruit. A mechanism for 'informal' consultation on these matters was established in 1990 with the formation of the Dublin Group (outlined in Chapter 3), linking CELAD to dialogue with Australia, Canada, Japan, Sweden and the United States.

The 'EC consensus' on anti-trafficking measures (for which read Trevi and MAG) thus became disseminated at the level of non-EC developed countries from this point in time, further reinforcing the enforcement-led priorities set by the Vienna Convention. A revised version of the European Plan to combat drugs was approved by the Edinburgh European Council of 11–12 December 1992. This version restated and updated the priorities of the 1990 plan, building on agreement reached in June 1992 via a draft Council regulation to set up a European Monitoring Centre for Drugs and Drug Addiction (EMCDDA). The regulation came into force on 30 October 1993, one month before the TEU itself (at which point CELAD was itself disbanded). Chapter 8 considers the EMCDDA in more detail.

Summary: comparing Trevi and CELAD

While CELAD established the basis for something resembling a consensual European drug policy framework, decisions on anti-trafficking measures were kept strictly outside Community competence. This can be clearly seen by examining the six areas outlined by the Commission in 1994 as priorities for joint action by member states to combat drug trafficking, as identified by the first two European Plans. Up until 1993, each priority had already been through a process of policy development via well-established (and clearly demarcated) intergovernmental 'sub-channels' (Commission, 1994: 39):

> Priorities 1 and 2:
>
> (1) reinforcement of drug controls at external borders; and,
> (2) cooperation and surveillance within Community borders.
> Channels: Trevi, MAG 92
>
> Priorities 3 and 4:
>
> (3) controlling manufacture of illicit drugs by preventing diversion of precursor and other chemicals; and

(4) measures against drug-related money laundering.
Channels: specialist G7-created Task Forces (CATF and FATF)[104]

Priority 5:

(5) strengthening of legal and judicial systems.
Channel: UN activity (supported by Council fora)

Of course, Community measures had begun to augment several of these areas: notably 3 (via a Regulation and Directive); and 4 (via a money laundering Directive).[105] Priority 6, provision of statistical information, was covered by the decision to establish the EMCDDA. Hence the framing and shaping of anti-trafficking measures was firmly retained in the hands of law enforcement officials and experts, exerting a powerful influence on how overall drug policy – and drug problems – were perceived in cause and effect terms.

Despite what he calls 'substantial limitations' in its scope of action, Estievenart (1995) argues that CELAD must be 'considered as a key factor in the political mobilization which has grown in parallel throughout Europe and the world' [on drugs] (p. 61). However, Elsen (1995) questions whether CELAD ever really took on the mission of 'essential coordination' within its original remit, which 'we would today regard as being above the "three pillars"' (p. 362). In this regard he notes that 'CELAD, by its origins and activities could not confine itself to areas to do with home affairs and justice: the greatest of its achievements (the European Plan to fight drugs, the Monitoring Centre, the European Prevention Week) are either entirely outside this framework or go considerably beyond it' (p. 366).

The form of intergovernmentalism represented by Trevi was thus fundamentally different to CELAD. At the root of this is the fundamental 'sanctity' of control by national governments over authority and control functions: while CELAD established a political framework for cooperation, Trevi exemplified the principle that law and order derives – and is indivisible – from national states. While governments are made up of transient political representatives, the apparatus of the state exudes continuity and permanence for which law enforcement officials are of great symbolic as well as practical significance. While Trevi can be said to be nominally accountable to political representatives, great freedom was allowed to law enforcement and bureaucratic officials to set policy parameters via their secret discussions.

The primacy of the Trevi position is illustrated by the reaction to the Cooney Report on drug trafficking and organized crime, commissioned by the European Parliament in 1991. Boekhout van Solinge (2002: 27) suggests that 'The subtext of the Cooney Report was that a new approach was needed', noting that it called for more attention to be paid to the demand side of the drugs problem as well as questioning the effectiveness of an approach based on repression in reducing the penetration of drugs into the EC. Boekhout van Solinge (2002: 27) also records that the report, published in 1992, somewhat undermined its recommendations by calling for unequivocal support for the three main UN drug conventions, despite the obvious contradiction in their provisions with many of the positions taken by the Report. The European Parliament resolution on the Report focused on calling for ratification of the UN conventions by member states, offering little challenge to the Trevi orthodoxy.

The entry into force of the TEU on 1 November 1993 brought with it a new institutional framework, resulting in the disbanding of both CELAD and Trevi. In placing the overall of significance of Trevi in context, den Boer and Wallace (2000) identify how the Trevi working arrangements influenced the institutional framework of the EU:

> Despite the lack of permanent secretariat, an extensive network had thus developed by 1991, which operated under the overall authority of the European Council on several political and executive levels, ranging from the responsible ministers through directors-general of the relevant ministries to middle-ranking civil servants and representatives of police forces and other agencies. (p. 495)

The Trevi *acquis* was to shape these structures far more than the work of CELAD. In the 1989–93 period the Coordinators' Group – Free Movement of Persons played a crucial role, with the Palma Document as its main basis for action (which, as has already been shown, was itself based fundamentally on the work and ideas emanating from Trevi and MAG). Following the negotiation of the TEU and as steps towards ratification proceeded, the crucial phase of transferring or adapting the pre-existing – and largely *ad hoc* – ways of working fell under the domain of this Group. It thus played a central role in developing the political rationale for the new post-Maastricht institutional decision-making structures. In December 1992 – a year after the agreement of the TEU – the Group submitted a report to the Edinburgh European Council meeting, reviewing progress since the Palma Document and, in its annex, proposing 'Work Structures for Title VI of the Treaty on European Union'. The annex (reproduced in Bunyan, 1997) illustrates how CELAD did not challenge the status quo (and the predominant consensus on the cognitive emphasis of drug policy at EC level), recording that 'As regards drugs issues within Title VI, the Coordinators had the benefit of advice from CELAD that drugs matters within Article K [matters of Justice and Home Affairs] would best be handled within the security law enforcement etc., sector' (p. 20).

The report concluded that the Coordinators 'agree with CELAD on that point' and as a consequence proposed that there should be a working group on drugs issues within Article K of the TEU under a steering group for this sector. At this point, the precise scope and terms of reference for the WG were felt to depend partly on further consideration of Article K.1.4 (relating to drug addiction matters).

One of the most striking features of the CELAD era is the absence of any criteria with which to evaluate the effectiveness of the different drug policy strands that it was responsible for advocating. Political consensus was indeed built during this phase, but the cognitive basis for the main emphasis of the approach (derived largely from work under the Trevi-MAG framework) did not incorporate empirical study on the effectiveness and impact of law enforcement on drug markets (particularly with regard to border controls). Instead it was rooted in normative expert testimonies which were based on a functional logic (supported by rhetorical statements and statistics of limited value) derived from inter-subjective, internally defined criteria for weighing and validating knowledge in these expert domains. As a consequence, the CELAD process did not represent a review but more a reordering and deeper institutionalization of drug policy, embedding the priorities arising out of prohibition-based strategies. It failed therefore to establish a basis for empirical review of the effectiveness over time of the multidisciplinary policy framework. This powerful cognitive position was carried forward into the new era of European Union. Chapter 8 now examines the transition phase to the TEU legal and institutional framework in more detail.

8
European Drug Policy and Maastricht: New Momentum, Familiar Priorities

One author – writing in the mid 1990s – described the entry into force of the Treaty on European Union in November 1993 as an event 'which enshrines and consolidates the political objective of the fight against the world-wide drugs issue' (Estievenart, 1995: 51). However, the period between the signing of the TEU in February 1992 and its entry into force – a period of around twenty months – saw important institutional developments closely associated with drugs policy. This period is notable for the emergence of two – quite different – institutions that owed their existence to the drugs issue in important ways: the European Police Office (Europol) and the European Monitoring Centre for Drugs and Drug Addiction (EMCDDA).

CELAD continued to operate throughout the TEU ratification period, producing (in 1992) the second and last of the two European Action Plans on Drugs for which it was responsible. The Trevi framework operated more or less unchanged during this period, with its working groups focused on the culmination of the aspects of the 1992 process within its remit along with the design and establishment of Europol. For the Trevi mechanisms it was more or less business as usual, albeit amid a certain amount of procedural innovation and inevitable bureaucratic manoeuvring as the new EU decision-making framework came closer to being realized. Analysis of this period also allows an assessment of the view that the TEU 'formalized the existing network of committees, without transforming the framework of authority and accountability' (den Boer and Wallace, 2000: 499). This chapter addresses this point in the context of assessing the implications of the TEU on the legal and procedural basis for European policy-making on drugs.

Drugs and the TEU

Transition

The TEU made drugs a so-called 'priority area' in each part of a new, unified institutional framework built around the so-called three pillars, outlined in Chapter 6. This framework is often cited as evidence of a political-level commitment to a multidisciplinary, integrated approach to drugs policy. At first glance, the institutional mode of handling drugs policy that was chosen does appear to reflect the 'global' approach to the problem advocated by CELAD and set out in the first action plan of 1990. However, from the outset it was difficult to see how the complex new 'pillarized' treaty arrangements (shown in Figure 8.1) would work in terms of generating a coordinated approach across and between the three pillars. Writing in 1993 – as the new structure began to take shape – Estievenart (1993) considered that 'The main consequence of this institutional choice is that it is difficult to read the Treaty from the drug angle. The Treaty has to be read "horizontally" and, accordingly, it is at the implementation level that the seeming lack of consistency may have to be compensated' (p. 12).

The horizontal structure of the Treaty was so constructed because the exact fields and precise ways of applying the powers given under the Treaty varied considerably across each of the three pillars. The new treaty structure thus required a new set of decision-making procedures and policy development mechanisms. The system that emerged was, in large part, a codification of what had been operating for some time (noticeably so in respect of the third [justice and home affairs] pillar, as we shall see). The text of the original TEU mentioned drugs by name in the first and third pillars, by implication only in the second, yet made no provision for a new body with specific responsibility for cross-pillar coordination of drugs issues (that is, an equivalent to CELAD or – as might have been expected – something akin to CELAD but with greater powers). In practice, responsibility for 'internal consistency' across the pillars was allocated to the Council and its organs: the Committee of Permanent Representatives (COREPER), a number of specialized working groups, and the Commission. In practice this meant that member states firmly retained (and in some respects tightened) control over decision-making, most evident in the areas relating to law enforcement under the third pillar.

Anti-trafficking measures were the only dimension of drugs policy that applied to all three pillars, although competences varied considerably in each. The most fiercely protected was police cooperation, exclusively

Fields for cooperation	PUBLIC HEALTH TRADE COOPERATION FIRST PILLAR	COMMON FOREIGN AND SECURITY POLICY SECOND PILLAR	JUSTICE AND HOME AFFAIRS THIRD PILLAR
Legal basis	Title II, Article 113 Article 235 Title X, Article 129	Title V, Article J	Title VI, Article K
Objectives	Preventing drug dependence, drugs as a priority in development aid	Fight against traffic in drugs [as set by Lisbon European Council decision, 1992]	Combating drug addiction; judicial and customs cooperation; police cooperation to prevent/combat drug trafficking
Legal instruments	Incentives Recommendations Decisions Regulations Directives	Joint actions Cooperation/coordination between member states	Joint actions Joint positions Conventions
Decision-making	Qualified majority voting (113/129) Unanimity (235)	Unanimity unless agreed	Unanimity unless agreed (or in procedural matters)
Right of initiative	European Commission	Member states, Commission only to be 'fully associated'	Member states only for matters involving judicial cooperation in civil and criminal matters, customs cooperation, and police cooperation

Figure 8.1 The Treaty on European Union and drug policy: legal basis, legal instruments, objectives, decision-making and right of initiative

located in the third pillar. Despite this, police cooperation in connection with drug trafficking warranted only a brief mention under Article K.1, point 9, in Title VI of the Treaty 'in connection with a European Police Office'. However, police cooperation received much more political attention than the brief mention in the Treaty text implies, highlighted by the fact that a 'Declaration on Police Cooperation' was annexed to the TEU (Fijnaut, 1996: 196).[106] Although the TEU added considerable momentum to the process of establishing Europol, the idea for its creation predated the negotiation of the TEU and discussion on an enabling convention was to run concurrently with the TEU ratification process: Trevi's 'Ad Hoc Working Group on Europol' (AHWGE) spanned the period between signing and ratification of the TEU.

The failure to create a body equivalent to CELAD within the TEU framework could also be seen as a reflection of the broader political agenda with which drugs were inextricably linked at this time. This is because, while the TEU provisions did not represent a rejection of the multidisciplinary principle for drugs policy-making embodied in CELAD, the principal focus lay in retaining the separation between intergovernmental and community decisions. In effect, the TEU process merely formalized the situation that applied during the CELAD era. As noted in Chapter 7, despite the avowed multidisciplinary character of CELAD, drug policy-making was effectively 'compartmentalized'. In practice CELAD merely rubber-stamped decisions taken in other *ad hoc* intergovernmental fora (that is Trevi and the Coordinators' Group). The TEU thus formally institutionalized this state of affairs. To substantiate this, let us look in more detail at the principal dynamics of drug policy under the TEU framework.

The legal basis

To recap, the first pillar of the EU preserved the *acquis communautaire* of the three Communities as well as introducing significant institutional changes and extending policy competence to the new EC in certain new areas (and strengthening some of the old ones). The first pillar was to utilize the 'Community method' of decision-making, in which Council reaches decisions only after the Commission has formulated a proposal (that is, the Commission has a 'right of initiative'). After proposals were formulated they would then be submitted to a relevant working party before going to Council for a final decision. In most cases, decisions would be made on the basis of qualified majority voting (qmv), although a growing number of areas came under a new 'co-decision procedure' in which the European Parliament gained the right of approval (see Nugent, 1999: 70–4).

Under the first pillar, specific reference to drugs was made in relation to Community competence in the field of public health. On the basis of the then Article 129 TEC [Treaty Establishing the European Community] (now Article 152 of the revised TEC[107]), the Community was given competence in relation to prevention of 'drug dependence'. In practice, this has meant that the Community has taken initiatives in relation to public information and education on drugs (the 1996–2000 programme of action on drug prevention, for example). Matters of this nature were to be dealt with by the Public Health Working Group (previously known as the Working Party on Health Questions prior to the TEU) and were to operate using the co-decision procedure.[108]

The first pillar also opened up the possibility of a range of other joint measures via its provisions in relation to the *acquis*, that is, Community actions that predated the TEU. This covered aspects of the drugs dossier already linked to aid and trade policy in relation to:

- development cooperation (North-South, Eastern Europe, and ACP countries)
- commercial policy (drug precursor substances, common customs tariff and money laundering).

Development cooperation and drug-related issues arose in the work of the first pillar External Relations Working Group. The TEU made it a specific treaty commitment for the first time that the Community should help developing countries, and provide multi-annual programmes to achieve this. In relation to commercial policy, Community competence arises because precursors relate to trade, while money laundering has an impact on the operation of the internal market.[109] These two areas were to be handled by the Economic Affairs and Finances working groups respectively. In fact, the Community had issued a directive on money laundering during 1991 and, in 1990, had issued a directive on control of chemical precursors, followed up by a regulation in 1992. However, these established competences should not be confused with control over the 'operative implementation of this EC legislation' (European Parliament, 2000a: 56). Prosecution of cases of money laundering and abuse of precursors was firmly left in the hands of police, customs authorities and judicial bodies of member states. As we shall see, the influence over measures relating to prosecuting drug trafficking offences was firmly restricted to the third pillar.

Specific measures designed to counter drug trafficking were thus embedded under the first pillar of the Treaty, thereby consolidating the role of the Commission that had been recognized after 1987 in building an integrated approach to the drugs problem.[110] In many ways the TEU formalized the 'bureaucratic territory' of the Commission, creating a domain of work to be defended and where possible extended. However, to restate, none of these measures had a direct impact on *how* member states would enforce more overtly security-related dimensions of drug policy. None the less, the role of the Commission was also given a boost in relation to drug policy under the second pillar (CFSP) created by the TEU, without the Commission actually having a right of initiative in this area. Title V, Article J of the original TEU set out the relationship between drugs and CFSP. However, the foreign policy aspect of anti-drugs measures was not specifically referred to under Title V, and measures of this nature (such as the inclusion of 'drugs clauses' in trade agreements) fell within the *acquis* element of the first pillar anyway.[111]

An important political decision was taken at the Lisbon European Council of 26–27 June 1992 – the first post-Maastricht summit, and well over a year before final ratification of the TEU – that 'the fight against the traffic in illicit drugs' was an area 'open to joint action *vis-à-vis* particular countries or groups of countries' (Estievenart, 1995: 88). The Lisbon verdict provided the definitive political interpretation of the legal possibilities provided for under the second pillar, deciding to identify 'even if only by way of guidance, traffic in illicit drugs as a "specific objective" in applying the CFSP' (Estievenart, 1993: 16). Largely as a result of this decision the Commission was given a more elevated role in trying to coordinate and ensure 'consistency' of drug policy between the three pillars. This arose out of two key provisions of the TEU: Article C conferred responsibility for ensuring the consistency of the external activities of the Union on the Council and the Commission while Article J.9 stated that the Commission should be 'fully associated' with work carried out in the CFSP field. Drugs issues were now systematically incorporated into virtually all diplomatic relations with third countries or regional organizations. However, the decision on the content of how to develop and implement *new* policy initiatives remained firmly defined by the legal platform under which priority sub-objectives were assigned to each of the three pillars. It is under the third pillar that the real significance of this factor becomes most apparent.

Chapter 6 gave a brief overview of third pillar activities, covering fields that prior to the TEU had always been intrinsically associated with national sovereignty, with varying degrees of intergovernmental coordination. Title VI, Article K of the TEU described actions in this field. Decision-making procedures under Title VI required unanimity for any measure to be passed, reflecting the high sensitivity of member states. Article K.1 took the important step of making the drug problem a cross-disciplinary priority:

> For the purposes of achieving the objectives of the Union, in particular the free movement of persons, and without prejudice to the powers of the European Community, member states shall regard the following as matters of common interest [*Note: items K.1 (1), (2), (3), (5), and (6) relate to non-drugs matters so are not included here*]
>
> (4) combating drug addiction in so far as this is not covered by (7) to (9);
> (7) judicial cooperation in criminal matters;
> (8) customs cooperation;
> (9) police cooperation for the purposes of preventing and combating terrorism, unlawful drug trafficking and other serious forms of international crime, including if necessary certain aspects of customs cooperation, in connection with the organization of a Union-wide system for exchanging information within a European Police Office (EUROPOL). (Council/Commission, 1992: 131–2)

A recent European Parliament report, reflecting on Article K.1(9), expressed the view that 'According to this formula, illegal drugs trafficking on whatever level of the illegal market is defined indiscriminately as serious crime' (European Parliament, 2000a: 54). As Estievenart (1995) points out, the provisions of Article K mandated *any* EU drugs action programme to include the following elements:

> (a) combating drug addiction, not including activities under Article 129 (prevention) [first pillar] and (b), (c) and (d) below;
> (b) judicial cooperation in criminal matters;
> (c) customs cooperation, not including activities which fall within the Community's competence (first pillar), particularly as regards precursors;
> (d) police cooperation, (preventing and clamping down on drug trafficking) in liaison with Europol (particularly the Europol Drugs Unit [see later in this chapter]), excepting again for activities under the first pillar (precursors, laundering). (p. 89)

For (a), competence is shared between member states and the Commission, whereas – and this is the crucial distinction – for (b), (c) and

(d) member states unambiguously have sole right of initiative via Council. Legal instruments adopted under the third pillar, where they are legally binding, are binding under international law and not Community law. As noted in Chapter 6, three possible types were made available under Article K.3 (2)(c) of Title VI. Of these, only conventions were seen as 'clearly indicative of a binding act of public international law' (House of Lords, 1997a: 46). The remaining two instruments – joint positions and joint actions – subsequently generated considerable debate as to their legal status.[112] The Council could also adopt non-binding resolutions and recommendations. With regard to items K.1 (7)–(9) the Commission was given no right of initiative. Also, under Article K.6, the European Parliament was to be merely 'kept informed' of Title VI discussions by the Presidency and the Commission 'as appropriate', but its powers were limited to the vague principle that its views must be 'duly taken into consideration'.

The TEU made the drug problem a priority area across all three pillars, providing a hitherto absent legal underpinning for an integrated approach. As has already been pointed out, this kind of approach required some form of overall action plan to be put in place, providing the Commission with a prominent role (as a kind of surrogate CELAD). As Estievenart (1995) has pointed out (p. 90), the 'main guidelines and milestones' for this process lay in the first two European plans to combat drugs, and not in the implementation of the Treaty itself. None the less, as the Lisbon European Council showed, the setting of drug policy objectives may actually emerge from the highest political level: political heads of member states. Given that the powers of the Commission, Council and European Parliament are different for each of the three pillars there is a clear risk that as a result drugs may become sub-categories of broader priority areas, however. In the case of the third pillar, matters concerned with drug enforcement were defined as matters on which member states retained full control and hence right of veto. It is equally important to consider the new institutional structures associated with the legal basis of the TEU with reference to how this related to the setting of priorities and their implementation in the context of an integrated policy framework. The key point here is to understand how policy initiatives and priorities were to be developed as part of a hierarchically ordered decision-making process within *each* pillar.

Institutional mechanics/dynamics

The pre-Maastricht *ad hoc* institutional structure was outlined in the previous chapter (shown graphically in Figure 7.1). If this is compared with the organizational structure under the TEU a remarkably high level of similarity is apparent. Figure 8.2 shows the initial TEU decision-making framework.

Existing Community regulations such as those on money laundering and precursors ensured an essentially procedural role for first pillar working groups, calibrating and monitoring the operation of measures in these areas. In the second pillar a new working party was established to deal with drug-related issues, with the responsibility of ensuring that first pillar 'external measures' (that is, trade and aid policies affecting third countries) were consistent and coordinated with CFSP measures. The Common Foreign and Security Policy Working Group on Drugs, better known by the acronym CODRO, had also to ensure that CFSP measures were in turn consistent with third pillar measures taken under cooperation in the field of justice and home affairs. The existence of a clear hierarchy skewed in the direction of the third pillar was confirmed by the fact that the CFSP working party was required to report to a new coordinating committee responsible for third pillar matters: the K.4 Committee (named after the clause in the TEU that mandated its existence). In fact, the K.4 Committee was a formalized version of the Coordinators' Group, established during the Trevi period in 1988. The K.4 Committee was in turn made responsible to COREPER for coordinating measures on drugs under the third pillar. Each member state has a national delegation – or Permanent Representation – based in Brussels, which acts effectively as an embassy to the EU. Delegations are normally headed by a Permanent Representative, who is generally a senior diplomat, and are staffed by officials seconded from specialist national ministries. As Nugent (1999: 149) points out: 'Of the many forums in which governments meet "in Council" below ministerial level, the most important is the Committee of Permanent Representatives (COREPER)'. There are in fact two COREPERs: COREPER I is made up of Deputy Permanent Representatives plus support staff, whereas the more senior COREPER II includes Permanent Representatives plus support staff.

The work of the Council of Ministers and of COREPER is filtered through a complex network of specialized committees and working parties. Figure 8.2 illustrates that COREPER sits above the three pillars, and as such was intended to provide general coordination on drugs issues under the TEU system (Estievenart, 1995: 91). However, the practical implementation of the TEU divided up the COREPER remit between the pillars, with third pillar activity solely under the domain of COREPER II. As originally envisaged, cooperation on third pillar matters was based on five decision-making levels, of which the Council was the most

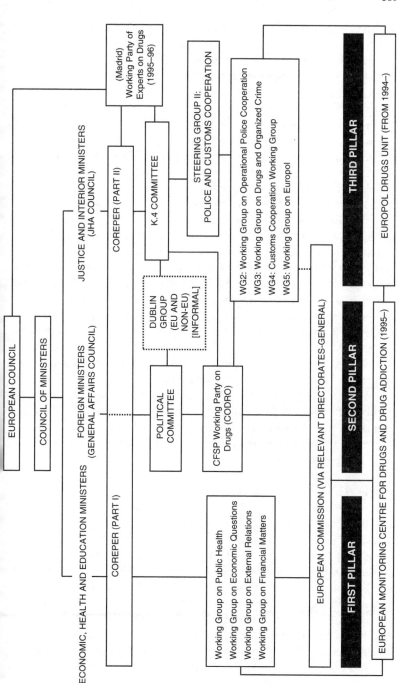

Figure 8.2 Drug policy-making institutional structure post European Union (1993–96)

senior (in this case the Justice and Home Affairs Council). The function of the K.4 Committee was to contribute alongside COREPER II in preparing work for the Council of Justice and Home Affairs Ministers. In practice, many third pillar proposals are wholly agreed at COREPER level, with European Council meetings becoming involved only when there is disagreement or to give political backing at the highest level. This reveals an important – and contentious – procedural feature of JHA Council decision-making. COREPER filters decisions into two main categories when preparing items for the agenda of JHA Council meetings (as a rule, there are two of these per Presidency period): matters with which COREPER is in full agreement (known as 'A points') and matters on which COREPER has been unable to reach agreement ('B points'). 'A point' items are agreed without debate between ministers. While there is an understandable need to streamline complex decisions, many 'A points' have concerned matters that have an impact on civil society and may potentially affect civil liberties, raising questions about the democratic accountability of decision-making at COREPER level and below (Chapters 9 and 10 return to this theme). However, to understand the 'classical' form of legislative process the structure needs to be examined in more detail. This reveals the extent to which expert deliberation determines policy proposals in advance of political decision-making.

As classically envisaged, a proposal would first be considered at the level of a working group, after which it would be referred upwards to one of three Steering Groups (SGs), then the K.4 Committee and then finally COREPER II before approval at JHA Council level.[113] Under the original third pillar structure three steering groups were tasked to report directly to the K.4 Committee, each responsible for proposing an annual work programme:

Steering Group I (Immigration and asylum)
Steering Group II (Police and customs cooperation)
Steering Group III (Judicial cooperation).

Drugs issues were not part of the remit of the first group so thus became an item to be discussed *inter alia* in work on police, customs and, on some occasions, judicial cooperation (in relation to international organized crime). A range of working groups reported to SGII, with Working Group 3 (directly equivalent to Trevi WGIII) tasked with drugs and organized crime matters. Another four groups were specified under SGII and it was clear that drugs issues would also be discussed in some form during the work of: WG 2 (operational police cooperation), WG 4 (customs), and WG 5 (Europol). In the case of the latter, as the next section shows, the issue of drug trafficking remained the primary rationale for the ongoing development of Europol. As with Trevi, the working groups provided for interaction between officials and senior law enforcement officers. This ensured that experts were given the initial responsibility to develop 'workable' policy ideas and rationale.

During its six-month tenure, the state holding the EU Presidency has the right to chair all meetings: in Council, COREPER, K.4 Committee and all working groups.[114] This also gives the Presidency state initiative through the power to nominate proposals. The pressure on Presidency states to show demonstrable 'progress' during what is a relatively short period makes for the inevitable consolidation of previously agreed measures (thus giving them *de facto* priority). Proposals that diverge from previous practice become 'radical' by definition. When a smaller state holds the Presidency it is forced to rely on the permanent Council Secretariat (DG H) far more than one the larger states.[115] This is particularly acute in the case of the third pillar, and tends to add a further layer of bureaucratic inertia whereby existing preferences and priorities are maintained. The net result of this process, allied to the legal and institutional factors already discussed, tends to result in inherent inflexibility with regard to the dynamics of EU drug policy making. Most bodies meet, on average, around once a month, although COREPER will tend to meet more frequently around the time of Council meetings and working groups may also convene more frequently if a large amount of business is being processed. It is exceptionally difficult to acquire details of the precise working methods of individual third pillar working groups, but it is self-evident that they generate the 'raw material' for decisions to be taken higher up the hierarchical chain of decision-making. This 'functional' role is made easier by the fact that broad policy parameters are clearly understood by all parties at working group level: their primary role is to develop specific measures in line with pre-set objectives.

While third pillar working groups are primarily made up of national civil servants, national law enforcement experts are sometimes also invited to participate. In practice, experts routinely have a more indirect input via briefings to national officials, particularly when an issue is deemed to have 'technical' law enforcement dimensions. In this way, national law enforcement preferences are likely to inform deliberations even when law enforcement experts are not present. External observers – and sometimes participants – may also be invited to specific working groups (see Chapters 9 and 10 on this point). An illustration of the degree to which participants in working groups may also be part of a broader international policy-making network external to the EC–EU framework is revealed in a quote from Jochen Meyer, Chairman of the Enforcement Committee of the World Customs Organization (WCO). Reflecting on the degree to which the work of his organization was coordinated with EC–EU work by the MAG and MAG 92 working groups, he observed (in 1994) that 'When all is said and done, if you look at the list of participants in all the meetings, those who go to MAG meetings also come to our meetings' (Meyer, quoted in European Parliament, 2000a: 84).

There is also a high level of 'networking' between specialists in COREPER and counterparts from national permanent representations to the EU. This informal contact is a highly significant part of the process whereby national positions are articulated and differences established outside of the more formal meetings.

Despite the high-profile political commitment to an integrated EU drugs policy, control of drug enforcement (aimed principally at trafficking) rested even more firmly in the hands of member states as a result of the TEU. By giving a more prominent role to permanent representatives of the member states, the institutional structure of the TEU consolidated and extended the authoritative claims to policy-relevant knowledge of law enforcement experts. It did this by drawing a line under the Trevi *acquis*, which was incorporated directly into the TEU without question, leaving 'political' decisions on the acceptability of new policy measures proposed by working and steering groups to COREPER. The TEU institutional structure marked a significant moment when enforcement action on drugs was given a higher degree of precedence than ever before, because it was now part of an integrated institutional framework whose overall political legitimacy could not be questioned in the way that *ad hoc* intergovernmental structures could be. The new structure also placed a greater emphasis on the 'efficiency' of policy-making, generating pressure for results-oriented policy-making over evaluation. The process has been characterized as follows:

> Unlike in the first pillar, where the disciplines of Commission proposals and parliamentary co-decision imposed a timetable, dossiers in the third pillar might move forward rapidly from initial draft to adoption, or change shape radically between first and final draft, as Presidency officials or *ad hoc* working groups sought consensual agreement. (den Boer and Wallace, 2000: 507)

The remainder of this chapter considers how both Europol and the EMCDDA evolved in the transition period between Maastricht and the entry into force of the TEU; at which point the decision-making structures described above became fully operational.

Emergence of Europol

The concept of a 'European police office' can be traced back to the 1970s (see Woodward, 1993: 11–14; Fijnaut, 1996: 198–200), but by the late 1980s a debate had emerged as to whether such an organization should be a fully fledged EC police force (as favoured by then German Chancellor Kohl) or an intelligence-gathering agency (preferred by the UK government at that time) (European Parliament, 2000: 91). The subsequent emergence of what we now know as Europol – which formally began operations on 1 July 1999 – was marked by a series of political compromises as well as concerns about the accountability of both the organization itself and, most pertinently, the policy-making process that led to its creation. Europol first emerged in 1993 in the shape of the 'Europol Drugs Unit' (EDU), which operated throughout the period while an enabling convention was ratified by member states.

The EDU exemplifies that drug trafficking has provided the principal rationale for Europol, even though the organization has steadily acquired a much broader set of competences to tackle other forms of crime. Political decision-making about Europol has been entirely intergovernmental, first under the ambit of the Trevi framework and subsequently under the third pillar arrangements brought in by the TEU. The establishment of the EDU in 1993 was the culmination of a process that had begun in 1987, with Trevi working groups instrumental in developing a rationale for the organization. The influence of Trevi working groups can be traced via a series of subtle terminological shifts in the name of the new organization. Initially, proposals envisaged a 'European Drugs Intelligence Unit' (EDIU), until the word intelligence was dropped from this name (see below). Writing in 1994, den Boer (1994: 175) speculated – presciently as it turned out – that this allowed a flexibility as to a broadening of the Europol remit beyond information and intelligence exchange (that is, the role indicated by Article K.1 (9) TEU) and into more 'operational' areas. Let us first trace the emergence of Europol in more detail and see how drug trafficking formed the principal rationale for its development.

During 1987, Trevi WG III proposed the posting of Drugs Liaison Officers (DLOs) outside Europe to gather information on producer and transit countries and recommended setting up National Drugs Intelligence Units (NDIUs) in each member state. Following the June 1989

'Palma Document' produced by the Coordinators' Group (notable for its request that the Trevi 92 working group draw up a report setting out the off-setting measures in anticipation of the removal of internal frontiers) national home affairs ministers adopted a Declaration at their Trevi meeting in Paris on 15 December 1989. The Declaration noted that the then 12 EEC member states had 'already agreed' to set up national intelligence units on drugs and 'to study the need for the possible extension at European level' (Declaration reproduced in Bunyan, 1997: 36).[116]

In June 1990, the Trevi 92 working group delivered a 'programme of action' to the Dublin European Council. The programme set out several points relating to the 'fight against drug trafficking', including a call to establish a network of drug liaison officers within the EEC as well as reinforcing and coordinating surveillance at external frontiers.[117] Although the Trevi document proposed only a study on the need for and conditions under which an EDIU be established, Trevi ministers chose to commit to the establishment of such an organization. A sub-group of Trevi WG III was established to consider the task of establishing an EDIU. In June 1991, Trevi ministers agreed guidelines for DLOs to work *within* the EC, collecting general crime information and coordinating intra-EC requests for operational data about drug crime (Woodward, 1993: 14). Soon afterwards, in a significant development, the German delegation submitted proposals to the Luxembourg European Council of 28 and 29 June 1991 on the establishment of a 'European Criminal Investigation Office'.

The German initiative appears to have been the catalyst for political agreement among heads of government on the rationale for 'a Europol'. Council instructed the WG III sub-group to examine the German proposals 'so that initial proposals for the establishment of Europol could be submitted to [the European Council] December meeting in Maastricht' (Trevi Ministers Report to Maastricht European Council, reproduced in Bunyan, 1997: 41). The Maastricht European Council of 9–10 December 1991 had a heavy agenda, hence the submission of a report from Trevi ministers in which they unanimously agreed that Europol should be established, beginning with a drugs intelligence unit, was unlikely to receive anything other than a rubber stamp of approval. As well as formally proposing that the first step in developing Europol should be the creation of a Europol Drugs Unit (note the subtle change in name) the report went so far as to say that the focus on drugs was essentially a 'stepping stone' as the scope of the organization would be progressively widened to include other crimes deemed to pose a threat to member states.

Woodward (1993) notes that the first stage of Europol entailed setting up the EDU, acting as the focal point for the NDIUs. The second stage required the setting up of centralized 'national criminal intelligence services' (the United Kingdom was among the first to follow this model, establishing the National Criminal Intelligence Service [NCIS] in April 1992), expressly designed to function as 'intelligence gatekeepers' between Europol and national police agencies. Finally, it was anticipated that a fully fledged Europol would emerge, analysing intelligence data on all forms of organized crime, not just drug trafficking. Although it was publicly denied for some time, the intention that the EDU was intended to cover all crimes from the outset was confirmed by the report (Bunyan, 1997: 40), which was not released into the public domain. The Maastricht summit fully endorsed the Trevi proposals and instructed that a new Trevi working group, the Ad Hoc Working Group on Europol (AHWGE) should be established, and that it should be chaired by the UK. Europol was then given a basis under treaty via Article K.1 (9) TEU.

The Portuguese Presidency in the first half of 1992 made the establishment of Europol a priority. The Trevi ministerial meeting at Lisbon of 11–12 June 1992 reached 'consensus' on the need to draw up a convention to bring Europol into operation (by the ambitious date of 1 January 1993) along with agreement to set up a 'project team' – to be chaired by Germany – tasked with establishing Europol. In their report to the Lisbon European Council of 26–27 June 1992, the Trevi ministers recorded that the AHWGE 'has carried out detailed work both on the establishment of the Europol Drugs Unit and also on the possible future expansion of Europol to cover areas of criminality other than drugs' (text of original report reproduced in Bunyan, 1997: 43). The report was endorsed by the European Council, which also called for a convention to be prepared to formally establish Europol. The report, in noting that remaining work on setting up the EDU mostly concerned 'technical and specialized matters', suggested this be allocated to the proposed new full-time project team. A small group of 15 (including high-ranking police officers with experience in drugs intelligence matters) was recruited and tasked with building the infrastructure of the new organization. All member states were entitled to nominate staff for what became known as 'Project Group Europol' (PGE), though only a limited number did so (Woodward (1993) notes that the UK sent representatives from NCIS and HM Customs and Excise). The appointed director of PGE was Jürgen Storbeck, from the German national police force, the Bundeskriminalamt (BKA). The PGE, which reported into the AHWGE, formally began work in September 1992.[118]

The AHWGE was assigned responsibility to draw up a convention establishing Europol. The Lisbon report also recorded that work via the AHWGE was proceeding to ensure that national criminal intelligence services were developed in all member states in order to support the operation of Europol, highlighting a considerable cross-fertilization of law enforcement practice between national and European levels (as well as mandating public expenditure). On 2 June 1993, Trevi ministers meeting in Copenhagen signed a Ministerial Agreement to set up the EDU, for which no ratification (or debate) was either required or undertaken in national parliaments.[119] This example again shows how ministerial approval frequently represents little more than a rubber stamp of expert deliberations, even on issues with potentially far-reaching implications. The Ministerial Agreement was thus a political compromise, allowing an embryonic Europol to begin operations on a limited basis while the implementing convention was prepared and then ratified, itself against the backdrop of the difficult passage of the TEU itself. As noted above, the AHWGE had primary responsibility for drafting the Europol Convention, but the minutes of the extraordinary Trevi ministers meeting in Copenhagen on 29 June 1993 reveal that the PGE had a direct input to this process:

> The Project Team will continue developmental work for the pre-conventional phase of EDU, particularly in the areas of intelligence and data processing ... and provide professional advice to the Ad Hoc Working Group on technical and practical matters related to the drafting of the convention establishing Europol. (Original minutes, reproduced in Bunyan, 1997: 45–6)

A combination of police officers and interior ministry officials were thus responsible for proposing the detailed terms of reference and powers for Europol. In October 1993, Council decided that Europol would be located in The Hague in The Netherlands. The EDU began operations at this location in January 1994.

The idea that Europol would have 'operational powers' (broadly in line with the original German vision of a 'European FBI') remained a contentious subject among member states. Despite this, the subsequent development of the EDU was to be characterized by a process of steady extension to the powers and remit of this nascent form of Europol. This process was conducted under a cloak of secrecy, with little effort given to informing national parliaments let alone civil society. Yet as early as 1992, the Civil Liberties and Internal Affairs Committee of the European

Parliament had questioned the choice of drug crime as the focus of the first stage of Europol, noting that 'Even many police officers are surprised that the Europol initiative is centred on drugs, given that so many initiatives already exist in this field. It would not appear to reflect operational requirements' (European Parliament, 1992: 16).

The Parliament's surprisingly strident viewpoint had negligible impact at the level of national political concerns, however. In June 1994, Jürgen Storbeck was formally appointed as Director of the EDU, even though the organization had actually been operating (with Storbeck in charge) in The Hague since January of that year. The EDU had been playing an active role in ongoing discussions regarding the Europol Convention as it participated in the new TEU Working Group on Europol (WG 5, the ex-AHWGE under Trevi) after November 1993. Agreement on the draft text of the Convention was proving difficult, even before the lengthy ratification process could begin, prompting Germany, which held the EU Presidency in the second half of 1994, to propose a joint action (under Title VI of the TEU) extending the range of crimes under the EDU remit. The joint action (95/73/JHA) agreed by the Council of Justice and Home Affairs Ministers on 10 March 1995 added the following criminal activities to the original EDU remit to tackle illicit drug trafficking (OJ L 62, 20 March 1995):

– Illicit trafficking in radioactive and nuclear substances;
– Crimes involving clandestine immigration networks; and
– Illicit vehicle trafficking.

In addition, the criminal organizations involved together with any associated money laundering were also brought within the ambit of Europol. Once again, no national parliamentary agreement was required for this extension of the EDU role beyond drug trafficking. The Europol Convention was finally signed in July 1995 (OJ C 316, 27 November 1995), although ratification proved a very slow process, with entry into force taking until 1 October 1998, although even then the organization did not begin 'full' operations until June 1999.[120] In the intervening years, while ratification dragged on, the EDU saw its role further extended by a series of joint actions during 1996 as well as in connection with a resolution aimed at curbing 'drug tourism' (see Chapter 9).[121] Although the EDU was supposed to be a non-operational organization, facilitating only the exchange and analysis of intelligence, it became involved in operations involving 'controlled delivery' of drugs at a relatively early stage of its existence.[122] This function was carried out by European Liaison Officers (ELOs) from national law enforcement agencies based at EDU, thereby blurring the notion of 'operational' work carried out by the EDU. Furthermore, the plan for Europol to be the hub of a computerized system of databases has taken on significant momentum in recent years (and was discussed well in advance of ratification), along with plans to develop the Europol mandate to allow participation in 'joint operational teams'.[123] These developments, assessed further in Chapter 10, have included a significant further extension in the range of crimes within the competence of Europol.

What is strikingly clear from the history of the EDU and what proved a seamless (albeit drawn out) transition into a fully fledged Europol is how the drugs issue has been accepted as providing a rationale 'beyond question' (the European Parliament's concerns never gained saliency here), emphasizing the cognitive dominance of the Trevi ideas framework. The ideological *leitmotif* of the drugs threat has provided a powerful means by which to minimize national democratic debate about the powers given to the evolving organization. An additional factor here – certainly in terms of elite level influence – was the independence allowed to the articulate director of the EDU (and now Europol), Jürgen Storbeck, who was prominent in placing the rationale for Europol on a broader footing and to a wider audience, particularly in the 1994–97 period (that is, immediately prior to the signing of the Convention and during the ratification stage).[124] Most of this discourse projected a much broader 'crime-fighting' role for Europol (a projection that has, in fact, become a reality) and served to further minimize questions regarding the efficacy of the organization's drug-related remit as well as wider issues regarding enforcement-led drug policies. Higher levels of informal as well as formal operational interaction and strategic dialogue unquestionably enhanced the cognitive authority of national law enforcement officials during this period.[125] It should also be recognized that the officials (including law enforcement professionals) who have played a key expert function might well have viewed the process as an opportunity for career enhancement. In being placed at the forefront of European drug enforcement policy it is clear that they would advocate a system that fulfilled – as a matter of priority – their professional vision. The next section examines the contrast between the establishment of Europol and an institution whose mandate is unambiguously associated with the drugs issue alone: the EMCDDA.

Origins and role of the EMCDDA

The case for a drugs 'monitoring centre' was made in the 1989 Mitterand proposals that established CELAD, the body that in turn was to do most of the preparatory work for the EMCDDA. The procedures through which the EMCDDA was created contrast strongly with Europol, however, as it did not impinge upon political sensitivities. A close association between the EMCDDA and the Commission is another illustration of the emergence of a more prominent role for the latter in terms of the overall drug policy development process in the post-TEU era.

The EMCDDA was established on the basis of a Council regulation in February 1993 (OJ L 36, 12 February 1993), following an initial Council decision in 1991, and became fully operational in 1995. The EMCDDA is a decentralized Community 'information agency' given the task of providing 'the Community and its Member States with objective, reliable and comparable information at European level concerning drugs and drug addiction and their consequences' (ibid.: 2). It was inevitable that the work of the EMCDDA would enter a politicized decision-making arena, although its role was carefully circumscribed in that the EMCDDA 'should not prejudice the allocation of powers between the Community and its member states with regard to the legislative provisions concerning drug supply and demand' (ibid.: 2). This seems to be a clear indication that the EMCDDA should avoid addressing 'controversial' issues; for example, the decriminalization or legalization debates. In 1997, the Council adopted a 'Joint Action concerning information exchange, risk assessment and the control of new synthetic drugs' (OJ L 167, 25 June 1997). One of the key provisions of this measure was a joint mandate given to both the EMCDDA and EDU to collect data and to produce a joint 'risk assessment' report, designed to provide a cognitive resource for member states to decide, ultimately through Council, whether or not to place new drugs under control. The EMCDDA was thus mandated to contribute to decision-making that may lead to enforcement actions, acting as the focal point for EU data drawn from the overall REITOX network, which facilitates the collation and discussion of scientific knowledge and expertise on ('illegal') drugs from national sources. The most novel feature of this procedure is the integration for the first time of both enforcement and epidemiological data in determining the threat from drugs. Actions relating to this have been a prominent part of both the current and previous (1998–2000) EMCDDA work programmes.

Much attention has been focused on the development of an 'early warning system' designed to ensure that new drugs are brought under control as quickly as possible. The system has three phases, the first of which requires information from national sources to be sent either to Europol or the EMCDDA, who in turn inform the Commission and the European Agency for the Evaluation of Medicinal Products (EMEA).

The second stage involves the EMCDDA Scientific Committee who, along with all other partners, agree a 'risk assessment report' for submission to the Horizontal Working Party on Drugs (HWPD), which has become an important Council working group (see Chapters 9 and 10). Finally, a Council decision will be taken; this will always be the JHA Council as the use of repressive measures is a possibility (hence unanimity will be required). This mechanism appears to offer some degree of balance in decision-making by involving a range of different forms of expertise, though the process is so designed primarily to reduce the time taken from the emergence of a new synthetic drug to when it can be criminalized. Nevertheless, it is perhaps the most interesting example whereby law enforcement, scientific and bureaucratic decision-makers interact with common purpose within the EU.

One of the most important aspects of EMCDDA work to date has been the creation of networks of interaction between groups of experts and in the stimulation of information flows between officials, academics and specialists at both governmental and non-governmental levels.[126] This 'universe' exemplifies the diversity of expertise on the drug phenomenon, and reflects a planned strategy to attempt to build consensus through specialist dialogue. It is difficult to generalize about the possible impact of this strategy over the medium to long term, although there is little doubt that the work of the EMCDDA to date has consistently represented the European drug phenomenon as multifaceted, without challenging the underlying basis of prohibition. The publications of the EMCDDA (most notably its annual reports, the first of which appeared in 1996) also provide a cognitive resource with regard to perceptions about the drugs problem from a European perspective, although it is difficult to gauge the impact of this process. The information collated, processed and disseminated by the EMCDDA is aimed at policy-makers, experts and – nominally – a general public audience. This forms a marked contrast with other sources of information about drugs in the EU that are unavailable even to specialist researchers, notably the deliberations of the working parties that advise the Council, and evidence from bodies such as EDU-Europol.[127]

With regard to how the EMCDDA may have begun to influence policy-making on a more direct basis, the evidence relates mostly to its relationships with six 'partner organizations', only one of which is restricted to EU member states. The two 'priority' partners are the Pompidou Group and EDU-Europol, along with the WHO, UNDCP, WCO and Interpol. The basis of cooperation ostensibly covers ways of improving comparability of drug-related data, although the type and content varies widely across the various partners. The WCO, for example, primarily produces data in relation to seizures from illicit trafficking, whereas the Pompidou Group has traditionally collected only epidemiological data. Co-working on the synthetic drugs early warning procedure may well have led to a more cordial working relationship between the EMCDDA and EDU-Europol than was apparent in the early years of EMCDDA operations (several EU-level policy actors made the point that the EMCDDA was almost certainly perceived as a 'Commission body', thereby limiting its influence initially).[128] Whereas EDU-Europol has been given almost complete freedom to attend third pillar meetings from the outset, the EMCDDA has had much more restricted access, although nominally it is represented by the Commission (which has observer status) at all times.

On one level, the EMCDDA can be viewed in straightforward functional terms, whereby moves towards Union have fostered a culture of uniformity for which agreement on problem definition (and the types of data used to support this) has become a prerequisite. Dehousse (1997) sets out the key arguments in this respect as well as considering the more general role of European agencies as providers of legitimacy. He makes the general argument that whatever power European agencies have been granted this has not been taken away from the 'political' institutions of the Community, but 'rather from obscure committees bringing together national and European officials' (Dehousse, 1997: 258). However, the area of drug enforcement is marked by a range of influential committees under the third pillar (and previously under Trevi), hence the establishment of the EMCDDA has not affected their role or influence (the EMCDDA is certainly not constructed so as it might challenge the legitimacy of their positions). While the EMCDDA has quickly established itself as an important information provider since 1995, other institutional developments have exerted a much greater influence on the overall substance of drug policy.

Summary

Both Europol and the EMCDDA can be described as 'knowledge brokers' in relation to EC–EU drugs policy (Dorn, 1996a). Both institutions were 'born' during the period of institutional realignment that was linked to the significant changes brought about by the TEU. The information provided by each of the two bodies reflects their location in the decision-making system: all substantive knowledge emanating from Europol is restricted to the intergovernmental sphere, whereas the

EMCDDA serves a broader Community function in relation to overall drug policy and makes its findings available to civil society. As 'police' and 'civil' institutions respectively, Europol and the EMCDDA exemplify the way that enforcement knowledge is a highly circumscribed commodity in relation to drug policy. While the initial rationale and legitimacy of Europol was founded on an anti-drug trafficking role it has been shown that this was partly an instrumental device in establishing what has become the lead institution in the building of a much broader EU security apparatus.

Between 1976 and 1993 cooperation on justice and home affairs between EC member states was governed by the *ad hoc* arrangements established under the Trevi framework, into which the drugs issue was introduced from 1985. The preceding analysis has shown the degree to which the negotiation and agreement of the TEU marked a period of significant emphasis on matters concerned with the enforcement aspects of drug policy, both constitutive of and reflecting the emphasis inherent within the design of the new institutional structure of the EU. Expert groups played a significant role in shaping and framing the development of both operational and strategic arguments underpinning political decision-making in this phase, notably so in terms of the emergence of Europol. Member states emphatically demonstrated that where authority and control issues were involved, intergovernmental structures were to be rigidly demarcated. This was also a period when the broader political backdrop created the conditions for a more 'technocratic' emphasis on the drugs issue at European level as political decision-makers were preoccupied with the wider implications of extended integration; the result was an institutionalized response focused on enforcement. Chapter 9 now examines how these structures evolved in the period 1993–99, that is, once the TEU was ratified and until a revised set of arrangements were brought in under the Treaty of Amsterdam in 1999 (covered in Chapter 10).

9
Expert Influence and
EU Drugs Policy, 1993–1999

The first significant initiative on drugs policy after the EU framework became operational emerged in June 1994. At this time the Commission presented a proposal to Council for a new 1995–99 European action plan to combat drugs (Commission, 1994).[129] The fact that the Commission submitted the proposal seemed to imply that it had acquired a new and more prominent role in drug policy development under the new structure. The proposed action plan was broken down into four areas:

1 measures to reduce demand for drugs
2 measures to combat drug trafficking
3 measures at international level
4 coordination.

However, initial impressions were misleading, as in formulating the proposal the Commission was to invoke a clear reaction from Council, unambiguously designed to establish the precedence of decision-making authority in relation to drugs. The first category from the action plan shown above appears to relate primarily to first pillar activities concerning education and public health under the new TEU structure. However, in response to the Commission proposal, a document setting out the position of Steering Group II (and agreed at K.4 Committee level) made it fundamentally clear that the Council took the view that third pillar competences should take a central role in drug policy development:

> Police prevention work, as well as that of other enforcement agencies, provides relevant experience in demand reduction, to which little attention has been paid in the action plan. The police and other

enforcement agencies have roles in the overall context of prevention which arise from their special expertise, their structure and organiza- tion and the particular task they perform. (Council, 1995a: 4)

This is a quite extraordinary claim for Council (that is, the member states) to make in the light of the fact that the overwhelming emphasis of police drug-related activity is 'of a repressive nature' (European Parliament, 1992a: 55). The Council document went on to conclude that it was the absence of Commission competence in the area of law enforcement that 'prevents the Commission's proposal from constituting a comprehensive outline of the different aspects of the fight against drugs' (Council, 1995a: 6).[130] The same document noted that the Working Party on Drugs and Organized Crime (WPDOC) – WG 3 in the new structure (formerly Trevi WG III) – favoured a single document 'which would no longer be the "Commission's proposal", but truly the Union's plan' (Council, 1995a: 6). However, a key statement and affirmation of where authoritative competence to develop policy was located can be found in a note from the K.4 Committee to Council and COREPER. This made clear that the WPDOC had authoritative status to develop policies and salient points for negotiation in this area:

The Justice and Home Affairs Council has called for a 'global strategy' to combat drug trafficking, to reduce demand and to act against producer and transit countries, focusing on the strengthening of con- trols at external frontiers and on measures to combat 'drug tourism', the Europol Drugs Unit to be made operational and the work in order to conclude the Europol Convention to be speeded up. The Working Party on Drugs and Organized Crime has taken on, *inter alia*, the task of framing the strategy. (Council, 1995a: 7)

This course of events shows that the Council working group most associated with drug enforcement policy development was quick to assert its authoritative claim to shape *overall* drug policy, including demand-side measures. For much of 1994, Council attention – and that of a number of other third pillar working groups – was focused on the attempt to reach agreement on a final draft of the Europol Convention, delayed by differences of opinion as to the role and remit of the European Court of Justice in connection with the new organization (in fact, COREPER did not sign the Convention until 26 July 1995). In the meantime, the Corfu European Council (24–25 June 1994), which first considered the 1995–99 Commission proposal, validated Council preferences (that is, the preference developed via the WPDOC) and formally assigned the task of developing the 'global strategy' to the WPDOC. The Essen European Council of 9–10 December 1994 called for this work to be completed by June 1995. Following its apparent defeat in the 'competence debate', the Commission focused on developing work relating to drug dependence via first pillar initiatives.

At the beginning of 1995 drugs issues were given a high political profile by the incoming French Presidency, due to a strong personal interest from President Jacques Chirac of France. Drug-related matters were prominent on the agendas of the two European Councils held in 1995: at Cannes (25–26 June) and, under the Spanish Presidency in the second half of the year, at Madrid (12–13 December). The Cannes European Council approved a work programme submitted by COREPER relating to what was now termed the 'European Global Plan of Action in the Fight against Drugs 1995–1999'. This work programme incorporated a set of 15 health-related measures developed under the first pillar (that is, within the Commission's area of competence). The Cannes European Council also decided to appoint a group of experts to produce a report 'outlining the steps needed to make the plan a reality' (EMCDDA, 1996b: Ch. 4, p. 11). The experts were convened under the title of the 'Working Party of Experts on Drugs', made up of relatively senior national civil servants (mostly from interior ministries) who had previously been working in other third pillar working groups (which may have included the WPDOC presumably). This gives us an insight into the meaning of the term 'expert' at EU level: here 'expert' means senior national civil servants with experience in justice and home affairs matters. At Cannes, the 15 health-related measures were not adopted by Council as part of the 'Global Plan', thereby ensuring that the remit of the new expert working party was exclusively focused on third pillar matters. At this point the 'power struggle' for competence between Council and the Commission was definitively resolved in favour of the former.

The Working Party of Experts on Drugs presented a report to the Madrid European Council containing 66 specific proposals, 15 of which concerned public health measures. Prior to Madrid, at a meeting of the Justice and Home Affairs Council (November 1995) it was recorded that 'The report was compiled with contributions from the fora responsible under the European Union's three pillars, i.e. the Health and Education Councils, CFSP and JHA. The Europol Drugs Unit and the European Monitoring Centre for Drugs and Drug Addiction also collaborated in preparing this report' (Council Press Release, 11720/95: Presse 332).

The 15 public health measures (that is, those prepared by the first pillar Health and Education Councils) were finally adopted in Madrid, only to be moved to what became the 'Community Action Programme on the Prevention of Drug Dependence 1996–2000' by the subsequent Italian Presidency. This, as one author has pointed out, highlights that 'the agreements made at successive European Councils were at the root of the distinction that was introduced between health-related and punitive aspects of drugs policy' (Boekhout van Solinge, 2002: 92). The political decisions taken by heads of state were of course informed by the opinions (that is, policy ideas) emanating from third pillar working groups, highlighting the dominance of overall thinking about the drugs issue by these groups. At Madrid, the heads of state called on the forthcoming Italian and Irish presidencies of the EU 'to prepare a concrete programme of activities on the basis of the [experts] report' (EMCDDA, 1996b: Ch. 4, p. 11). The authority and policy-relevance of this report – and by implication those that would compile it – was thus assured in advance by this statement.

The Presidency conclusions from the Madrid European Council note that the meeting approved the report of the Working Party of Experts on Drugs and stressed 'the urgency of translating the guidelines into precise, coordinated operational activities within the Union' (*EU Bulletin*, 12-1995: 16). After Madrid the Working Party became known as the 'Madrid Group of experts on drugs' (henceforth in this volume: 'Madrid Experts'). Concurrent with the high level of Council attention to drugs issues, the Commission (in conjunction with the European Parliament and the Spanish Presidency) had convened a Conference on Drugs Policy in Europe which was held in Brussels on 7 and 8 December 1995. This brought together over 170 'drug experts' drawn principally from national civil servants working in interior, foreign and health ministries. Once again, the term 'expert' is used but in a different (and this time broader) context in relation to drug policy.[131] The Conference at least helped to give the impression that the Commission had an input into overall drug policy thinking (if only narrow competence), shown by the direct transmission of the Conference findings into the policy-making process, particularly the ideas from a follow-up workshop (in March 1996) on the application of national drugs legislation.

The Madrid Experts' report

During 1995, the influence of third pillar working groups was highly significant in providing a rationale for what the primary emphasis of EU drug policy 'should be', and in building a 'consensual' knowledge base (that is, in constructing a normative framework). The frame of reference within which the Madrid Experts worked was clearly defined both in terms of a bureaucratic location and in having a clear functional goal. That goal was to find ways of implementing the recommendations contained in the 1995–99 'global plan' rather than examination of the efficacy of particular strategies. However, the decision-making parameters had already been pre-set by specialist working groups, particularly so in relation to anti-trafficking measures. This was a direct consequence of the institutional machinery set up under the TEU (that is, a formalized Trevi structure).

It has already been shown that the WPDOC (also sometimes referred to as the Drugs and Organized Crime Working Group, or DOCWG) was given responsibility for developing a strategy to counter trafficking while the Customs Cooperation Working Group, or CCWG (WG 4 under the TEU structure, formerly MAG under Trevi) was given responsibility for designing a strategy concerning external borders.[132] The second pillar working party on drugs, responsible for promoting 'external compliance' (principally to meet supply reduction objectives) had a more limited role (that is, supporting implementation rather than developing policy as such) and reported directly to the third pillar K.4 Committee. In line with the Presidency decision at Cannes to assign responsibility to the competent bodies in each pillar, a draft report from the WPDOC was submitted to Steering Group II on 8 November 1995 on 'the third pillar contribution to combating drug trafficking' (Council, 1995c). The document recorded that it was 'understood that Member States could invite their experts in fields not usually covered by this group such as police and judicial cooperation to attend meetings of the Group to contribute to [the] draft report' (Council, 1995c: 2). The draft report 'should be considered as the detailed contribution of the Third Pillar to the strategy and actions in [the draft report of the Group of Experts on Drugs]' (Council, 1995c: 3). The WPDOC report was clear in emphasizing that the 'concrete measures' proposed were aimed at reducing the supply of drugs, stressing that legislation that admits intervention against the drug problem 'in all its parts' was desirable (citing the three UN Conventions), adding that 'It is obvious that all forms of legalization of drugs are incompatible with these efforts' (Council, 1995c: 9).[133] We see here that the Madrid Experts were given what amounted to an ultimatum with regard to so-called supply-side measures, emphasizing that prohibition was a completely non-negotiable parameter. The proposal also made recommendations on measures targeted at specific countries, highlighting how

CFSP action under the second pillar was seen as purely an implementation device for enforcement-led decisions taken under the third pillar.

The report of the Madrid Experts to the Madrid European Council stressed the mandate given by the Cannes European Council 'recommending that steps should be taken to ensure practical implementation of the strategy involving reducing supply, combating trafficking and international co-operation'.[134] The report gave an account of the size and nature of the drugs problem, drawing on existing data and new reports from the EMCDDA and EDU on EU drug consumption trends and the 'general drugs situation' respectively. The EDU material described the main sources of drug supply, using drug seizure statistics as supporting evidence, as well as – somewhat incongruously – a non-contextualized table of drug-related deaths across the EU. No attempt was made to differentiate between the various drugs described with regard to the extent or type of threat that they pose.[135] Part II of the report stressed the need for a multidisciplinary approach, including the statement that 'the struggle against drugs must be based on interaction between preventive measures, control and suppression of illicit production and trafficking, as well as care and treatment for drug addicts' (Council, 1995d: 11).

The 15 measures covering demand reduction set out in Chapter III of the Madrid Experts' report were taken directly from first pillar discussions on drug dependence (these 15 measures later formed the 1996–2000 plan on this area). Here, implementation was viewed as a matter purely for national-level bodies to decide, and no recommendations were made on public funding of the programmes suggested. In contrast, Chapter IV – on the reduction of illicit trafficking – laid out a much more detailed set of recommendations, calling for greater intergovernmental coordination of law enforcement activity and for the strengthening of the legal basis for this. Chapter V of the report elaborated on the role of international cooperation in the achievement of a coordinated approach, reiterating the instruments available and stressing the UN framework as a desirable model in this respect. The final section of the report highlighted law enforcement coordination between national authorities. The European Council was invited to mandate COREPER to consider the creation of a permanent mechanism of cross-pillar coordination 'possibly consisting of national drugs coordinators' (Council, 1995d: 24). This can only be interpreted as a self-perpetuating mandate.

While the Madrid Experts' report formally expressed commitment to a balanced perspective on drugs, it devoted the majority of its detailed and substantive recommendations to law enforcement measures, amalgamating a set of policy ideas developed in expert working groups (mostly in the third pillar). The real significance of the report – in effect a composite of reports submitted by other third pillar expert working groups – lay in the extent to which it successfully mobilized and provided a mandate for political action from the time it was delivered to senior decision-makers. In approving the report, the Madrid European Council also:

- requested the incoming Italian Presidency, the Council and the Commission to prepare a report with the member states, the EDU and EMCDDA on a 'precise programme of activities' based on the experts report; this was to be prepared by December 1996
- requested the Council and the Commission to prepare a report and action proposal in the area of cooperation with Latin America and the Caribbean regarding drugs, setting up an *ad hoc* working party for this purpose
- called on the Council and the Commission to consider 'the extent to which harmonization of laws could contribute to a reduction in the consumption of drugs and unlawful trafficking in the EU'. (EMCDDA, 1997a: 111)

The Madrid Council also agreed with the recommendation that a new Ad Hoc Working Party on Drugs (AHWPD) should be established to oversee and develop these matters.[136] This decision thereby placed the Madrid Group on a more permanent institutional footing, for the AHWPD was to be made up of essentially the same national experts (civil servants). The AHWPD met seven times in 1996 and then nine times in the first half of 1997.[137] The group is also sometimes referred to as the 'expert group on drugs' in official documents, confirming the impression that it was seen as having the same status as the Madrid Group. The AHWPD began to take on a *de facto* priority status in the coordination of work from other drug-related working groups, although the work of the third pillar WPDOC retained an independent competence (this group met more frequently than the AHWPD; for example, it met 11 times during 1995, 22 times during 1996 and 11 times in the first half of 1997). In line with the Madrid mandate, the AHWPD submitted an interim report to the Florence European Council (21–22 June 1996).[138] As the high volume of working group meetings suggests, this was a very intensive period of activity on drugs matters during which time the groups became the focal point of discussion covering a wide range of legislative actions. The second half of 1996 saw the incumbent Irish Presidency make drugs a clear priority in its overall programme, leading to a highly significant period of drugs policy development.

New political momentum: the 1996 Irish Presidency

In the second half of 1996 the new Irish Presidency made the control of drugs and cooperation against drug trafficking the highest priority in its programme, prompted by domestic concern about the issue at this time. den Boer (1997: 5) suggests that this was a good example of how the short-term focus of the JHA agenda is often contingent on domestic factors in the state holding the Presidency (in this case, the murder of an Irish journalist, Veronica Guerin, who had been investigating drug traffickers in Dublin). This political momentum was to lead directly to some 18 drug-related initiatives taken by the Council of Ministers after September 1996 (listed in EMCDDA, 1997a: 111–12). By far the majority of these covered justice and home affairs cooperation, aimed at formalizing the legal, police and customs aspects of the Madrid Experts' report.

The most significant legislative outcome of the Irish Presidency came shortly after the Dublin European Council (13–14 December 1996). A 'Joint Action concerning the approximation of the laws and practices of the Member States of the EU to combat drug addiction and to prevent and combat illegal drug trafficking' was agreed on 17 December 1996 (OJ L 342, 31 December 1996). A Council 'Resolution on sentencing for serious illicit drug trafficking' soon followed, on 20 December (OJ C 10, 11 January 1997). These measures heralded a concerted effort to both harmonize and toughen anti-drugs measures across the EU at this time. The Conference on Drug Policy in Europe had previously drawn the conclusion that there was already a fairly high degree of similarity between the laws and legal practices of EU states in relation to drug trafficking. None the less, the joint action implied a preference for further harmonization of laws and practices designed to make cooperation more effective in the 'common determination to *put an end* to illegal drug trafficking' (OJ L 342: 6; emphasis added). In fact, the measure encapsulated the tension between attitudes to trafficking and to harm reduction across the member states (notably ongoing French criticism of the Dutch 'coffee shops' policy and relatively more tolerant approach to cannabis use). The primary objective of the measure was aimed at making police, customs services and judicial authorities more compatible with each other with regard to their procedures against trafficking (Article 2). However, Article 3 of the joint action stated: 'Member States shall undertake to combat illicit movements of narcotic drugs and psychotropic substances within the community, including drug "tourism"' (OJ L 342: 7). This reveals a second, more contentious, dimension to the Joint Action, reflecting formal criticism of Dutch drugs policy.[139]

In the face of strong pressure to harmonize legislation from other member states (principally from France), the Dutch successfully held out against the inclusion of a clause in the original text which they claimed would have forced them to close the 'coffee shops'.[140] This compromise came after a pointed 'Resolution on measures to address the "drug tourism" problem within the European Union' (96/C 375/02) was passed by Council on 29 November 1996, reflecting the predominance of views favouring a repressive approach over the more liberal, harm-reduction strategy long pursued by The Netherlands (OJ C 375, 12 December 1996). A limited range of tougher enforcement measures based on bilateral cooperation between France and The Netherlands was the result. Council resolutions can be seen as an expression of what we might term the 'political temperature' at the time they are passed, as well as being intended to bolster adherence to relatively 'soft' measures such as TEU-era joint actions. The Resolution on sentencing for serious illicit drugs trafficking was overtly aimed at harmonizing a tougher approach, stating that, 'Member States will ensure that their national laws provide for the possibility of custodial sentences for serious illicit trafficking in drugs which are within the range of the most severe custodial penalties imposed by their respective criminal law for crimes of comparable gravity' (OJ C 10, 11 January 1997: 4).

The resolution was significant as a tacit statement of legitimacy for a situation whereby – in relation to drug enforcement – 'the executive authorities of the Member States in the Council adopt positions on which their respective Parliaments and in certain cases the courts must decide' (European Parliament, 2000a: 56). In at least one member state, criminal justice practice had already adopted the approach favoured in the Resolution.[141] The harmonization strand running through the Irish Presidency period represents the most concerted attempt so far to ensure that both the substance and character of *national* repressive anti-drugs measures are set at EU level. The joint action also created a process whereby developments in the national laws and strategies of the national police and customs authorities of member states had to be regularly reported both to Council and to European Council meetings. Viewed critically, 'This measure clearly goes beyond cooperation alone and infringes on the area of national legislation. It allows the Council or the working groups of the Council to oversee the work of national Parliaments and makes this collection of national executive authorities a kind of "super legislator"' (European Parliament, 2000a: 57).

The previous points highlight the deeply politicized nature of decision-making about drugs at this time and the critical role of expert groups in finding a formula around which consensus could converge while still permitting different national interpretations. This process is evident with regard to the role played by the Group of Experts in developing a rationale for specific actions in support of the broader harmonization objective. The Dublin European Council received a COREPER-endorsed report summarizing EU drugs action and progress made during 1996. The report included an annex containing a sub-report by the 'Group of Experts on Drugs' (that is, the AHWPD) regarding harmonization of drug laws, in which the group expressed support for 'ongoing work', especially in the fields of

- police, customs and judicial cooperation
- role of liaison officers
- controlled deliveries
- intelligence services and the role of Europol
- relations with Central and Eastern European countries
- effective cooperation in respect of seizure of assets of drug traffickers.
  (Council, 1996d: 26)

The report also noted that the Group of Experts considered the (then proposed) Joint Action to be a significant step 'given that harmonization cannot be attained at present' (Council, 1996d: 26). Despite the avowed purpose of the Joint Action being to combat both illegal trafficking and drug addiction, no specific measures regarding the latter were identified or advocated by the AHWPD. The Group thus validated an approach predicated on strengthening enforcement-based measures, advocating closer cooperation on working practices between enforcement agencies as a strategy to achieve this. This exposed the dichotomy at the heart of EU states' drug policy: normative intergovernmental consensus on enforcement alongside acceptance of different preferences on other ways of tackling drug problems. The report also contained the viewpoint that 'Harmonization is not a feasible objective as it should be based on common elements in the setting of priorities (which does not exist at the moment)' (Council, 1996d: 32).

In fact, this was the conclusion that had been drawn at the March 1996 workshop on the application of national drugs legislation. The workshop had also found that the legislation of all member states was actually in compliance with the three main UN Conventions. The message coming out of the AHWPD was clear: it had no remit to enquire into the reasons for the lack of consensus on drug policy priorities. This is because its role was limited and prescribed by the original remit set by

Council for the Madrid Experts. The Group of Experts thus facilitated the transmission of a broader cognitive framework, rationalizing and adding legitimacy to the extension of action in areas where consensus could be most easily generated (that is, enforcement approaches). However, its legitimacy – and authoritative claim to policy-relevant knowledge – was fundamentally related to a tacit agreement that national preferences would not be challenged. Viewed in this way, the role of the Group of Experts becomes a more functional and instrumental one in which a significant part of its authoritative status was based on the tacit understanding that it would avoid actions (or questions) that impinged upon or challenged state sovereignty. Given that the Group was composed of *national* officials, this highlights the extent to which EU notions of expertise and the supposedly 'functional' role of experts is an inherently politicized phenomenon.

The Dublin European Council stressed that continued examination of further (formal) harmonization of laws would continue 'in so far as an agreed need for it is identified' (*EU Bulletin*, 12-1996: 14), again hinting at the lack of consensus around movements in this direction. This was also an implicit acknowledgement of a reference to synthetic drugs contained in the Joint Action. It contained a commitment to endeavour to draft convergent legislation 'to the extent necessary to make up legal ground or fill legal vacuums'. The report to the European Council had recorded growing concern over synthetic drugs and also revealed that 'US experts' had participated in the deliberations of Council working groups (under the Transatlantic Agenda framework).[142] Advocating special attention for the problem of synthetic drugs during 1997, the report supported a strategy on this matter based solely on a repressive framework, without recognizing the existence or possible contribution from other approaches. The conclusions of the document advocated that the synthetic drugs problem 'needs to be tackled at three levels: (a) legislation; (b) practical cooperation against production and trafficking including improved cooperation between national authorities and the chemical industry and (c) international cooperation' (Council, 1996d: 8). This fitted into a broader call to enhance cooperation between law enforcement agencies to combat trafficking 'in particular through further strengthening of the external frontiers of the member States' (Council, 1996d: 9). In short, the synthetic drugs problem was conceptualized as above all a law enforcement problem. This symbolized the new heightened level of political concern about 'new drug threats' generated during the Irish Presidency. Drug policy development during most of 1996 and into 1997 took place against a backdrop of the IGC that had begun to examine the operation of the TEU in March 1996, due to culminate at the Amsterdam European Council in June 1997. The possibility of transferring parts of the existing third pillar to community competence under a new treaty were certainly open for discussion by the IGC, but this did not seem likely to include decision-making on drugs issues.[143]

Cross-pillar coordination, third pillar priorities

At the start of 1997, the incoming Dutch Presidency felt that the failure to create a cross-pillar body for coordinating drugs policy was becoming a weakness (implicitly criticizing the role played by COREPER to this effect since the disbanding of CELAD).[144] This prompted the creation of what was to be known as the Horizontal Drugs Group (HDG), although what this decision amounted to in practice was a decision to give the AHWPD permanent status and a clear remit.[145] Like most working groups, the HDG was not intended to have a fixed membership, with different experts (that is, national civil servants) attending based on the specific issues on the agenda (prepared by the Presidency in conjunction with the Council Secretariat). The HDG was immediately tasked with reporting to Council and COREPER on cross-pillar drugs matters and given the authority to advise on the 'appropriate' allocation of work among the working groups operating in the other pillars (for example, in the second pillar CFSP Working Party, CODRO). The agendas for the meetings of the group during 1997 show that it became the focal point for drug policy development, in particular the establishment of an 'early warning system' on new synthetic drugs, leading to the Joint Action described in Chapter 8 (based on joint EMCDDA-EDU input). The agendas for HDG meetings from this period show an increasing number of references to Central Asia, Latin America-Caribbean, and joint dialogue on drugs matters with the United States (for example with reference to an EU–US Summit meeting held in The Hague on 28 May 1997). Throughout 1997, references to first pillar activities were noticeably absent from these agendas. This is a further illustration of the predominance and prioritization of JHA concerns in respect of drug policy, despite the formal commitment to cross-pillar coordination that had emerged. The case studies in Chapter 11 look at this point and at the emergent role of the HDG.

After the flurry of initiatives and legal instruments related to drug enforcement in 1996, 1997 could be described in overall terms as a year of consolidation. With the exception of the Joint Action on the evaluation of risk from synthetic drugs, attention shifted towards matters concerned with transnational organized crime, although drug trafficking was consistently highlighted as a principal part of the rationale for action in this field.[146] The Dublin European Council had agreed with a proposal to establish a 'High Level Group on Organized Crime'. It can reasonably be assumed that the 'high-level' appellation meant that the group would have a slightly higher seniority level than a 'standard' working party. A little over four months (and six meetings) later, in April 1997, the High Level Group submitted an 'action plan to combat organized crime' to Council, with the intention of seeking endorsement by the Amsterdam European Council meeting (16 and 17 June 1997). The Action Plan contained 15 'political guidelines' and 30 specific recommendations in the form of a work plan ranging from prevention, legal instruments for combating organized crime, practical cooperation between police, judicial authorities and customs, the scope of Europol's remit, and the combating of money laundering and confiscation of the profits of crime. Somewhat surprisingly, no specific reference was made to drugs in the plan but they were discussed *inter alia* (such as giving support to the involvement of the EDU in support of joint 'operational actions' by 'competent authorities' of member states).[147] None the less the action plan had a direct impact on the way that drugs issues were handled institutionally under the third pillar. The action plan recommended that a multidisciplinary Working Party on Organized Crime should be established to 'coordinate the fight against organized crime' (political guideline number 9). As part of this change, point 22 of the action plan recommended that the third pillar WPDOC should 'either limit its remit to drugs issues relevant to tasks performed in accordance with Article K of the Treaty or be abolished'.

The Amsterdam European Council was inevitably dominated by the search for political agreement on the new treaty that would revise the TEU. Agreement was reached on an outline Treaty of Amsterdam, which was then finalized before formal signing took place in October 1997. The period of ratification commenced thereafter, culminating in the entry into force of the Treaty in May 1999. The provisions of the Treaty as they affected the legal basis of drug policy are outlined in Chapter 10, together with an assessment of its impact on institutional arrangements and policy development after its entry into force. The Amsterdam European Council approved the action plan of the High Level Group and agreed with its recommendation that a 'Multidisciplinary Group on Organized Crime' (MDG) be established. Figure 9.1 illustrates the decision-making arrangements at this point in time. The remit and composition of the MDG is

136

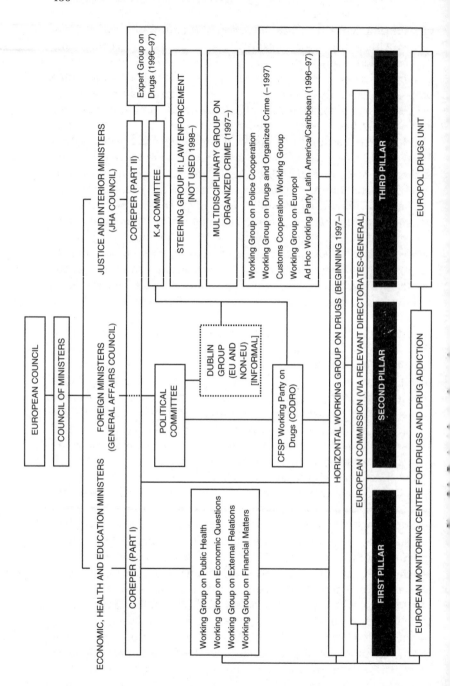

considered in Chapter 11 in connection with the case study of the 1998 UK Presidency. Other work related to preparation for the entry into force of the Europol Convention and on updating mutual assistance and cooperation between customs administrations. A joint action (97/372/JHA) was adopted by Council on 9 June 1997, designed to encourage customs authorities to improve 'targeting criteria' and the collection and exchange of information in the fight against drug trafficking (OJ L 159, 17 June 1997). A new Convention on Mutual Assistance between Customs Administrations (generally known Naples II) was eventually signed in December 1997. Primary responsibility for the development of these measures lay with the Customs Cooperation Working Group.

Luxembourg took on the Presidency for the second half of 1997, and the conclusions of the Luxembourg European Council expressed satisfaction with the 'substantial progress' made in the various areas covered by the report on drugs requested in Dublin, preceded by an interim report in Amsterdam (Commission, 1998: 360). Both reports were produced by the HDG, confirming that it had quickly acquired a pivotal role, with the MDG also emerging as a source of authoritative competence on specific matters relating to drugs and organized crime. Amid the emphasis on enforcement, one small development during the Luxembourg Presidency stands out. On 4 December 1997, ministers from the JHA and Health Councils undertook joint discussions on drugs issues for the first time ever. This fact is a revealing illustration of the deep institutional demarcations apparent in EU policy-making on drugs. This discussion merely took the form of a 'working lunch' and had no formal agenda, and no official account of proceedings was recorded. This highlights yet again that the third pillar was the focus of EU drug policy development and that the focus of HDG activity at this time was based on giving precedence to measures in this area. The incoming UK Presidency in the first half of 1998 sought to reinvigorate the political prominence of the drugs issue, and this period is examined in the second case study in Chapter 11. By this time Council was beginning to assess how the provisions of the new treaty would impact upon third pillar decision-making. During the Austrian Presidency, the Vienna European Council (11 and 12 December 1998) sought to define a set of objectives in the form of an action plan on 'how best to implement the provisions of the Amsterdam Treaty establishing an area of freedom, security and justice' (commonly referred to as the Vienna action plan). Perhaps because of the expected 'new opportunities' that would be presented by the Treaty of Amsterdam, no significant legal instruments with a direct bearing on drug enforcement were enacted during 1998 or 1999.

Summary

The course of European drug policy from 1993 to 1999 was dominated by policy-making carried out under the third pillar and the specialist working groups that operated within this framework. In reviewing this first 'operational' phase of the European Union under the original TEU provisions it is important to be aware of the wider context for drug policy development. Looked at in the broader sense, the third pillar became an 'encapsulated world', in which 'Interior ministries, judicial authorities, and law enforcement agencies have begun to combine efforts and share expertise in what had previously been regarded as a core area of national sovereignty, in a way that has insulated their collective decisions from parliamentary and judicial review at both national and EU levels' (den Boer and Wallace, 2000: 518).

Decision-making under the TEU inherited the hierarchical Trevi system, reliant on strong control by Council and by COREPER, but the continued expansion of European integration and the inevitable broadening of the range of issues under consideration placed greater emphasis on the working group level (given the more limited time available for discussion at the higher levels). It is here that agreement was reached on many proposals and where consensus was achieved. Although it is difficult to generalize about the role of 'national experts', it is clear that civil servants – rather than representatives of executive agencies – have done most of the negotiation at working group level. However, many of the initiatives put in place have given police and customs professionals a significantly expanded range of opportunities through which to express their views, leading to the development of what den Boer and Wallace (2000) have called an 'intense intergovernmental network' between interior ministries and police. This has also been matched by a significant growth in international conferences, training courses and informal contacts, particularly between police officials, affording numerous opportunities for informal networking (p. 505).

The use of 'expert' knowledge to address specific policy requirements was a feature of the evolution of ideas around EU drug policy after 1993; the influential 'Madrid Experts' shaped and framed the course of policy significantly. It was in 1996 that legislative action on drug enforcement was most apparent, under an Irish Presidency that gave drugs a high political profile, highlighting how the rhythm of policy development is often heavily influenced by the rotating six-month Presidency. By 1997, the institutional structure did not seem to be functioning as planned, and as a result two 'horizontal' working groups were born: the HDG and the MDG. The latter marked a new shift towards a more generic policy against organized crime, with drugs seen as a *de facto* element of actions in this area. Despite an apparent broadening of the drug experts' mandate through the establishment of the HDG, 'For the first two years the Group focused primarily on third pillar subjects ... and most of its delegates came from the ministries of Justice and Home Affairs' (Boekhout van Solinge, 2000: 51). The working practices of the HDG were to change during 1999. Chapter 10 now examines the period after the entry into force of the Amsterdam Treaty.

10
EU Drug Policy-Making under the Amsterdam Treaty

The entry into force of the Treaty of Amsterdam on 1 May 1999 brought justice and home affairs policies firmly to the centre of the European political stage. In July 1998, the then Commission President, Jacques Santer, had proposed the idea of a special European Council purely to discuss JHA issues in order to assess the implications of the Treaty of Amsterdam in this respect. This proposal ultimately led to the special JHA European Council at Tampere, Finland, on 15–16 October 1999. At this meeting heads of state expressed their commitment to the creation of 'an area of freedom, security and justice' in the European Union. The breadth of this concept, incorporating an avowed 'unionwide fight against crime', marked an attempt to provide a single rationale and legitimacy for measures in the JHA field that had previously been absent. At this time, the full JHA *acquis* was given political legitimacy: measures from the Schengen, Trevi and Maastricht eras were formally unified and consolidated. As a result, a wide range of security measures that included (or at least had at some stage included) drugs as a significant part of their rationale were now legitimized within a broader conception of internal security for the EU.

The decision to incorporate the Schengen *acquis* into the new Treaty focused attention on the Schengen Information System (SIS) and how this might be integrated with both the Europol computer system and the Customs Information System (CIS).[148] A draft convention on a European Information System (EIS) had been considered since 1995 but was now superseded by the decision to incorporate the Schengen *acquis*.[149] In December 2001, Council adopted a decision to give the director of Europol authority to conduct negotiations with third states and bodies not related to the EU (OJ C 358, 15 December 2001). At the same time, it was decided to extend the Europol mandate to a broader range of crimes.[150] This extension, which took effect on 1 January 2002 in common with previous extensions of the Europol mandate, took place 'without any prior objective assessment of [Europol's] efforts and achievements' (Hayes, 2002: 8). Political agreement was also reached on a new cross-border legal assistance unit, Eurojust (already operating in provisional form as 'pro-Eurojust'), and on proposals to establish a common 'European arrest warrant' for arrest and extradition.[151]

The terrorist attacks on the US in September 2001 unquestionably added political momentum to decision-making on this complex array of JHA measures, creating pressure for unprecedented speed in their introduction. This raised particular concerns that civil liberties issues would not be given adequate consideration. It was perhaps inevitable then that at this time the drugs issue was less 'visible' on the EU political agenda than at any time in the recent past. However, the post-Amsterdam policy agenda included a number of significant initiatives that were directly associated with drug enforcement. In calling for increased cooperation in investigating cross-border crime the Tampere conclusions gave political support to the establishment of joint investigative teams (a measure already included in the Treaty provisions) 'to combat trafficking in drugs and human beings as well as terrorism' (Commission, 1999b, para. 43). The idea of joint investigative teams (that is, Europol officers working alongside national law enforcement officers) has steadily gained momentum via a variety of political and legislative decisions. A draft Convention on Mutual Assistance in Criminal Matters, agreed in 1998, was given renewed momentum and a final version was agreed in May 2000.[152] Many of the law enforcement techniques covered in this convention have been rationalized principally on the basis of anti-drugs operations (modelled on the Schengen provisions in this area). Finally, apart from a call for harmonization of certain national criminal laws, including those on drug trafficking, the most specific reference to drugs in the Tampere Conclusions was a call to Council to adopt the then proposed 2000–2004 European strategy against drugs (ibid, paras. 49 and 50). Before considering the development of this strategy let us first consider the impact of the Amsterdam Treaty on the legal basis and institutional process for policy-making on drugs issues.

Drugs and the Treaty of Amsterdam

The legal basis

The broad changes to the third pillar brought in by the Treaty were outlined in Chapter 6. Activities under the revised Title VI (the third pillar) are now concerned with 'Provisions on police and judicial cooperation in criminal matters'. In general, the Treaty preserved the division of drug policy between the three pillars. However, in procedural terms,

> The Commission now has the right of initiative in all areas of intergovernmental cooperation. Whereas the Parliament under the Maastricht Treaty only had to be informed (which it rarely was), it is now consulted also on issues concerning the Second and Third pillars. Of course, as before, only the Council makes decisions. In the main, it takes decisions unanimously, only implementing actions can be set up by majority vote. The Parliament's position is slightly better. It does, however, not have powers of co-decision under the Second and Third Pillars. (European Parliament, 2000a: 54)

On an explanatory note, readers should be aware that a decision was taken to 'consolidate' all of the relevant European treaties as a result of the changes agreed at Amsterdam. The practical effect of this decision has meant that the original TEU articles have been renumbered, from 1 to 53 rather than from A to S. Article 29 of the consolidated TEU (Article K.1 of the original TEU) stated that the EU should have the objective of providing its citizens with a high level of safety within an area of freedom, security and justice by developing common action in the fields of police and judicial cooperation. It went on to say: 'That objective shall be achieved by preventing and combating crime, *organized or otherwise*, in particular terrorism, trafficking in persons and offences against children, illicit drug trafficking, corruption and fraud' (OJ C 340, 10 November 1997; emphasis added).

Three methods were set out to achieve this:

1 closer cooperation between police forces, customs authorities and other 'competent authorities' in the member states, both directly and through Europol
2 closer cooperation between 'judicial and other competent authorities' of the member states
3 approximation, 'where necessary', of rules on criminal matters in member states.

Articles 30 and 32 provide details of the elements that method 1 'shall include', ranging from 'operational cooperation' among law enforcement bodies in preventing, detecting and investigating criminal offences to information exchange ('in particular through Europol') and cooperation via training, exchange of liaison officers and common evaluation of investigative techniques in relation to detection of 'serious forms of organized crime'. Article 30(2) mandates the Council to promote cooperation through Europol, setting a timetable of five years after the entry into force of the Treaty for actions enabling Europol to support preparation and 'encourage coordination' involving operational actions of joint teams, including representatives of Europol 'in a support capacity'. Furthermore, within this same period a slightly less firm commitment is made to 'promote' liaison arrangements between prosecuting and investigating officials specializing in the fight against organized crime 'in close cooperation with Europol'. Article 32 took the highly significant step of giving Council the authority to lay down conditions under which 'competent authorities' may operate in the territory of another member state. This means that, depending on the national political culture in member states, such measures could be enacted by a decision taken by JHA ministers meeting in Council and without the requirement for any debate in national parliaments. It is possible, indeed likely, that the terms and basis for such a decision would be formulated and agreed in a third pillar working group before reaching COREPER for approval. In relation to method 2, Article 31 specified common action on judicial cooperation in criminal matters, including a specific reference to drug trafficking. Significantly, this reference is specifically linked to method 3: Article 31(e) states that common action on police cooperation shall include 'Progressively adopting measures establishing minimum rules relating to the constituent elements of criminal acts and to penalties in the fields of organized crime, terrorism and illicit drug trafficking'. The new Treaty thus maintained the broad thrust of the TEU but, with Europol in operation, it shifted the emphasis away from information exchange to an overt commitment to operational action involving Europol (compare with Article K.1(9) of the original TEU).

The reference to 'approximating' rules in Article 31 seems to preserve the option of harmonization objective of drug trafficking laws while abandoning the objective of the 1996 Joint Action aimed at approximating laws in relation to both trafficking and drug addiction. In contrast to the careful wording under the new Title VI, allowing for a wide range of police and judicial cooperation against drug trafficking, a revised Article 129 of the original treaty (now Article 152) did little to clarify Community competence in relation to harm reduction measures. The original Article 129 (which was itself contentious) went some way to establishing drug addiction as a field for Community action in relation to public health. Article 152 refers to Community action to complement member states' actions 'in reducing drugs-related health damage', which appears to open up more scope for harm reduction initiatives as 'preventive' health measures. So far, this has not led to significant changes, but this almost certainly reflects the fact that all member states have introduced extensive national-level programmes in this area in recent years.

Community competence in relation to precursors and money laundering was unchanged by the Treaty of Amsterdam and, although more provision for Commission right of initiative has been made in relation to the second pillar, this seems unlikely to lead to significant changes. In relation to external drug initiatives of the EU, the Commission will still operate in a framework in which the substance of any agreements is developed under the third pillar (or falls under the existing *acquis* in this field). The Commission has certainly grasped the opportunity to propose initiatives in relation to third pillar matters in the Amsterdam era, but this development must be seen in a context of what is now an already comprehensive set of measures and institutions in the third pillar area. While the bureaucratic status of the Commission has certainly been elevated, real decision-making power still rests firmly with the Council.

Institutional mechanics/dynamics

The most noticeable change in the post-Amsterdam institutional landscape was the absorption of the parallel working groups and sub-groups from the Schengen system. These groups were given the task of integrating the Schengen *acquis* into the wider EU framework. As Figure 10.1 shows, four new working groups were established, but it was envisaged that a large number of existing groups would also examine the implications of the *acquis* for their specific area. A new Working Party on Drug Trafficking was created with the intention that this group would look at drug trafficking in relation to the Schengen *acquis*. This group was to be subordinate to the HDG, to which it had to report. The HDG continued to have first, second and third pillar coordination responsibilities in relation to drug policy. Equally, the MDG had been given a mandate to design and monitor the implementation of EU strategies and polices in the prevention and control of organized crime.[153] The HDG is unusual in having both scrutiny and implementation functions, and reports directly to COREPER rather than the Article 36 Committee.

One author has observed that in the course of 1999 the HDG gradually acquired 'a more cross-pillar character', discussing more first and second pillar matters as well as third until – in 2000 – 'delegates from health and social affairs ministries came to dominate the forum'

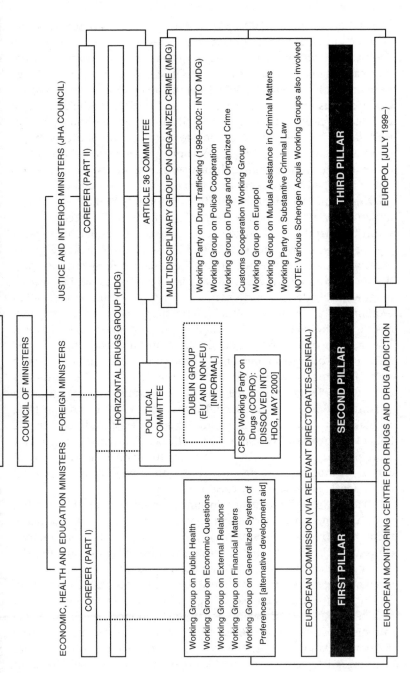

Figure 10.1 Drug policy-making institutional structure after the Treaty of Amsterdam

(Boekhout van Solinge, 2002: 51). In setting out its proposed work programme in the JHA area, the Portuguese Presidency (first half of 2000)
revealed that part of the HDG role at this time was 'to present the activities carried out by the "Health", "CODRO" and "Drug Trafficking"
Working Parties' (Council, 2000). Later in 2000, CODRO was in fact dissolved and its functions incorporated into the HDG. By the first half of
2002 it was clear that the HDG had taken on this role and that other
working groups would be responsible for development of the more specialized dimensions of policy. In a document summarizing the results of
its six-month tenure, the incumbent Spanish Presidency recorded at this
time that it had been 'determined to reinforce the coordinating role of
the Horizontal Working Party on Drugs, informing it of all drug-related
initiatives by other Working Parties' (Council 2002b: 3). It seems rather
surprising that the HDG would not be aware of such initiatives, suggesting that a degree of autonomy operates in relation to policy development work by other working groups. The Spanish Presidency revealed
that other working groups had been involved in developing specific
drug-related matters during its period in office: the Customs Cooperation
Working Party (a draft Convention on the suppression of illicit drug trafficking on the high seas); the Working Party on Substantive Criminal
Law (a proposal for a framework decision on drug trafficking); and the
MDG (the work programme on the prevention of urban crime, youth
crime and drug use via the Crime Prevention Network).[154] In December
2001, COREPER had instituted a review to examine the reorganization
of JHA working parties. It concluded that the Working Party on Drug
Trafficking should be dissolved and its activities spread between the
Police Cooperation Working Party, the Substantive Criminal Law
Working Party and the MDG. This seems to highlight a narrowing of
debate on drugs at working party level into a more technical process,
implementing or fine-tuning existing strategies.

   What the Spanish Presidency document reveals is not just a snapshot
of the contemporary institutional dynamics of EU drug policy development but that action remains predominantly focused on matters
concerned with and developed within the third pillar. In particular, the
document shows that work was heavily focused on supply control and
international cooperation. With regard to the former, the Working Party
on Drug Trafficking examined a range of initiatives in addition to work
related to its 'long-term work programme' (Council, 2002b: 5). These
initiatives covered several Council recommendations, including the
'Recommendation on the need to enhance cooperation and exchanges
of information between the various operational units specializing in

combating trafficking in precursors in the Member States of the European Union' (adopted by the JHA Council on 25 April 2002).[155] This clearly illustrates how first pillar competence remains subordinate to third pillar decision-making in practice. In second pillar matters, attention was focused on Latin America and the Caribbean, and the candidate countries. An 'Extraordinary Meeting' of the HDG was held on 6 June 2002 in Brussels, attended by national drug policy representatives from the candidate countries. A number of meetings were also held on the troika principle, with the United States, with Russia and with Iran.

A final point on the matter of institutional mechanics and dynamics concerns the less formal processes through which policy development – and ideas – may emerge. Based on a recommendation from the MDG, a European Police Chiefs Task Force was established in 2000. The rationale for this body, which has subsequently met once per Presidency, was to exchange 'in cooperation with Europol, experience, best practices and information on current trends in cross-border crime and contribute to the planning of operative actions' (Commission, 1999b, para. 44). In many respects, the Task Force symbolizes how dialogue in the form of personal links between law enforcement specialists has now become institutionalized.[156] When informal contacts are added in – three conferences on supply control issues were held during the Spanish Presidency alone – it is inevitable that few participants in the policy process will consider matters or submit ideas that are not 'technical' (that is, relate purely to their professional competence). In summary, the post-Amsterdam institutional mechanics and dynamics perpetuate – and have been designed to perpetuate – the drug policy preferences embedded in the existing system.

The European Union Drugs Strategy 2000–2004

In June 1998, under the UK Presidency, the Cardiff European Council endorsed the broad principles of a post-1999 EU drugs strategy, which had been developed under the auspices of the HDG and CODRO (see Case Study 2, Chapter 11 for an account of this period). This strategy was to supersede the 1995–99 'global plan' on drugs. However, not until late 1999 (under the Finnish Presidency) was a final proposal for a 'European Union Drugs Strategy 2000–2004' submitted by the HDG to COREPER (Council, 1999). The Helsinki European Council of 10–11 December 1999 endorsed the plan, after which a detailed EU Action Plan on Drugs (2000–2004) was prepared and subsequently endorsed at the Santa Maria de Feira European Council of 19–20 June 2000. This rather drawn-out process was undoubtedly due to the gradual emergence of a new post-Amsterdam policy environment in which the Commission was to take a more active day-to-day part in the process of drug policy development. The lead Directorate-General on these matters was the newly formed DG for Justice and Home Affairs, under Commissioner António Vitorino.[157] On 8 June 1999 the Commission submitted a proposal to Council for a European Action Plan to Combat Drugs (2000–2004). The existence of *two* plans led to a degree of confusion around this time, even for participants in the policy-making process. By the time of the Helsinki meeting this had been resolved: the strategy endorsed in Helsinki had a stronger emphasis on repressive measures than the Commission plan, which had emphasized a more preventive approach (Boekhout van Solinge, 2002: 127). However, in a sign of political compromise, it was the Commission that was to emerge with eventual responsibility for monitoring the implementation of the strategy.

The final 2000–2004 strategy submitted to Council by the HDG contained a section on 'the new possibilities provided by the Treaty of Amsterdam' (Commission, 1999: 5). The strategy was based on 11 principles and objectives, including a commitment to 'continue' a multidisciplinary, integrated and balanced strategy and to give greater priority to drug prevention and demand reduction. The fifth principle expressed commitment to 'Reinforce the fight against organized crime, illicit drug trafficking and related organized crime as well as other drug-related crime, and to step up police, customs and judicial cooperation between member states' (ibid: 5). The document set six targets for the strategy; to:

1 reduce significantly over five years the prevalence of illicit drug use, as well as new recruitment to it, particularly among young people under 18 years of age
2 reduce substantially over five years the incidence of drug-related health damage (HIV, hepatitis B and C, TB, etc.) and the number of drug-related deaths
3 increase substantially the number of successfully treated addicts
4 reduce substantially over five years the availability of illicit drugs
5 reduce substantially over five years the number of drug related crimes
6 reduce substantially over five years money laundering and illicit trafficking of precursors. (Council, 1999: 6)

The proposal did not suggest any criteria on which these targets would or should be evaluated, raising questions as to their purpose and value.

The strategy document set out three main areas for action: demand reduction, supply reduction and international action. A further section covered information and evaluation, and expressed the view that 'In the past Member States and the Commission have given insufficient priority to evaluation of anti-drugs activity' (ibid: 18). The subsequent EU Action Plan on Drugs (2000–2004) 'translated the aims and targets into roughly one hundred concrete activities' for implementation over the period of the plan (Commission, 2001b: 2). The Commission emerged with responsibility for reviewing the implementation of the Action Plan after proposing a methodology for this process in 2001.[158] Although this is essentially a bureaucratic function, the Commission had acquired a formal right of initiative on third pillar drugs matters and the Action Plan explicitly gave the Commission responsibility 'to propose measures establishing minimum rules relating to the constituent elements and penalties for illicit trafficking in drugs' (Commission, 2001b: 30, Point 4.2.4).[159] The Commission responded to this right of initiative with a proposal for a Council framework decision, an instrument intended to generate alignment in the laws and regulations of member states (Commission, 2001a). The long-running issue of harmonization was thus firmly back on the policy agenda. The measure was subsequently discussed in various working groups, including, as the previous section noted, the Working Party on Substantive Criminal Law. Despite this 'technical' discussion, political agreement among member states has proved difficult to reach once again.[160]

Summary

The initial post-Amsterdam phase has seen little that could be described as innovation in EU drug policy. However, by linking drug strategy to the notion of safety within an area of freedom, security and justice, the Amsterdam Treaty consolidated and legitimized the idea that drug policy is predominantly within the field of justice and home affairs at EU level. In practice, this has far more relevance to participants in the decision-making framework than to the content of the 2000–2004 EU Drugs Strategy which continues to advocate a balanced, multidisciplinary approach. The Commission is now more active (tellingly, led by the DG on JHA) in the policy development and implementation process, but this is amid an enormous range of ongoing drug programmes and measures that were agreed in the post-Maastricht era. Unequivocally, Council remains the authoritative decision-making body on drugs policy matters, and in the post-Amsterdam era attention has been focused on third pillar matters and the international implementation of agreements that are predominantly based on repressive strategies.

At the working group level, the drugs–organized crime nexus has meant that a slightly wider range of WGs have addressed issues with a drug trafficking orientation. These WGs have responsibility for agreeing 'technical' details, in fulfilment of the broader political agenda that has seen the culmination and expansion of a number of measures and institutions involving law enforcement cooperation that were rationalized as essential components in anti-drugs activity. Prominent in this process has been the extension of the Europol mandate and remit, the Convention on Mutual Assistance in Criminal Matters, and the establishment of a nascent Eurojust. Finally, renewed political consensus has emerged around the strategy of harmonizing laws and penalties on drug trafficking, highlighting that post-Amsterdam EU drug policy shows signs of entering a mature phase.

11
Case Studies

Introduction

This chapter presents material in the form of two case studies from the post Maastricht era. The examples provided show how the notion of expertise has a broad range of meanings in the context of EU drug policy development. They also illustrate how the flow of ideas derived from designated experts enters the decision-making process, and highlight the complexity and range of factors that may affect how ideas become translated into specific policy development.

The first case study examines three so-called 'drug expert missions of the EU': to the Caribbean, Latin America and Central Asia. Each mission was tasked with developing strategic policy recommendations with regard to drug problems associated with these regions. Each case looks at how experts were initially selected and how their backgrounds were relevant to this process, and makes an assessment of the factors that determined their terms of reference. In each case an account is provided of how the findings of the mission were disseminated and how the influence of the views they contained can be traced over time. The Caribbean case is examined in most depth as it had a particularly interesting evolution and because it was to prove the model for the subsequent missions to Latin America and Central Asia.

The second case study looks at how drugs issues were handled at EU level during the first half of 1998 when the United Kingdom held the Presidency of the EU. This affords an opportunity to look at preliminary work on the post-1999 EU action plan to combat drugs and the input of specialist working groups to this process.

Case study 1: EU drug expert missions to the Caribbean, Latin America and Central Asia (1996–1997)

Political context to the missions

In June 1996, the Florence European Council designated three EU 'priority' areas for coordinated bilateral and multilateral action against drugs:

1 Latin America and the Caribbean
2 Central and Eastern Europe
3 Russia.

This decision had its roots in an Anglo-French initiative of the previous year, focused on the Caribbean. In early 1995 the then Prime Minister of Barbados (Owen Arthur) made a direct appeal to the then UK Prime Minister (John Major) for special assistance to cope with drugs issues in the region. Subsequent Anglo-French dialogue quickly generated a joint declaration between the UK and France (signed by Major and President Chirac of France) committing the two governments to an increase in regional assistance levels regarding drugs control (in the context of the longstanding interests of the UK and France in the region as former colonial powers). Further support was canvassed via a letter from Major and Chirac to Jacques Santer (then President of the Commission) calling for consultative measures at EU level. After gaining further support (notably from The Netherlands, another country with a former colonial interest in the region) the matter was raised at the Madrid European Council (December 1995). Fellow heads of state agreed that priority should be given to the establishment of a mechanism for cooperation between the EU and the Caribbean to combat drugs, but proposed that this be extended to include Latin America as well as the Caribbean (*EU Bulletin* 12-1995: 16).[161] The decision to broaden the geographical scope of the initiative reflected an acknowledgement of wider political concerns, particularly the strong Spanish interest in Latin American matters.

The Madrid European Council called for a report to be prepared by April 1996 on the drug situation in Latin America, including the Caribbean, and that it be accompanied by a set of recommendations. Based on the TEU framework this would have seemed a natural second pillar task, principally involving issues of international cooperation. However, a decision was taken by COREPER to set up a new, dedicated working group to operate under the third pillar: the *ad hoc* Working Party on Latin America and the Caribbean (Drugs) [WPLAC].[162] On one hand, this decision can be interpreted as a tacit assumption that discussion would predominantly cover trafficking-related matters. On the other, it could equally be read as a normative expression of a dominant cognitive position on the dynamics and underlying causes of drug problems as they affect countries outside the EU. However, empirical assessment of the decisions for which the working party was subsequently to be the locus reveals a much more nuanced process. One of the first decisions taken by the WPLAC was to decide that an 'expert mission' should be sent first to the Caribbean in order to provide a basis on which to make decisions regarding any future programmes. This decision was almost certainly taken under pressure from the UK and France, and in spite of Spanish preferences. However, there were a number of factors that worked in favour of making the Caribbean a discrete region for EU action. One of the most important of these relates to the jurisdiction of the Commission, as the next section explains.

The Caribbean Drugs Initiative

The countries of the Caribbean region are not significant producers of illegal drug crops (in fact only cannabis, an indigenous plant, is grown on some Caribbean islands).[163] However, their close geographical proximity to Latin America and the wide variation in jurisdictions and law enforcement capabilities across the region have contributed to high levels of drugs transhipment activity and associated money laundering, which expanded significantly during the 1990s. Although France, the Netherlands, Spain and the UK had all engaged in bilateral anti-drugs initiatives of one form or another for some time, most activities of this type had been led by the United States, frequently with UNDCP support. All these factors were identified in the analysis contained in the introductory section of the report produced by an 'EU Experts Group on Drugs' who were sent on a mission to the Caribbean. The Group submitted a report in March 1996 that proved highly influential, containing detailed recommendations on how to address the drug-related problems affecting the region. Before analysing this influence it is important to understand the context in which the group of experts came to be formed and the process of selection, in which the Commission had a more prominent role than might have been expected.

The fourth ACP-EEC Convention, better known as Lomé IV, was signed in 1989 and subsequently provided an overall framework for relations between the EU and the African, Caribbean and Pacific (ACP) countries of the developing world. The Convention came into force in

1991 and included provisions for financing drug control measures in two respects: Article 154(3) made general provisions in the area of public health while Article 159(k) allowed for the scope of regional cooperation to include 'assistance to ACP States to help combat drug trafficking at regional and inter-regional levels' (OJ L 229, 17 August 1991: 57). However, the June 1994 communication from the Commission on a 1995–99 EU drugs action plan noted that such provisions 'have not yet been exploited by the authorities in those countries' (Commission, 1994: 21).[164] It also called for dialogue with the 'most seriously affected' countries to 'make them see the extent of the problem and the impact it is having on their development' (ibid.). In fact, preparatory work in relation to this was already taking place under the auspices of the Commission's Directorate-General for Development (then DGVIII).[165] The lead official in this respect had a background in foreign affairs and drugs issues within her home government before joining DGVIII in 1993 and – based on this experience – almost immediately began to initiate research projects to assess the extent of drug problems and their impact on the development of the ACP countries. Drug projects were widely seen as a relatively low priority in development terms at this time, and in the Caribbean region drug issues were generally perceived as enforcement rather than development matters (almost certainly due to the enforcement emphasis of high-profile US initiatives in the region). None the less, in the context of preparing the next five-year aid programme for the period 1995–2000 (European Development Fund IV), a consensus had begun to build in favour of introducing some small-scale drug demand reduction activities. In this regard, DGVIII had recruited an ex-UNDCP offi-cial (Michel Amiot) to run a new EC drugs bureau in the Caribbean following a DGVIII mission to the region in June 1995.[166] This was to become the European Commission Drug Control Office (ECDCO) in Barbados.

Amidst a high profile for drugs issues within the EU at this time, the Anglo-French initiative and backing from the Madrid Council added significant political momentum to the work already undertaken by DGVIII from a development perspective. It was for this reason that the Commission was keen to participate in the new initiative and, on the basis of the work by DGVIII, it had a strong and logical reason for being actively involved. The Commission also expressed a willingness to provide funds for the proposed expert mission. As a result, while member states retained the prerogative in nominating experts for the mission, the Commission was given an important coordination role. An eight-person team of experts was selected for the mission (see appendix),

Case Studies   155

made up of two individuals from each of France, The Netherlands and the UK, together with a Spaniard and, finally, Michel Amiot representing the Commission. The majority of the team were predominantly from a law enforcement or judicial background (including police and customs officials, a public prosecutor and a money laundering specialist from the EDU) but also included a senior UK diplomat (formerly Governor of the British Virgin Islands). The law-enforcement oriented composition of the team caused some private concern within DGVIII at the time, particularly as it was set against a backdrop of tension between France and The Netherlands in connection with Schengen and the issue of drugs (described in Chapter 9).

However, the selection of the individuals who made up the expert team was clearly itself the result of politicized process. First, the selection criteria for each member state varied depending on how drug policy was organized at the domestic level. There are different traditions as to which ministry takes the lead on drug issues across the EU as well as cases where a cross-ministry approach exists.[167] Second, although the Caribbean mission was a *collective* EU exercise, only countries with a regional interest (including France and Britain who had proposed the initial move) provided personnel, with other member states diplomatically choosing not to nominate candidates even though they were entitled to do so.[168] The law enforcement bias evident in the nominations affirms dominant (institutionalized and normative) preferences regarding drug policy, but this does not mean that individuals from such backgrounds cannot hold or express views that look beyond such preferences. The final report of the EU Experts Group on Drugs provides a good illustration of this point.

The mission visited the region from 12 February to 12 March 1996, in which time consultations took place with a large number and range of officials from Caribbean governments and regional representatives of EU member states, as well as international organizations with a regional presence and remit (plus a visit to talk with US officials in Miami).[169] The final report was submitted in March 1996 and contained a total of 60 recommendations with regard to the following aspects of drug policy:

- law enforcement
- information and intelligence
- legislation/judicial system
- money laundering and freezing, seizing and forfeiture of assets
- precursors and essential chemicals
- cultivation and production

- demand reduction
- coordination.

It should also be noted that the document itself bore no internal EU affiliation, making it seem neither a Commission nor Council 'product', thereby helping to project an image of objective neutrality on the part of the experts. The recommendations could certainly be described as multidisciplinary, although only 7 of the 60 were related to factors linked to positive-control measures, that is, had regard either to cultivation, production or demand reduction. None the less, the authors did not avoid adopting what they were bound to realize would be controversial viewpoints. In the introduction to the report, the regional strategy pursued by the countries of Europe and North America for almost 20 years in trying 'to interdict, repress and enforce a reduction of supply [of illegal drugs] almost essentially through law enforcement means' was described as having achieved 'little success' (Caribbean Experts Report, 1996: 2). This kind of critical analysis renders redundant any simplistic idea that a collection of individuals whose professional background is related to law enforcement will automatically give primacy to repressive policy instruments. It is not possible to tell whether any of the experts had a greater influence than the others on the inclusion of particular points or emphases in the report, however. The interpersonal dynamics of expert groups of this kind are clearly an important influence on the ideas that emerge as different backgrounds and experiences interact and the mix of personalities and characters leads to individuals taking an overall lead or having particular authority with regard to certain aspects of the analysis (by dint of force of personality, or specific experience). The search for consensus inherent to this process is particularly likely to hinge on interpersonal relationships. In this specific case the resultant report was both nuanced and pragmatic, evidenced by the inclusion of a second controversial recommendation, to the effect that 'the eradication of ganja [marijuana] and the arrest for simple possession of ganja should be given lower priority compared with the other law enforcement efforts against the drugs problem, particularly those related to the trafficking of cocaine' (Caribbean Experts Report, 1996: 41). Such an opinion contradicted avowed US policy in the region, causing a certain amount of friction when the report was released. This surfaced in May 1996 when the experts report (having received Council-level approval) was put forward to a UNDCP meeting held in Barbados. However, despite significant US misgivings about the point on ganja, the meeting launched the 'Barbados Plan of Action', for which the

60 recommendations in the experts report were widely credited as providing the basis.

Careful diplomatic handling of the 29 Caribbean countries as well as the broad donor community (bringing in the US, Australia, and Canada as well as regional and international organizations, in addition to the interested EU states and the Commission) was needed to ensure that the EU was not seen as 'muscling in' by any of the other parties. Hence what became known as the EU Caribbean Drugs Initiative (CDI) was born as an important component of a broader five-year 'UNDCP Barbados Plan'.

Implementation of the Caribbean Drugs Initiative

The recommendations contained in the experts report quickly became the template for implementing the CDI. Funding was derived partly from Community funds and partly from bilateral funds originating from member states. From May 1996 a series of feasibility studies were commissioned covering five specialist areas:

1 equipment and training needs
2 secure communications for the exchange of intelligence
3 maritime cooperation
4 forensic laboratory upgrading
5 money laundering.

Work was also initiated in relation to legislation and drugs councils, demand reduction and treatment and rehabilitation, but 'feasibility studies' were not commissioned for these matters. This meant that the next stage of the implementation process was focused on law enforcement measures. Small teams of experts with highly specialized law enforcement qualifications were commissioned to undertake the feasibility studies.[170] These studies provided the basis for a programme of specific projects and work plans. Experts from the United States were involved in the production of reports on maritime cooperation, intelligence and money laundering. The funding of the resultant projects was split largely along 'pillar' lines: institution building was largely covered out of Commission funds whereas equipment was generally covered by member states bilateral funding, together with 'third pillar' money channelled through the Commission's 'JHA Task Force'. This process was managed primarily through an 'informal' Council working group coordinated by DGVIII which met every couple of months or so, often on the day before a formal Council meeting, undertaking technical discussion and allocating work responsibilities (and monitoring progress over time). Initially, the group included the original experts who had been part of the mission, (although by 1998 only one remained) supplemented by 'home-based' officials from the lead ministries of contributing member states; for example, the UK Foreign and Commonwealth Office (FCO). Several participants in this process stressed during interview that the informal character of the group had greatly helped its effectiveness, allowing potential problems to be discussed outside of more formal channels.

Reviewing the Caribbean Drugs Initiative

The CDI ran from 1997 to 2001 and (according to figures published by the UK FCO) was supported by a budget of 35 million Euros. It represents an interesting example of the kind of complex interaction of policy specialists that occurs within the drugs field, as well as illustrating how expertise can be deployed to provide authoritative support for a common policy enterprise. However, one of the most interesting features of the CDI was the apparent absence of any formal method or criteria by which to measure the efficacy of the strategy. Interviews with participants in the policy-making process revealed that this was largely because different participants had different expectations about the purpose and rationale for the project. DGVIII, with its ACP development remit, viewed the 'success' of the CDI as an already apparent phenomenon even by 1997, having been instrumental in making the project a reality. DGVIII saw the CDI as a positive example of cooperation between the Commission and member states; as an example of broader EU–US cooperation; and also as having achieved the objective of generating both policy and political consensus via pragmatic project management. There seems to be strong *prima facie* evidence to support this view, but perhaps the most notable absence from the DGVIII perspective is the notion that the aim of the CDI might be primarily to stop drugs reaching Europe. By contrast, the UK FCO saw this as the primary objective for success, yet privately recognized the difficulty of measuring achievements in this regard. Nevertheless, the UK FCO shared many of the same objectives as DGVIII, particularly with regard to the successful implementation of national drug 'master plans' by Caribbean countries. Unquestionably, an important factor behind the rapid implementation of the CDI was the fact that a framework for regional cooperation (that is, CARICOM) was already well established.

What the CDI clearly shows is the way that first pillar development instruments played a part in what in other instances have clearly been regarded as third pillar prerogatives, enmeshed with bilateral initiatives undertaken by member states (in conjunction with other regional actors, including IGOs). Within the EU policy arena, the CDI project became a symbol of the need for cross-pillar coordination on drugs matters, drawing as it did on all three pillars. Participants in the CDI noted the growing role of the Horizontal Drugs Group (which supplanted the work of the WPLAC during 1997) in providing a forum in which the focus of drug policy moved away from a purely 'internal focus' to consider the wider international context of drug problems and their causes. The real impact of this process on third pillar policy-making does not seem to have led to a significant shift in the balance of drug policy, however. What is clear, though, is that the expert mission played a pivotal role in creating a shared policy enterprise around which various viewpoints were able to converge.

EU drug expert mission to Latin America

The June 1996 Florence European Council accepted the report of the drug experts on the Caribbean and also called for proposals covering the whole of Latin America. Based on a proposal from the WPLAC, 'COREPER agreed to send an evaluation mission' for this purpose (Council, 1996c: 5). The geographical terms of reference for the mission were set by the WPLAC on 6 September 1996, in which it 'considered it advisable to have the mission visit the Andean countries – Venezuela, Colombia, Ecuador, Peru and Bolivia – and Brazil and Costa Rica' (Council, 1996c: 5). The WPLAC thus became the principal driving force in developing a rationale for EU action on controlling drugs in Latin America. The Latin America group of experts, like the Caribbean mission, also showed a majority of members from a law enforcement background (see appendix for details), with three of the five members having police or drug liaison credentials.

The Group of Experts visited Latin America in September and October 1996, submitting a *Report on drugs in Latin America* (Council, 1996c) on 4 November 1996 simultaneously with both the WPLAC and the DOCWG. Although the report was modelled on the Caribbean report both in terms of methodology and the range of measures on which it made recommendations, it was not as concise. This was almost certainly a reflection of the difficulty of producing innovative ideas, given the large number of existing regional drug control initiatives, most notably the Inter-American Drug Abuse Control Commission (CICAD) of the Organization of American States (OAS), established in 1988. Although the report made 66 multidisciplinary recommendations, the mechanism for implementation clearly envisaged heavy reliance on existing institutional and political cooperation. The experts were thus unable to mobilize support for a more substantive EU-led initiative comparable to the CDI. Part of the reason for this can be seen in the very different role played by the Commission in this case.

Latin American issues were the responsibility of a different Directorate-General: DG1B.[171] Unlike DGVIII, the DG1B remit covered external relations for territories as diverse as the Middle East and Southeast Asia as well as Latin America. Given that existing mechanisms between Latin American states and the EU on drug precursor control were already in place it was perhaps inevitable that the political impetus to undertake new actions was relatively weak within DG1B. As a consequence, the Latin American initiative was characterized by attempts to build and consolidate institutionalized dialogue. Even before the report was submitted for European Council level approval (Dublin, December 1996), development of the rather vague-sounding 'mechanism to combat drug abuse in Latin America, including the Caribbean' had already been placed on a list of priorities for cooperation *in the field of justice and home affairs* for the period from 1 July 1996 to 30 June 1998 (OJ C 319, 26 October 1996: 2).

By the time a revised Council Resolution on JHA priorities was made on 18 December 1997 the emphasis had shifted to implementing the action plan for the Caribbean and 'the recommendations made for Latin America by the European Council in Dublin' (OJ C 11, 15 January 1998: 2). Despite the lack of an institutional framework through which to implement the ideas contained in the expert report, the report became the definitive source of ideas for cooperation on drugs with Latin America after it was submitted to Council.[172] The decision to make implementation of the recommendations a third pillar matter marginalized ideas concerning alternative development, and prevention and rehabilitation included in the report. The third pillar status of the WPLAC meant that any decisions would be sanctioned only via third pillar mechanisms.

The expert groups and new political cooperation (EU–LAC)

Despite the contrasting outcomes from the two drug expert missions to the Caribbean and to Latin America, both were instrumental in building a basis for what has developed into a framework for political dialogue and cooperation between the EU and the combined Latin America and Caribbean (LAC) on drugs issues. The Panama Action Plan, adopted in Panama City in April 1999 and ratified at the first ever summit between Latin America and the Caribbean and the European Union held in Rio on 28 and 29 June 1999, established the framework of the 'EU–LAC Cooperation and Coordination Mechanism against drugs'. By this time a 'high-level' meeting had already been held in Brussels (March 1998) and three further meetings had taken place by March 2002).

EU drug expert mission to Central Asia

Approximately half of the illicit opiates and heroin being sold in the EU are believed to originate in Afghanistan and in neighbouring areas in Central Asia.[173] The Republics of Central Asia have increasingly been identified as key transit routes through which drugs reach Europe. A year after submitting their proposal on the Caribbean in Madrid, Prime Minister Major and President Chirac called for an examination of ways to assist Central Asian republics, utilizing the TACIS programme, to fight transit in and production of drugs (*EU Bulletin*, 12-1996: 14).[174] The Dublin European Council endorsed this proposal and decided to send an EU drugs expert mission to the region.

The setting up of this mission is a particularly interesting example of the politicized context in which expert missions are often appointed and given terms of reference. In this case, the decision to look at Central Asia came after a decision had already been taken to send a mission – under the auspices of DG1A of the Commission – to the New Independent States (NIS) to examine cooperation via the TACIS programme on areas related to justice and home affairs. Drug trafficking was included alongside nuclear material smuggling, illegal immigration, money laundering and organized crime in this regard. The drugs mission to Central Asia was, in effect, 'bolted-on' as a subordinate part of the wider mission. The Commission had already drafted a set of terms of reference (TOR) for the TACIS JHA mission, but then revised them to allow for a 'sub-mission' to Central Asia specializing in drugs issues. At this time, the standard procedure was that TOR were sent to 'K.4 national contact points' (national ministry officials) to solicit candidates as national experts. As instigators of the initial proposal only the UK and France were asked to propose drugs experts for the 'sub-mission'. The team of four chosen included two former ambassadors, reflecting the political sensitivity of the mission. The other two members of the team were law enforcement specialists, from a police background (France) and customs (UK).[175] An 'observer' from DG1A of the Commission also accompanied the team but is not named in the list of participants. The team visited Uzbekistan and Turkmenistan in March 1997 and Kirgizstan and Kazakhstan two months later.

The mission submitted its report in July 1997 to DG1A at the same time as the wider JHA-related report (which also included drugs recommendations for the NIS) although Council did not act on its findings until the autumn. Before considering the content of the report and how it has been used to create policy action it is important to consider the frame of reference within which the expert group was working. The TOR for the overall mission prepared by the Commission contained very specific guidelines with regard to drugs. The guidelines also made the relationship of the sub-mission to the JHA mission very clear, with annexes setting out specific criteria in relation to 'narcotic drugs' for the overall mission (Annex 1) alongside a specific brief covering 'Drugs – Central Asia' (Annex 5) and a more general 'Tasks of the Drug Mission in Central Asia' (Annex 6). Point 5.3.3 specified that all relevant tasks and aspects of Annex 1 should be taken account of and integrated into the report.[176] The sub-mission thus became a sub-JHA mission, working 'in the frame of the overall terms of reference' (Point 6.2.1). Point 5.2 specified what the Central Asia report should contain: 5.2.2 stated that 'The report shall identify the best means by which the EU can help the republics of Central Asia to strengthen cooperation between their government and law enforcement bodies and so to enhance their capacity to counter traffic in and production of drugs and precursors'. The group were also instructed to make contact with the UNDCP as a 'major source of information' (point 6.3).

In this case it was thus the Commission who specified both the type of expertise considered relevant for the mission and framed its terms of reference. Reading the TOR document in conjunction with the final report shows how closely the field of reference specified in the TOR shaped the parameters of its findings. Of course, this is not to express any judgement on the validity of those findings, but simply to point out that the authoritative nature of any conclusions drawn were the product of a broader normative framework that matched existing policy preferences to the assessment framework. The mission did have a fairly specific task in this case, but the depth of any consideration of non-enforcement issues was inevitably curtailed. In its conclusions the expert report recommended that 'a number of practical steps could and should be taken to strengthen the capabilities and resources of the regional governments, particularly in fighting the flow of illegal narcotics' (main report p. 15). Only brief mention is made of 'non-trafficking' issues, with the report concentrating on making recommendations in relation to specific projects. In this regard the experts' report was responsible for generating a further six project-based missions (all of which covered technical law enforcement areas), some of which then later submitted further reports.

In common with the Latin America mission, the Central Asia recommendations could not be incorporated into a wider political framework, such as ACP, and had also to be set against work already underway in the region, including work by Germany, the US and the UNDCP. The politicized nature of the process was striking, beginning with the initial proposal from the UK and France and continuing in the expert selection phase. The Commission played a strong role, illustrating the role of funding in giving project management responsibility: DG1A led the project, despite the sensitivity of JHA matters among member states. It is perhaps a rare example of third pillar action in which the Commission has had a leading role, but it must not be forgotten that the broader mission was about implementation of JHA priorities established under the third pillar. The influence of the drug experts' report lay mostly in providing a rationale for specialized *ad hoc* law enforcement projects. This case thus provides a different example of how expertise is assigned and utilized in a EU context, this time in a way that overtly linked drugs to the JHA priorities of the EU as a whole in the context of its external relations with the former Soviet states.

Case study 2: The handling of drugs issues during the 1998 UK Presidency of the EU

Presidency objectives on drugs issues

The United Kingdom held the Presidency of the EU in the first half of 1998. This period was interesting for several reasons: drugs were made a priority issue by this Presidency; the institutional mechanisms set up under the TEU framework to handle drugs issues were in a state of transition; and a new post-1999 EU drugs strategy was at a formative stage of development. Additionally, the UN General Assembly Special Session on Drugs (UNGASS) was held during this Presidency on June 8–10 1998, raising the political profile of drugs issues considerably.

With regard to the institutional framework for handling drugs issues, one of the most noticeable points set out in the document proposing the work programme on drugs and drug-related issues for the UK Presidency was the 'pivotal role' given to the Horizontal Drugs Group (HDG) working party 'in coordinating and, where necessary, initiating, taking forward and overseeing appropriate activity' (Council, 1998b: 2). This point affords an opportunity to assess the practical significance of this emphasis, and to assess earlier observations about a built-in bias towards third pillar decision-making in relation to the HDG. First, it is important to examine the objectives set out by the UK Presidency with regard to drugs.

The UK set out five objectives for its work programme on drugs and drug-related issues (Council, 1998b: 2); to:

- progress further implementation of the EU drugs strategy with a focus on practical activity, aimed at enhancing cooperation, and taking full account of measures agreed at the Luxembourg European Council on 12–13 December 1997
- begin consideration of the main elements of a post-1999 EU drugs strategy
- ensure effective EU coordination for the UN General Assembly Special Session on Drugs
- ensure effective coordination of drug-related activity between the EU and G-8 Countries[177]
- promote practical and effective implementation of the EU/Caribbean/ Latin America and EU/Central Asian drugs initiatives.

Prior to issuing this specific drugs work programme the UK Presidency had submitted a proposed JHA matters work programme to the K.4 Committee for its consideration on 15 December 1997 (Council, 1997b). This document highlights how the UK viewed its drugs agenda as a third pillar agenda, as the proposed work areas were identical to the five objectives above with the exception of the reference to EU-G8 coordination (Council, 1997b: 8). Given the overt emphasis placed on the role of the HDG it is reasonable to infer that the UK Presidency viewed the principal remit of the HDG as relating to third pillar matters.

Institutions, pillars and experts

The UK made it clear that it saw the role of the HDG as ensuring coordination of drugs measures 'in conjunction with other appropriate Council working groups in all three pillars, in particular the Customs Cooperation Working Group [CCWG] and the Second Pillar CODRO' (Council, 1997b: 8).[178] The UK chose not to hold any Steering Group meetings during its Presidency, reflecting a belief that institutional changes – principally the new Multidisciplinary Group on Organized Crime (MDG) and the HDG – had largely supplanted the role of the steering groups. Implementing the MDG action plan was seen as a 'major JHA priority' for the UK, focused upon pursuing the strategic programme of 30 recommendations for tackling international organized crime 'which will, of course, impact on action against drug trafficking' (Council, 1998b: 2). This is in spite of the aforementioned observation that the 30 recommendations contained hardly any reference to drugs. The MDG ostensibly took over the functions of the third pillar DOCWG (which fell into abeyance at this point) but residual work from the DOCWG was allocated to the HDG and CCWG. The HDG was assigned the task of complementing and assisting the work of the MDG 'as necessary'. A more detailed insight into the working remit of the HDG was also outlined in the drugs work programme. The measures listed included a number of law enforcement measures: implementation of the joint actions on new synthetic drugs and on the approximation of drugs laws and practices, along with consideration of a new joint action on practical measures regarding cooperation on asset confiscation, and work on 'practical measures' to tackle drug trafficking from Latin America and heroin trafficking along the Balkan route. The HDG was given the role of launching initial consideration of the main elements of a post-1999 EU drugs strategy and (as a minor point) following up the joint JHA/Health Councils discussion held in December 1997. A series of measures for the HDG to work in conjunction with the second pillar CODRO were also identified. First on this list was coordination of common positions in relation to the UNGASS. The Presidency submitted a document that it intended to form the basis of the Council (and EU) position on drugs at the UNGASS and which 'emphasized law enforcement' (Boekhout van Solinge, 2002: 65). The Commission submitted its own document (Commission, 1998a) which generated a certain amount of friction that was later to re-emerge in connection with the plans for a post-1999 EU drugs strategy. In addition to this matter, the HDG and CODRO were given further tasks related to the drugs initiatives in the Caribbean, Latin America and Central Asia. This affirms the view developed in the first case study in this chapter: that member states viewed these initiatives principally as third pillar matters.

During the UK Presidency the HDG was made up of second and third pillar experts, alongside Commission representation. On 5 February 1998 the 'first-ever' CFSP-CODRO troika meeting with the USA took place, which 'focused on preparations for UNGASS and anti-drugs cooperation in the Western Hemisphere' (Council, 1998e: 10), showing how diplomatic initiatives were a high priority in developing consensus in relation to drugs matters.[179] The drugs work programme document also laid out other areas of action seen as not falling under the direct HDG remit, namely: precursors, prevention of drug dependency, and relations with third countries. With regard to drug dependency, proposed action was covered by a brief and relatively noncommittal statement to the effect that 'Further work will be taken forward on the Community Action Programme on the prevention of drug dependency' (Council, 1998b: 6). The lack of a clearly outlined programme contrasts strongly with the detailed measures set out in relation to the HDG remit.

Developing a post-1999 EU drugs strategy

In keeping with the objectives originally set out in the K.4 Committee work programme the Presidency submitted a paper on 7 January 1998 to the HDG making suggestions as to the main elements of a post-1999 EU drugs strategy (Council, 1998a). The introduction to this document affirmed the importance of the Madrid Experts' report as a significant basis for action. The paper invited member states and the Commission to 'identify and put forward their preliminary views on those elements they consider to be areas for priority action at EU level' (Council, 1998a: 2). The paper proposed that the 5 March 1998 meeting of the HDG discuss these matters, and asked that answers be submitted based on four questions (the first of which asked 'What do you consider to be the main strengths or weaknesses of the existing EU drugs strategy?'). These contributions were then put forward by the Presidency to the HDG, which 'considered them in detail'. The exercise was claimed to 'reflect the consensus view of the Horizontal Drugs Group that the new strategy should ensure a proper balance of law enforcement and demand reduction (particularly prevention) aims and activities' (Council, 1998e: 3).

The document submitted and endorsed at the Cardiff European Council (Council, 1998e) included an annex identifying the 'key elements' of a 2000–2004 EU drugs strategy. The introduction to the document recognized that 'the problem of illicit drugs' had not diminished despite extensive EU efforts. A total of 13 key elements for the new strategy were then identified, the second of which re-emphasized commitment to a balanced approach between demand and supply reduction 'so that each reinforces the other ... across the three pillars of the European Union' (Council, 1998e: 13). The most notable of all was the seventh point, which advocated that the strategy should 'recognize the relationship between drug abuse and wider social disadvantage, such as poverty, deprivation, unemployment, homelessness, exclusion etc., and the links between drug abuse, delinquency and crime' (Council, 1998e: 14).

The document also identified that 'effective coordination against drugs and the implementation of existing drugs strategies has been hindered by a plethora of working groups' (Council, 1998e: 17). In response, the revised remit of the HDG was seen as having ensured more effective coordination. The future role of the HDG was also promoted; it was tasked with considering how to 'maximise the effectiveness and transparency of existing structures ... while avoiding, where possible, the creation of additional working groups' (Council, 1998e: 17). Once again, implicit criticism was made of previous working group arrangements.

In May 1998, ministers responsible for JHA matters in EU applicant countries signed a Pre-Accession Pact committing them to parallel legislative measures (that is, adoption of the EU *acquis*) and crime prevention projects as a condition of their future membership. Acceptance of all previous EU measures and agreements on drugs were thus made a legally binding condition of membership for the EU candidate countries. The MDG (via a specialist Pre-Accession Pact Expert Group, PAPEG) played a key role in this and, as a Council press release revealed, 'has promoted cooperation with key countries and bodies outside the EU: in the margins of its meetings discussions took place with representatives of the USA, Canada and the Council of Europe' (Council Press Release No. 8856, Presse 170, 29 May 1998). The role of the MDG in drug policy making was thus subtler, though no less important, than the HDG at this point in time.

Summary of the UK Presidency

The UK Presidency took the initiative on drugs issues, attempting to build an embryonic 2000–2004 EU drugs strategy in line with its own drug policy preferences. The strategy that subsequently emerged was outlined in the previous chapter. The UK Presidency period showed a degree of institutional innovation as this was the period in which the Horizontal Drugs Group began to emerge as the main forum for coordinating the overall drug policy framework; as such, the HDG is somewhat unique in being both a working group and a 'coordinating committee'. Despite the multidisciplinary language that was a feature of documentary outputs during the UK Presidency, the work of the HDG was clearly focused on third pillar matters and the majority of HDG delegates were JHA officials. The coordination work of the HDG also extended to close supervision of external relations discussions and initiatives involving drugs. Without exception, these programmes were heavily focused on the implementation of repressive strategies at this time.

Part III
Conclusions

12
Experts, Technocracy and European Drug Enforcement Policies

.

The Single European Act has been somewhat overshadowed by subsequent treaties that have set the course of European integration, but neither Maastricht nor Amsterdam (or even Nice and its commitment to significant enlargement of the EU) have had anything approaching its impact in psychological terms. That is because, in signing the SEA in 1986, heads of state and government were conceding that their borders – one of the most symbolic aspects of statehood – would in future be shared in ways that would require acceptance of a modified form of sovereign control. The so-called 1992 project created a febrile atmosphere of change and accompanying uncertainty. In the political declaration attached to the SEA, political leaders formally expressed their belief that the introduction of free movement of persons necessitated cooperative measures to cope with the threats associated with a defined set of activities: terrorism, crime, the traffic in drugs, and illicit trading in works of art and antiques, as well as controls on the entry, movement and residence of nationals of non-EEC countries. The declaration was careful to preserve the right of each state to take whatever measures it felt necessary for dealing with these matters, however. We have seen that the Trevi Group was the source of the underlying rationale for these commitments.

At this point, anti-drug trafficking policies became part of a broader normative policy framework based on the idea that 'removing' internal borders would increase crime and that the most effective way to address this was through 'compensatory' law enforcement measures. A year before the SEA was signed, the 1985 Schengen Agreement established the principle of formal, treaty-based cooperation between a subset of member states in relation to combating cross-border crime. The Schengen Agreement made provision for a wide-ranging set of cross-border law enforcement activities and for the sharing of information on crime and on criminal suspects in computerized databases. At this time, law enforcement professionals were thus placed at the forefront of political change in Europe; it was imperative that the new system would operate without problems. This process significantly enhanced the professional competence and authoritative claim to policy-relevant knowledge of law enforcement experts. However, the precedent for bringing law enforcement experts together in specialist fora had been set some time before this. As early as 1972, the formation of a Customs Mutual Assistance Group (MAG) established the principle that direct dialogue between experts (specialist officials and practitioners) was the best way for strategic thinking and practical ideas regarding European law enforcement cooperation to be developed and agreed. The significant point here is that national actors were given authority to develop a basis for *international* cooperation and to propose specific activities around this before submitting them for political approval. This blueprint for policy-making has subsequently proved remarkably influential in relation to the course of law enforcement policy development in Europe, especially in relation to anti-drugs actions.

Around 1985, drug trafficking and related 'serious crime' became a central concern of the Trevi Group. Trevi was an intergovernmental mechanism for dialogue between senior law enforcement officials and practitioners from member states. Policy ideas were developed within small specialist groups, or 'working parties'. We thus see that – within the confines of secretive transnational policy-making fora – a rationale was generated for increased law enforcement measures to combat rising levels of drug trafficking. A transnational law enforcement policy network thus began to emerge, facilitated by the Trevi framework, as well as a growing interaction between interior ministries in this burgeoning area of policy development. In short, the basis for a common policy enterprise had been founded, bringing together experts from the home affairs ministries of national administrations and senior law enforcement officers from national policing, customs and security agencies. Liaison officers posted to other member states in order to facilitate drug trafficking cooperation and information exchange were first appointed in the late 1980s as first the Schengen framework, then the Europol Drugs Unit and eventually Europol made this practice commonplace, heralding what has been a transformation in the working practices of national law enforcement bodies in Europe.

The Maastricht Treaty marked the political legitimization of the Trevi era and all of the decisions and agreements made at that time. It also formalized and institutionalized the Trevi decision-making framework without introducing a new system of transparency or accountability for the highly secretive form of policy-making characteristic of the Trevi era. The Treaty of Amsterdam incorporated the decisions and practices that were part of the Schengen system (including the far-reaching police cooperation arrangements that had evolved). This complex accumulation of precedents, preferences and political validation has shown a consistent pattern whereby expert knowledge has been used to validate particular courses of action. This book has described the evolution of European drug enforcement policies, and has examined the influence of expert actors at all stages of this process. Let us now consider the extent to which this reflects the influence of epistemic communities, along with wider questions about technocracy in relation to this policy area.

Epistemic communities

The concept of epistemic communities is concerned with trying to understand the role played by networks of 'knowledge-based experts' in articulating the cause-and-effect relationships of complex problems, helping states identify their interests, framing the issues for collective debate, proposing specific policies and identifying salient points for negotiation. The concept directs our attention to how knowledge and ideas influence the course of international policy development. This takes us beyond interest-based explanations that tend to view international cooperation as simply a rational response to the forces of globalization. The epistemic communities concept is actor based, so we are naturally directed towards questions about the *source* of ideas. We have seen that law enforcement expertise has played a dominant role in framing and shaping ideas that have influenced the overall direction of drugs policy in Europe. To what extent does the concept of epistemic communities inform our understanding of this?

The Trevi Group performed the kind of uncertainty-reducing role claimed to be typical of an epistemic community when the idea of free movement within a common European space became a serious possibility, driven by powerful political and economic forces. In the process, a set of causal ideas about drug problems were propagated, based on the notion of expanded threat arising from the removal of internal border controls. Senior national police officials made public statements that reinforced the idea that the 'new threat' from drugs required new and increased levels of enforcement. Dire warnings from senior police officers in the United Kingdom about an impending 'tide' of crack cocaine around 1989 provide a good example of how threat was given added saliency by delivering this message to a public audience. It has been suggested that the origin of this argument came directly from dialogue within Trevi (Dorn, 1993). A steady process of professionalizing national law enforcement undertaken by most liberal democratic governments gave law enforcement institutions, and practitioners working within them, an enhanced claim to policy-relevant knowledge.

The power of an epistemic community is claimed to lie in its ability to influence policy innovation, which it does by framing the range of political controversy around an issue, by defining state interests and by setting standards for policy implementation and evaluation. The Trevi framework facilitated direct access to decision-making channels for law enforcement experts and stimulated both formal and informal dialogue between experts on a personal working basis. However, we must be clear that Trevi was a mechanism based fundamentally on intergovernmental dialogue between national officials from interior ministries. However, by drawing practitioners into policy debate – notably senior police officers – the basis for shared causal beliefs to emerge, derived from common frames of analysis of practices in the professional domain, was made possible. Haas (1992b) suggests that it is this factor that serves as the basis for elucidating the multiple linkages between possible policy actions and desired outcomes. But most importantly of all, a common policy enterprise was to emerge out of this process that would consolidate the causal idea that drug trafficking was an activity driven predominantly by freedom of movement: the building of Europol. The rationale for building national drug intelligence units, followed by a European-level coordinating unit, became part of the blueprint for a radical new police organization. Law enforcement experts designed this process and set the terms for the new organization, founded on a convention that was developed in secret intergovernmental working parties before EU justice ministers agreed it politically.

The Trevi working methods were seamlessly adopted and formalized as the TEU entered force, but from this point national ministries took a much closer interest in the broadening agenda of EU Justice and Home Affairs (JHA) and the process became more bureaucratic in nature. None the less, by retaining the emphasis on developing drug policy within the JHA policy arena, law enforcement expertise retained the highest saliency in developing policy ideas. By 1995, the influential report of the Madrid Experts on Drugs illustrated how policy ideas developed in specialist enforcement working groups were accepted without any question of the wider rationale for action (that is, prohibition). A more mature phase, in which epistemic influence retained its saliency but ideological argument became increasingly replaced by a more technocratic style of policy development, seems apparent here. The specialist drug missions (described in Chapter 11) sent to evaluate drug issues in designated regions with specific drug problems were predominantly made up of individuals with law enforcement expertise. This reflected a normative preference on the part of political decision-makers rather than evidence of a cohesive epistemic community. In fact, the ebb and flow of policy-making has not been marked by significant phases of new uncertainty about drug enforcement, suggesting that the preference for law enforcement has been deeply assimilated. Drugs have still been a *leitmotif* for a broad range of law enforcement measures but cast in a broader set of uncertainties involving transnational organized crime. The post-Amsterdam era affirms this, with an institutionalized set of normative preferences apparent in the decision-making during this period. We must look beyond the epistemic communities model to understand this, but by keeping the focus on expertise and ideas it is of great assistance as a heuristic device.

Technocratic legitimacy

The concept of technocracy, or 'government by experts', is most frequently used to characterize the most bureaucratic of the supranational European institutions, the Commission. The concept has a number of drawbacks, however, not least the fact that it has both empirical and ideological aspects. The notion of 'technocratic legitimacy' has been used to describe the situation in which the Commission is able to utilize its powers to achieve a form of legitimacy that applies in connection with the internal policy-making process of the EU, whereby all policy is ultimately sanctioned by the Council of Ministers (Radaelli, 1999). The same process may lack democratic legitimacy, but national political elites take on the task of rationalizing within their own countries those actions that arise from their participation in the EU. Many of those actions may have low political salience while others are extremely sensitive. In relation to European drug enforcement policy we have seen that the Commission has played only a limited role; only since the Amsterdam Treaty has it had the right to initiate proposals in this area, and even then this is limited by the extent and orientation of the range of measures that are already in place. Drug enforcement policy (that is, measures pertaining to police and customs cooperation) has remained the most intergovernmental of all EU policy areas. A number of implications have arisen from this.

In preserving 'sovereign' control over joint enforcement decisions, national political elites have been keen to project that they retain control over the means to implement those decisions that are agreed at an intergovernmental level. Decision-making on law enforcement is thus an intrinsically and intensely politicized activity within the EU, meaning that expert involvement in decision-making is directly affected by political factors. Political elites have relied on a mixture of rhetoric and public anxiety to legitimize virtually any measure designed ostensibly to 'fight drugs'. The principal interaction of expert actors in the development of drug policy has been through a combination of national officials (from justice ministries) and law enforcement practitioners (police and customs officials). The former have a bureaucratic function while the latter have more domain-specific 'technical' knowledge. Radaelli (1999) argues that technocracy operates in policy domains with high uncertainty and low political salience, where experts stabilize the policy-making process by providing assumptions, rules and models. This is an interesting view but rather a static conception of the dynamics of policy development. The more independent voice allowed to senior police figures across Europe allowed them to both participate in the policy process – introducing ideas – as well as being able to influence it through a direct call to public opinion. This shows how expertise may contribute to the lowering of uncertainty (for decision-makers) at one point in time, reducing the political salience of action on that issue in a subsequent time period. This does not mean that expert authority has declined in influence; quite the reverse, it has become more deeply institutionalized. The crucial point about technocratic legitimacy here is that although specific types of expertise are intrinsically politicized, political elites legitimize their involvement by delegating policy development to functional areas *without* the external influences that are more typical of other areas of EU policy-making (where, ironically, it is the Commission that plays the leading role). Actor-based models thus help direct us to the question of why particular experts are considered to have authoritative knowledge in a given policy domain while alternative views may be marginalized. Drug enforcement highlights that 'common' understandings, such as shared disciplinary training and professional acculturation, are themselves socially generated. Hence, networks of law enforcement experts do not operate on a neutral, objective basis when they give advice; they do so based on preconceived ideas about causal relationships involving social processes observed in their professional domain. Haas (1992b) recognizes that another characteristic of epistemic community members may be a shared aversion to policy agendas outside of their common policy enterprise, or to policies based on explanations they do not accept. Adler and Haas (1992) explicitly recognize that epistemic advice can be used to justify particular state policy and to legitimize state power in the process.

Neither the epistemic communities model nor technocratic ideas give us a complete view of the policy evolution described in this book, yet both point to the role of experts. Technocracy may well be more about the politics of expertise in the modern idiom, and epistemic communities highlight the normative basis of decision-making. The final chapter addresses the relationship between knowledge and political power and, in the light of European drug enforcement policy, assesses what this reveals about the nature of the modern state in the particular context of the European Union.

13
Drugs, the State and the Political System of the European Union

The process of European integration has produced a new and complex political system which has involved a redefinition of the role of the state in Europe (Hix, 1999). This has generated considerable debate around questions of whether or not this is indicative of – or indeed might require – changes in the territorial organization of the state. In the course of this debate it has been observed that 'The EU does not have a monopoly on the legitimate use of coercion. As a result, the EU is not a "state" in the traditional Weberian meaning of the word. The power of coercion, through police and security forces, remains the exclusive prerogative of the national governments of the EU member states' (Hix, 1999: 4). Decisions taken by justice ministers from member states, meeting in Council, have cumulatively led to the construction of a complex security apparatus designed to control threats to member states and the citizens of those states. The central feature of this process is harmonization: of law enforcement practices, and both hard and soft law measures.[180] As well as a broad range of legislative measures, it has also involved the creation of institutions designed to facilitate transnational cooperation between law enforcement and justice agencies (for example, Europol and Eurojust) along with computerized systems capable of storing data on crime and criminal suspects (for example, SIS, and CIS). Based on the evidence of its evolution so far, Europol represents a significant step toward acceptance of a modified system of territorial jurisdiction in relation to coercive powers. This raises the question of whether this represents a modification of the norms of sovereignty in relation to the authority and control functions of the state. Drug trafficking has provided an important legitimizing principle for the building of a European security apparatus at a formative stage in its development. A clause included in a Council recommendation passed in 2002 encapsulates the contemporary rationale for collective European controls on drug trafficking: 'Illicit drug trafficking generates vast fortunes which allow drug-related crime to adversely affect society in general; for that reason, depriving such organizations of the enormous profits obtained from their illicit activities, as well as seizing the drugs, causes them serious damage, thus thwarting and preventing their resurgence' (OJ C 114, 15 May 2002: 1).[181] This shows us several cognitive aspects to the political support underpinning contemporary anti-drugs enforcement in Europe.[182] First, without providing a definition, it is implied that *all* 'drug-related crime' is believed to adversely affect society *in general*, a very vague notion indeed. Second, it is claimed that law enforcement based on interdiction and asset seizure is intrinsically an effective strategy in reducing and *preventing* drug trafficking. Substantive evidence to support either claim is not apparent either in public domain material emanating from European institutions or in the discourse of internal policy deliberations. The logic of prohibition dictates an enforcement response, but it is extraordinary how little evidence is available as to the efficacy of this approach.

The survey of the evolution of European drug policy that this book contains is a story both of the changing political landscape of 'integrated Europe' and of the extent to which this is one element in the response to a more fluid and complex transnational environment. All assessments of drug policy need to be understood in the context of the evolution of the global drug prohibition regime described in Chapter 3. What has been revealed is a policy-making process that is rooted in intergovernmental prerogative and the desire to preserve two of the most fundamental tenets of statehood: authority and control. The consequences of this process affect the citizens of EU member states and also the citizens of states who wish to join, trade with or receive aid from the EU (particularly applicant countries and developing countries).[183] This is because the EU systematically brings drugs issues into dialogue with third countries and makes compliance with EU preferences a condition of cooperation. Why do political leaders continue to have faith in increased drug enforcement to reduce the problems created in our societies by drugs? To what extent does 'drug threat' provide a basis on which to develop and justify a broader security framework? What impact does this have on standards of political accountability and transparency, civil rights, and on the rights of criminal suspects?

Drug enforcement as a European political project

The idea that drug policy is fundamentally a matter of law enforcement runs deeply through political and social life. Political decisions have reinforced this progressively through the emphasis given to repressive measures. Derks and van Kalmthout (1995) suggest that this had led to the strengthening of an 'integrative' model of criminal justice which has united a range of designated agencies and organizations in the pursuit of a superordinate goal: the eradication of drugs and drug problems. The same authors set the terms for an important debate when they ask: 'What makes drugs, and drug control, so attractive for state and international policies? Why is more control sought, and what consequences are likely to result from increasing levels of repression in our societies in general, and for individual and societal drug problems in particular?' (Derks and van Kalmthout, 1995: 100). They quite correctly identify that the answers to these questions are not 'readily available', suggesting that they can only be found within the scope of an international perspective. This book focuses on the nexus between internal and external state policy that arises in the shaping of drug enforcement policy through collective negotiation at European level. The second chapter of this book sketched the broader context of changing transnational forces that have been seen as a challenge to state power and state sovereignty. Whilst there have been many claims that state managers are in a generally weaker position, the response to a range of 'new' security threats has seen increased delegation of responsibility to expert groups working on a transnational basis to develop policy responses. Ideological (liberal) perspectives legitimize such actions on the grounds that the state is acting unambiguously in the interests of society. Putting aside the questions around this notion for the time being, the contemporary EU reveals the extent to which state sovereignty is a negotiated form of meaning that allows for selective sharing of sovereign control. Using the analytical framework provided by Thomson (1995), sovereignty can be understood as the means through which states claim – and have the recognized 'right' – to define the political: a concept she terms meta-political authority. Mutual recognition of this 'right' is validated by interaction between state managers (political elites) in the form of intergovernmental dialogue. Meta-political authority is intrinsically related to the state functions of authority and control, the latter of which concerns the ability to enforce and make good authority claims, that is, policing or law enforcement activities.

The notion of large-scale drugs threat rationalizes and legitimizes a high level of policing against drug trafficking and is often accompanied by a heavily rhetorical political discourse. The conflation of different kinds of transnational security threats has seen drug trafficking steadily become positioned as part of a broader set of problems on the argument that it is a significant component in an *integrated* pattern of activities undertaken by organized criminals. To meet this more generic threat, European states appear to be moving towards acceptance of a partial homogenization of their authority claims through the creation of Europol. The initial rationale for Europol was to provide an information exchange for criminal intelligence about drug trafficking organizations. The Europol Convention clearly reveals how this was a pretext for a much broader future remit; the remit and competence of Europol has been steadily extended, to the point where it now covers virtually all forms of 'serious crime'.[184] Alongside this, a steady extension in powers is also apparent, with strong political momentum for Europol to be involved in joint operational teams. This provides a basis for Europol to be involved in cross-border surveillance and covert operations, nominally as a facilitator.[185] However, there are concerns about this prospective shift towards operational powers: 'Member States have always been quick to state that Europol is not a police force with powers of arrest. But this distinction between initiating, pursuing and setting up arrests (Europol) and the actual arrest (national police) is irrelevant when it comes to the rights of suspects on trial' (European Parliament, 2000a: 100).

The evolution of Europol, with the intention that it should be the fulcrum of a range of computerized criminal intelligence databases in the EU, mirrors a rise in the overall surveillance capacity of national police forces.[186] Hebenton and Thomas (1992: 8) point out how trends towards centralization and specialization of policing in England and Wales during the 1980s generated so-called 'proactive policing' practices, reliant on information and intelligence gathering. This evolution is no coincidence: all advanced industrialized states are building a more extensive apparatus of control which is designed to control all forms of threat to the state, rationalized on the grounds that a threat to the state is a threat to society more generally. This engenders and deepens the perception that new forms of law enforcement are not only imperative but also capable of disarming threat, which in turn contributes to the 'solving' of crime-related problems. Politically, intergovernmental decisions at EU level clearly indicate a joint commitment to reinforce meta-political authority but within a reconstructed notion of territoriality. The link between authority and sovereignty is retained but in modified form: the monopoly on legitimate coercion is becoming more loosely grounded in a single state and made part of an evolving sense of collective statehood for member states of the EU. While this has significant consequences for academic thinking about the contemporary meaning of state forms, why should it concern us in terms of a direct impact on civil society?

Serious threats to the safety of citizens exist, many of which are stimulated by greater transnational fluidity. Illicit drug trafficking is unquestionably an undesirable activity with a range of negative consequences, but it has become *reflexively* seen as a threat to the state or, more accurately, positioned as a threat to state control. Drug traffickers have become a significant element in a revised post Cold War compendium of threat, evident in political decisions taken at EU level. Such a culture has particularly important consequences for thinking about drug problems.

Almost any form of action against drug traffickers has become 'legitimate' (consider the example that the scale of punishment for drug traffickers now exceeds that for murder in some EU countries). All of these factors have contributed to building legitimacy for the efficacy of international cooperation in support of higher levels of drug enforcement; that is, deepening the culture of prohibition. The EU is formally committed to a multidisciplinary approach to drug policy. However, the dichotomy at the heart of European drug policy remains as strong as ever: harmonization and toughening of enforcement measures alongside acceptance of alternative approaches to the issue of harm reduction. None of these points should be seen as ignoring the salient fact that drug enforcement is so deeply entrenched at all institutional levels – social, political and legal – that decision-making on drugs obviously cannot easily abandon the enforcement dimension. This book is concerned to understand the reasons why governments favour the kind of extended state control described by Derks and van Kalmthout (1995), moving beyond normative notions of protecting society from the 'evil' of drugs to consider these actions as deeper reflections on contemporary state forms and practices. An important aspect of this book is its emphasis on knowledge and how this is institutionalized, creating normative understandings and reflecting particular power relationships. The EU provides a powerful illustration of these phenomena.

Anti-drugs enforcement and the politics of expediency

If European political decision-makers base their preferences for anti-drugs policy on expert assessment of social phenomena, then it is important that this is conducted with the highest standards of political accountability and transparency. However, the institutionalized model of decision-making described in this book is secretive and has limited accountability. The model also has both bureaucratic and technocratic features in which a clear normative preference for law enforcement expertise is apparent. A common policy enterprise is now shared between the working practices of national interior ministries and police forces, generating an intense transgovernmental network (den Boer and Wallace, 2000). The classic method of constraining the power of technocrats – that is, strengthening the role of parliaments in the control of the executive – has been effectively sidelined in favour of strengthened intergovernmental decision-making.

A series of weaknesses have become apparent in the way that the broad range of justice and home affairs policies are set. Critical accounts point to the low political visibility and accountability of the essentially bureaucratic system and the absence of mechanisms for ensuring national ratification of what has been agreed (den Boer and Wallace, 2000). With drug policy, we see the emergence of an essentially techno-cratic process in which participants accept and work to a circumscribed set of policy parameters of policy-making, allowing specialist law enforcement experts to develop ideas and furnish agreement before political approval is granted. Political approval is then often perfunc-tory, as time constraints restrict the practical ability of national JHA ministers to evaluate each decision: the fact that it is justice ministers making these decisions limits the frame of reference in any case, such that many decisions are frequently 'rubber stamps' giving political legit-imacy to expert proposals.[187] Inevitably, this system precludes funda-mental review of wider policy objectives or the rationales behind them.

What is also relevant here is to say that on the *acquis* principle decision-making becomes deeply and progressively institutionalized: debate does not re-evaluate the wider principles on which action is based.[188] This is despite manifest democratic shortcomings of the process through which many of these measures were agreed: the Europol Convention is the most prominent example of a far-reaching step that systematically denied the national parliaments of member states and the European Parliament the right to challenge the content of the Convention (the original draft of which was drawn up by a special-ist group of law enforcement experts). Despite this, questions as to the legitimacy of this process had low saliency in civil society, challenged only by NGOs such as the UK-based Statewatch, which monitors civil liberties in the EU. As a result, we can observe that the policy agenda reached a point whereby a far-reaching measure has low political salience despite the fact that it is linked to what is nominally a high salience issue: drug crime was cited as the principal rationale for estab-lishing Europol, which has since acquired jurisdiction to cover almost every possible type of crime. This example encapsulates both the secrecy of the policy-making process and the degree to which measures legit-imized on an anti-drugs approach have become part of broader security objectives.

Hence, there is a danger that the civil liberties implications of asset seizure laws or the data protection implications of holding large amounts of computerized data on criminal suspects are subject to debate only in the narrow 'technical' decision-making structures of the third pillar. As more powers are given to support an integrative model of criminal justice developed through intergovernmental agreement, this exposes a risk, as Derks and van Kalmthout (1995) presciently point out, that traditional safeguards on power are being abandoned. This form of policy-making culture also rationalizes the pursuit of the goal of drug eradication, legit-imizing new control-based measures such as compulsory workplace drug testing in precedence to a more pragmatic appraisal of strategies designed to minimize drug use and harm. Any discussion of the causal relations that generate drug crime and how this may relate to prohibition are systematically marginalized (particularly in terms of funding).

This work has shown how particular forms of normative knowledge serve to reinforce state functions of authority and control; functions which have been directly challenged by the forces of globalization. In Europe, this has deepened a dichotomy between harmonization of repressive strategies and acceptance of diversity in 'harm reduction' measures, in an overall context of political support for drug prohibition. It has also seen the creation of a state-facilitated system of policy devel-opment that has come to resemble a transnational technocracy. The Treaty of Amsterdam contained the objective of providing citizens with a high level of safety within an area of freedom, security and justice, for which 'The fight against drugs is an inseparable objective' (Commission, 1999a: 2). As membership of the European Union probably expands to 25 states in 2004 (with perhaps more to follow) it is vitally important that efforts are made to ensure transparency of existing measures (particularly where justice issues are at stake) and to review the wider rationale for drug enforcement policy. Academic research must endeavour to be at the forefront of this scrutiny process.

Appendix: Participants in EU Drug Expert Missions

1. Mission to the Caribbean, February–March 1996

European Commission

Michel Amiot
Technical Adviser on Drugs
Caribbean Region
Bridgetown, Barbados

France

Professeur Paul Lafargue
Chargé de Mission auprés du Premier Ministre
Comité Interministeriél pour les questions de Coopération
Economique Européenne Secrétariat Général
Paris

Alain Tourre
Contrôleur Géneral
Chef de la Mission de Lutte Anti-Drogue, Police Nationale
Ministère de l'Intérieur
Paris

The Netherlands

Robert Tjalkens
Project leader: Money Laundering
Europol Drugs Unit
The Hague

Elisabeth Horstink-Von Meyenfeldt
Public Prosecutor
The Hague

United Kingdom

Peter A. Penfold (CMG, OBE)
Special Advisor on drugs in the Caribbean
London

Alan Pamplin
Her Majesty's Customs & Excise
Drugs Liaison Officer
Kingston, Jamaica

Spain

Miguel Alonso Rodriguez
Unidad Central de Estupefacientes
Brigada de Investigacion
Grupo de relaciones Internacionales
Madrid

2. Mission to Latin America, September–October 1996

European Commission

Alastair White
Consultor
Banbury, Oxon.
United Kingdom

Spain

Modesto Garcia
Justice and Interior Secretary
Permanent Representation of Spain to the EU
Brussels

Juan Antonio Denis
Police Inspector
National Drug Plan
Spanish Ministry of the Interior

United Kingdom

Duncan Stewart
Drugs Liaison Officer
British Embassy
Caracas
Venezuela

Republic of Ireland

John McGroarty
Superintendent of Police

3. Mission to Central Asia, March/May 1997

France

Francois-Marcel Plaisant
(Former) Ambassador de France
Ministere des Affaires Etrangeres

Serge Antony
Commissaire Prinicipal
Direction Générale de la Police National

United Kingdom

Richard Christopher Samuel
(Former) Ambassador
Foreign & Commonwealth Office
London

Roy Affleck
Her Majesty's Customs & Excise
National Investigation Service
London

Notes

Notes to Chapter 2

1   Perhaps the definitive statement of this orthodoxy was made by then President Clinton of the United States in his address to the United Nations on 22 October 1995, when he suggested: 'We can't free our own neighbourhoods from drug-related crime without the help of countries where the drugs are produced. We can't track down terrorists without the assistance of other governments. We can't prosper or preserve the environment unless sustainable development is a reality for all nations.' Cited in Alexander F. Watson (US Assistant Secretary for Inter-American Affairs), 'The Americas in the 21st Century: Defining U.S. Interests', *U.S. Department of State Dispatch*, January 1996, vol. 7, nos. 1–3: 6.
2   See Held (1995b), especially pp. 99–101 and 135–6.
3   See Thomson and Krasner (1989), p. 216.
4   See Litfin (1994: 1).
5   I use the term state managers as it provides a useful heuristic device. It identifies that states are not homogenous, people-like entities but that they do have personnel whose nominal function is to manage and take decisions about resource allocation in respect of a defined territorially based structure. In some instances it may be useful to focus solely on executive functionaries within governments, but such an approach risks reinforcing normative concepts of power. Bureaucratic or regulatory power may be highly influential at an operational level. Hence the author expresses a preference for empirically based research to identify the role and power of state managers in specific areas, recognizing the highly complex nature of modern state apparatuses as well as the compartmentalized nature of much state decision-making (itself a corollary of the breadth of modern state activity).
6   See Thomson, 1995, p. 223.
7   This does not mean that other states will not try to bring pressure to bear on other states to comply with favoured norms or policies but that this dialogue is conducted chiefly through diplomatic channels, either privately or through a combination of private bilateral communication and public comment reported in the mass media.
8   Krasner's influential definition of regimes from 1983 remains salient here. He defines norms as 'standards of behaviour defined in terms of rights and obligations' (Krasner, 1983: 2). Norms are thus distinct from, though in some way related to, the more formal concept of rules (as represented primarily by laws) defined as 'specific prescriptions or proscriptions for action'. See Kratochwil (1989) for a more in-depth discussion of rules and norms.
9   The emergence of an embryonic interstate European police force (Europol) represents an interesting development in this respect. The evolution of Europol and the issues raised by this development are discussed in Parts II and III of this book.

10 German sociologist Ulrich Beck provided an influential account of the broader consequences of what he termed the 'risk society' in his 1992 book of the same name.

11 Will Hutton, 'The familiar shape of things to come', *Guardian*, 28 December 1995.

12 International prohibition of drugs provides a good example. It is the condition of prohibition that attracts criminals to drugs in the first place, because if demand is high then high prices (and thus profits) apply. See Stevenson (1994) for a good basic introduction to this argument.

13 See the introductory chapter by Smith and Baylis in their edited collection, *The Globalization of World Politics* (1997) for an illustration of this.

14 A good collection of perspectives can be found in Held and McGrew (2000). Earlier work by McGrew (1992) provides a good summary of the 'traditions' that were most influential in shaping ideas about globalization in what was a formative period of thinking about the issue.

15 In Britain, the national security intelligence agency MI5 was given powers to attempt to combat 'serious crime' in 1996. For a summary of the issues surrounding this decision at the time see: Richard Norton-Taylor and Nick Davies, 'On Her Majesty's Secret Service', *Guardian*, 29 January 1996.

16 The idea of 'stretching' is derived from Giddens' notion of time–space distanciation, or the conditions under which time and space are organized so as to connect presence and absence. Giddens (1990: 64) argues that, in the modern era, the level of time–space distanciation is higher than in any previous period, such that 'relations between local and distant social forms and events become correspondingly 'stretched' ... Globalization refers essentially to that stretching process, in so far as the modes of connection between different social contexts or regions become networked across the earth's surface as a whole. ... [it] can thus be defined as the intensification of worldwide social relations which link distant localities in such a way that local happenings are shaped by events occurring many miles away and vice versa'.

17 Giddens (1990: 1) defines modernity as referring to 'the modes of social life or organization which emerged in Europe from about the seventeenth century onwards and which subsequently became more or less worldwide in their influence'.

Notes to Chapter 3

18 Public international law provides a common framework that specifies the types of drugs for which control is deemed to be necessary, but a very wide range of criminal sanctions and modes of classification still exist at national level. Such variation exists even between the member states of the European Union. Details available online via http: <http://www.eldd.emcdda.eu.int> (accessed 24 November 2002).

19 The principal botanically derived drugs (from cannabis, coca and the opium poppy) grow predominantly in specific regions of the world (see Stares, 1996: 2 for details), requiring them to be shipped to and via other countries for processing and eventual sale (the main markets tending to be outside of these regions). A major sub-theme of prohibition has been the difficult

balancing act of trying to live by the fundamental principle of national sovereignty, and the desire to apply legal sanctions across borders and to foreign nationals involved in the illicit drug trade. This has led to a progressive attempt to universalize principles favoured by leading states: see Nadelmann (1993, especially Chapter 4) for an in-depth commentary on the attempts of successive US administrations to ensure that the methods and practices favoured by the US have become adopted as widely as possible.

20   For a systematic analysis of these factors see Stares (1996: 47–79).

21   See the edited volume by W. O. Walker (1996) for a series of articles that provide an interesting commentary on the cultural, social and economic role played by coca in the Andean region, illustrating that this predates the Spanish conquest of the area by two millennia.

22   Berridge and Edwards (1981: 259) define informal controls as 'a complex amalgam of manners, conventions, traditions and folkways, accompanied by systems of disapprobation for infringement of these rules and expectations which, in combination, generate social expectations about individual social behaviour'. The implication is that, over time, although such controls have become in a large sense superseded by formal controls they may continue to coexist as mediating and reflective devices to inform individual moral behaviour in relation to legally based rule frameworks.

23   See Nadelmann (1990: 506–7), and Musto (1987) reproduced in Coomber (1994: 85–6) for a range of observations on this factor in a US context.

24   Bruun et al. (1975: 9) note the significance of the founding, in Britain in 1874, of the Society for the Suppression of the Opium Trade, leading thereafter to steady pressure on the British Parliament to end British involvement in the trade.

25   See Nadelmann (1990: 505–10).

26   See Nadelmann (1990: 480).

27   See Nadelmann (1990: 507) and Bayer and Ghodse (1999: 3).

28   The 'Drug Supervisory Body' was set up to compile an annual statement of estimated world requirements for these purposes (Bayer and Ghodse, 1999: 5).

29   Bayer and Ghodse (1999: 4).

30   See Bayer and Ghodse (1999: 6) for a list of the original terms of reference for the CND.

31   See Bayer and Ghodse (1999: 6–8) for a more detailed description of the 1946, 1948 and 1953 Protocols. A key provision of the 1948 Protocol was the obligation that it placed on parties to inform the Secretary-General of any drug used or capable of being used for medical or scientific purposes that the party considers capable of producing harmful effects. Bayer and Ghodse view this as the birth of the 'similarity concept' whereby any addiction-forming drug, whether already discovered or to be discovered in future, should in principle be brought under international control.

32   See Nadelmann (1990: 508–9) and, in more detail, Bruun et al. (1975: 181–203).

33   Bruun et al. (1975: 17).

34   See Stares (1996: 26–7).

35   See Nadelmann (1993: 106–7).

36 Stares (1996: 30–4) traces the political economy of Colombian cocaine trafficking in relation to the US during this period.

37 The US presidents in office during this period, Ronald Reagan and George Bush senior, reinvigorated the Nixon-inspired concept of a 'War on Drugs', organizing a series of summit meetings with the leaders of Latin American states and committing vast amounts of US resources, including the military, to this end. At times, world attention was so concentrated on US actions that the drug problem was perceived as essentially an adversarial contest with two combatants: the US government versus the drug 'cartels'. A vast, often fascinating, literature provides a largely critical account of this period, notably 1989–92: see Baum (1997), Levitsky (1992), Mabry (1989), Musto (1994), Nadelmann (1989), Perl (1994), Reuter (1994), Scott and Marshall (1991), Walker, W. (1993 and 1994).

38 See Ruggiero and South (1995), especially Chapters 2 and 3, for a survey of the changing patterns of drug use and trafficking in the wider Europe.

39 The dynamics of the global drug market and the notion of law enforcement as a 'crime tariff' or 'criminalization tax' are both analysed by Stares (1996: 47–8).

40 Stares (1996: 37) also notes that the convention committed signatories to share law enforcement evidence and provide mutual legal assistance, relax bank secrecy laws, and extradite individuals charged in connection with drugs offences: that is to say selective – though important – moderation of the rigid constraints arising from national sovereignty over such areas.

41 For comparison, as of 1 October 2002, out of a total UN membership of 189 countries at this time 179 states had ratified the 1961 Single Convention (or the Convention as modified by the 1972 Protocol) and 172 states had ratified the 1971 Convention on Psychotropic Substances.

42 In 1997, the UNDCP was brought together with the United Nations Centre for Crime Prevention (CICP) to form the United Nations Office for Drug Control and Crime Prevention (ODCCP). The UNDCP underwent significant upheaval around this time. One of the very first tasks of the then incoming Secretary General, Kofi Annan, was to request the resignation of the programme director and 23 other officials, calling the effectiveness of the organization into question (see: 'Heads roll at the UN', *Guardian*, 11 January 1997). Despite these changes, the CND still establishes the main parameters of drug policy as it provides for a direct contribution from member states. The UNDCP is responsible for the implementation and administration of UN drug policies, however, and undertakes independent programmes to this end. It also acts as the secretariat for the INCB, which monitors compliance with UN drug control conventions.

43 The EMCDDA has also produced an annual report on the state of the drugs problem in the European Union since 1996. For an independent and more general overview of the 'emerging' drug markets 1989–95, see Stares (1996: 37–45).

44 A note on sources and limitations of data at the end of the report counsels that data presented therein 'should be treated with caution' (UNDCP, 2002: 281). It also states that information on trafficking (and partly on manufacture) is mainly derived from annual reports questionnaires submitted by governments to UNDCP.

45   The carefully polished language of the Political Declaration contained a commitment by UN member states to *eliminate* or *reduce significantly* 'the illicit manufacture, marketing and trafficking of psychotropic substances, including synthetic drugs, and the diversion of precursors' (UN General Assembly Resolution A/RES/S-20/2, 10 June 1998).

46   For an assessment of new trends in synthetic drugs in EU countries, see EMCDDA 1997c.

47   This reflected a higher than usual opium harvest in Afghanistan in 1999, after the Taliban authorities controlling most of the country at that time placed a ban on opium production in areas under their control in July 2000 (following negotiations with the UNDCP). The forcible removal of the Taliban authorities following the terrorist attacks on the United States in September 2001 is almost certain to have an effect on future opium production in Afghanistan but this will take some time to become clear, along with the implications for alternative sources of opium.

48   A 1996 UN report provided a graphic picture of the worldwide availability of ATS (see UNDCP, 1996). See also 'Stimulants, Next Century's Major Drug Problem', *UNDCP Information Letter*, December 1996, p.1.

49   A succinct analysis of this 'new drug trend' in European Union countries is contained in EMCDDA, 1997c (especially pp. 48–60). Social and cultural development is assessed alongside supply issues and other influential factors such as commerce and the media.

50   See Kleiman (1997) for a commentary on US experiences in this regard.

51   The 1998 UNGASS led to the creation of a UN Action Plan on Demand Reduction in 1999, establishing common principles for this aspect of drug policy but lacking the binding force of an international treaty.

52   On the origins and remit of the G-7 generally, see Lewis (1991) and Degenhardt (1986).

53   Using the work of the CATF as a basis for action, the US Government convened a conference on Chemical Control Operations at Lyons, France in September 1991 in association with the INCB, the Customs Cooperation Council and Interpol. This provided a basis on which to establish mechanisms for sharing information between the databases of those organizations and the establishment of procedures to verify the authenticity of applications for export authorizations. The CATF was thus a catalyst for a much broader set of initiatives.

54   By 2002, FIUs from a total of 69 states belonged to the Egmont Group.

55   See Taylor (1997: 290–2) on the political economy of the drug trade.

56   This is particularly acute where international decision-making is concerned. Stares (1996: 36–7) makes this point when he says that 'The 1988 convention represented a significant extension of existing international drug controls, but the global drug trade was already expanding in new areas and new ways even before the convention formally took effect'.

57   A short summary of the arguments for and against legalization of illicit drugs as an alternative to prohibition is provided in Stevenson (1994). For a wider series of viewpoints see: Nadelmann (1989), Nadelmann and Wenner (1994), and the chapters by Mishan, Wilson and Szasz in Coomber (1994: 338–82). Stares (1996: 105–21) also provides a pragmatic assessment of the future direction of drug control and the issue of legalization.

Notes to Chapter 4

58 For comparative purposes, see the articles by Mathews (1997) and Slaughter (1997). For a more in-depth and empirically grounded critical assessment, see Picciotto (1996).
59 Slaughter (1997: 184) lists 'today's international problems' as: terrorism, organized crime, environmental degradation, money laundering, bank failure and securities fraud. The notion that such a list is definitive is both fanciful and normative. Slaughter does not concern herself with understanding the criteria that determine which issues appear on such a list. For instance, several issues do not appear despite their demonstrable impact on human welfare (for example: levels of poverty, illiteracy, or rates of water-borne disease). What are here termed 'today's' international problems might be better described as issues seen as representing transnational threat to AICs. The rapid prioritization of terrorist threat after the attacks on the United States in September 2001 highlights the shifting prioritization inherent to this process as well as emphasizing the proscribed and normative nature of the list of international problems at any point in time.
60 The 'drugs problem' is a classic illustration. The scale of the institutional and bureaucratic machinery that is responsible for carrying out the actions designed to further enforcement aspects of drug policy is so vast that it works against the conceptualization of the problem in any other sense.
61 See Chapter 5 for a discussion on the nexus between science and social processes, and how this shapes understanding of both problems and solutions for 'technical' problems with socially located cause and effect relationships.
62 The idea that international treaties are always subject to rigorous scrutiny is open to question. The constitutional arrangements under which international treaties are ratified vary quite considerably between countries and although ratification may be slow it does not necessarily involve extensive democratic oversight. This is particularly so with regard to certain types of EU law. For example, in the United Kingdom the Europol Convention that established Europol was approved with only a minimal amount of parliamentary scrutiny (see Chapter 8 for more detail on this episode).
63 The exact nature and extent of this cooperation remains shrouded in secrecy. It was first revealed in 1997 in *Statewatch Bulletin*, vol. 7, no. 1, January–February 1997, pp. 1–4.

Notes to Chapter 5

64 For more detail on these concepts see Sabatier (1998) and Kingdon (1984).
65 The term itself originates with Holzner and Marx (1979: 107–11) although their use is both broader and more specifically related to the 'scientific community' as a whole.
66 Haas (1992b) provides an overview of the emergence of the 'modern administrative state' (pp. 7–12). He argues that a broadly based 'knowledge elite' has emerged, founded on the possession of scientific and technical skills.
67 The emergence of a 'knowledge elite' echoes Weberian notions of the rationality inherent to the modern bureaucratic state in which politics as a 'lived',

participatory experience is increasingly and 'inevitably' replaced by the condition of faith in expert systems.

68   In order to assess these points it is necessary to have an understanding of positivism, which is associated with a belief in the existence of an independent natural reality (within the context of science). The key question to ask about epistemic community members is how do their 'independent' causal beliefs relate to their interpretation of social processes?

69   For the positivist, science is an attempt to gain predictive and explanatory knowledge of the outside world. To do this, theories must be constructed that contain general statements that enable both prediction and explanation of phenomena, discovered through systematic observation and experiment. To 'explain' something here is to show that it is an instance of these regularities and that predictions can only be made on this basis (Keat and Urry, 1982: 4).

70   This relates to 'the logic of science' developed through positivist thought. As Keat and Urry point out (1982: 22–6), positivists conceive of the logic of science as dealing with issues of rational evaluation and justification. Related to this is the idea that the philosophy of science entails an analysis of science which does not depend on the actual and varying contents of specific scientific theories 'but which is conducted at a "higher" or "meta" level' (Keat and Urry, 1982: 25). Hence, on such logic is founded the appeal to external, rational standards in settling disputes between rival theories or explanations: a logic which is claimed to be the only logic underlying science and to which any intellectual activity that aspires to be 'scientific' must comply. A deep and enduring influence on advanced industrialized societies is revealed through this account.

71   Haas cites A. M. Carr-Saunders's definition of a profession: 'What we now call a profession emerges when a number of persons can be found to be practising a definite technique founded upon specialized training' (Haas, 1992b: 19, fn. 40).

Notes to Chapter 6

72   A vast literature provides an in-depth account of the development of the EU, its principal actors, institutional features and antecedents. For a good general introduction see Nugent (1999). For more specialized accounts of EU policy-making see Cram, Dinan and Nugent (1999), Richardson (2001) and Wallace and Wallace (2000).

73   The two treaties signed in Rome on 25 March 1957 entered force on 1 January 1958.

74   For a broader discussion of these points see Radaelli (1999: 30–52).

75   In fact, Pompidou initiated the formation of an expert consultative committee in 1972. The group has carried his name to this day, becoming known as the Pompidou Group, meeting informally at first and then – from 1980 – within the framework of the Council of Europe. Chapter 7 places the Pompidou Group in context in relation to the course of European drug policy development.

76   For a full description of the measures envisaged in the White Paper see Estievenart (1995: 57).

77 As Estievenart points out, this runs counter to the frequent public perception that physical internal frontiers formed the main barrier for intercepting drugs and drug traffickers.

78 The Pompidou Group was able to operate outside of the formal structures of the EEC on the basis of EPC for example.

79 A detailed account of Schengen cannot be provided here, unfortunately. For detailed accounts see Anderson et al. (1995: 56–63) den Boer (1996: 396–401).

80 SIRENE provides a facility for bilateral and multilateral exchange of mainly supplementary information about persons or objects registered in the SIS. Despite being developed alongside SIS, SIRENE is not mentioned at all in the Schengen Convention. See Mathiesen (1999: especially 4–19).

81 A secret proposal that Europol should have access to SIS data was first made in 1997, despite this being some two years before the ratification of the enabling Convention that formally established it (see Chapter 8).

82 European Council meetings have become an increasingly important part of EU decision-making since the early 1980s, especially in terms of setting policy priorities (see Nugent, 1999: 118–99). See Glossary.

83 At this point in time all member states, with the exception of Ireland and the United Kingdom, had signed the Schengen Agreement. Both Ireland and the United Kingdom chose to opt out of the Schengen Protocol, although the UK has subsequently sought to gain access to Schengen data via a selective 'opt-in' to the Protocol.

Notes to Chapter 7

84 The full title of the Naples Convention is 'The Convention of the Member States of the European Economic Community on the provision of mutual assistance by their customs authorities'. The Convention is to be replaced by the 1997 'Convention on Mutual Assistance and Co-operation between Customs Administrations' (also known as 'Naples II') (OJ C 189, 17 June 1998). The Convention was signed by the member states on 18 December 1997 and is based on Article K.3 of the TEU. It provides for enhanced administrative cooperation in relation to customs offences and also for special forms of cross-border cooperation. The Convention will come into force 90 days after the last EU member state has notified that it has completed its constitutional procedures for its adoption. However, in the interim any member states that have completed these procedures may declare that the Convention will govern their relations. On the date of its entry into force the Convention will repeal the Naples Convention. This illustrates a case of how legislative instruments build a web of cooperative arrangements over time, in which existing practices are merely adjusted rather than subject to a review of their effectiveness in relation to overall policy goals. No official account has provided any evidence on the effectiveness of the cooperation brought about via the original 1967 Naples Convention.

85 Elsen (1995: 360) recalls Pompidou's statement that 'It is the duty of leaders to grasp the problem and organize the defence of young people against a temptation whose dangers they fail to measure, which the traffickers excite,

sustain and shamelessly exploit, all too often with impunity'. The comments reveal a rhetoric that both rationalized and prioritized measures against trafficking. Causal analysis of this kind was undoubtedly fuelled by the emergence of the so-called 'French connection' involving opium trafficking from Turkey, refined into heroin in the Marseilles area and then re-exported to the US (and which captured public attention, inspiring the 1971 film of the same name, itself adding a layer of resonance to Pompidou's words at the level of popular culture). Anderson (1989: 152) records how in 1971 this prompted a cooperative bilateral agreement between France and the US to exchange law enforcement officials.

86   A 1990 UK Government report summed up the reasoning: 'Although all member states of the EC are members of Trevi, Trevi is strictly outside the framework of the EC. The EC has no direct police competence, and the British Government's view that Trevi is independent of the EC is supported by all EC member states' (House of Commons, 1990a: xxi).

87   This study considers only those aspects of the work of the Trevi Group that relate to drugs. For a full account of its broader ambit and workings, see: Benyon et al. (1993) (see pp. 152–68); Bunyan (1993a, 1997); Woodward (1993). Exemplifying the secretive nature of the Group's activities, Benyon et al. (1993: 152) note that even the origin of the Group's name remains the source of some dispute.

88   Schengen embodied an attempt to balance free movement of goods, persons and services with more intense cross-border police cooperation. den Boer (1996: 396) notes that the five Schengen countries already had experience of bilateral and multilateral agreements relating to police cooperation and the treatment of individuals regarding their common borders (for examples see her fn. 6, p. 408). A Schengen Implementing Convention was signed on 19 June 1990. For details of the Schengen process see Anderson et al. (1995: 56–63).

89   In addition, a general declaration was made on the subject of Articles 13 to 19 of the SEA to the effect that nothing in those provisions affected the right of member states to take such measures as they consider necessary for the purpose of controlling immigration from third countries and to combat terrorism, crime, the traffic in drugs and illicit trading in works of art and antiques (Commission, 1988).

90   Elsen notes how the Treaty gave more latitude with respect to the health aspects of the drugs problem but even then generated only a partial compromise that allowed the Commission observer status to meetings covering these issues. Again, sovereign sensitivity clearly underpinned this rigid interpretation of the Treaty.

91   This feature is hardly new: A. R. Lindesmith (1968: 240), writing a postscript to his classic text, notes how legislatures have long viewed the police as the final authority on 'most aspects' of the drugs problem. Prohibition, by definition, affords a leading role to law enforcement, but this does not explain why it should persist in the face of mounting evidence of the failure of law enforcement to reduce the scale of the problem despite large increases in resources (both legislative and material).

92   An important feature of WG III was how, from the outset, anti-drugs activities were discussed 'in the round' with other criminal activities, namely armed robbery, stolen vehicles, environmental crime, money laundering and illicit traffic in works of art (Benyon et al., 1993: 155), replicating the elements cited

in the SEA political declaration. Drugs were not differentiated since a common causal logic was deemed to apply to all of the criminal activities at hand in the sense that the impending removal of internal border controls was taken to be a kind of 'traffickers charter'. A further aspect of the Group's work involved identification of 'national contacts' (in policing authorities) designated to then make specialist contributions when discussions covered their area of expertise. A Memorandum submitted by the Metropolitan Police Special Branch to the Home Affairs Select Committee gave only a perfunctory list of the UK participants in WG III, describing them simply as: 'Home Office (F3), [and] Police' (House of Commons, 1990b: 43).

93 With regard to Trevi as a whole, from the UK perspective 'senior officials' included Home Office and police personnel, as well as the security services (House of Commons, 1990b: 43).

94 Criticism has generally centred on the lack of direct accountability of the officials involved in the process, as well as highlighting how information about the activities of the Group were largely dependent on the degree of openness inherent to national political cultures (which shows wide variation across Europe). See Bunyan (1993b: 38–40), and Benyon et al. (1993: 167–8).

95 Bunyan (1993c: 180) notes that three other countries were 'briefed' on Trevi activities by EEC states: Argentina (by Spain), Finland – which later joined the EU in 1995 (by Denmark), and Hungary (by Germany).

96 Membership of the Coordinators' Group consisted of 'high level civil servants from the 12 Interior Ministries' (Bunyan, 1993c: 174). The Group met at Palma de Mallorca on 4–6 June 1989 and had previously met on five occasions since February 1989 in Brussels. The Palma document names the fourteen members of the Group and their respective countries (the United Kingdom had two representatives). This reveals that a very senior official represented the Commission, in the form of its then Vice-President, Martin Bangemann (original document reproduced in Bunyan, 1997: 12–16).

97 For details of the specific measures concerning 'Action in Connection with Combating Drug Trafficking' see Bunyan (1997: 15). Once again, the Metropolitan Police Special Branch was no more forthcoming in detailing the UK participation in Trevi 92 than they were with WG III. Participants were listed baldly as 'Home Office (F4), Police and other agencies as required' (House of Commons, 1990b: 43).

98 The UK Home Office went on record to say that 'the group [MAG 92] is establishing contacts with other working groups [including Trevi 92] ... with a view to exploring areas of common concern and cooperation e.g. common information systems' (House of Commons, 1990b: 7).

99 Dorn (1993: 34) suggests that Trevi was the initial source of support for this proposition.

100 The significance of this institutional framework is discussed in more detail in the case study included in Chapter 11 on the EU Caribbean Drugs Initiative.

101 Estievenart (1995) lists the seven recommendations in full (pp. 58–9). They also included a call to step up controls at the external borders. The persons designated to serve as national coordinators were also expected to work 'in close conjunction' with the Coordinators' Group.

102 Elsen (1995: 361) records that CELAD actually met for first time on 1 December 1989, one week before its existence was formally approved.
103 A progress report from CELAD to the European Council covering guidelines for a European plan to combat drugs was included as an annex to the Presidency conclusions from the 1990 Dublin European Council. The full document is contained in Commission/EMCDDA (1993: 40–60).
104 It is noted that 'The European Community has also participated actively in the drafting and implementation of international drug control strategies and in the work of ... the CATF and the FATF' (Commission, 1994: 42). The relative contribution of Commission officials – as compared to national officials – in the work of the CATF and FATF is not revealed.
105 All of these measures were incorporated into the TEU on an *acquis* basis. Chapter 8 examines this in more detail.

Notes to Chapter 8

106 Fijnaut (1996: 197) records that the Declaration summed up the functions that it was envisaged Europol would at some stage fulfil, including 'support for national criminal investigation and security authorities; creation of databases; central analysis and assessment of information' and various research and training functions.
107 As part of the Treaty of Amsterdam it was felt that the existing treaties, including the TEU as well as the TEC, should be consolidated, that is, renumbered to make the numbering system more logical (given that a significant number of repealed articles had been removed and new articles added).
108 For a more detailed account see: Estievenart (1993: 12–14), and Hunter and Wasbauer (1995: 330–40).
109 Both of these issues came under the *acquis* relating to the broad framework of the E(E)C Customs Union, completed as long ago as 1970.
110 See Commission/EMCDDA (1993) for a summary of the relevant *acquis* measures.
111 Drugs clauses generally hinge around adherence to the main UN drugs Conventions as well as requiring more specific activities to be undertaken by signatories.
112 The ambiguity of these instruments highlights the cautious approach to measures in this area. This ambiguity was hardly improved by a comment in the UK House of Lords report (1997a: 46): 'The question whether or not an act in the form of a joint action (or joint position) is binding international law will primarily depend upon the intention of the parties and the terms of the act itself.'
113 Of course, in practice some proposals would be passed backwards and forwards several times between the various levels, depending on the degree of difference between the positions of different member states. The JHA Council in general acts on the basis of unanimity, although there are small technical exceptions to this (see House of Lords, 1997a: 45).
114 The K.4 Committee and (when operational) the Steering Groups are composed of one representative from each of the member states plus a Commission observer, supported by DG H of the Council Secretariat. Working groups are made up of nominees of the member states, assisted by

the Council Secretariat and Council legal service, together with Commission representatives (House of Lords, 1997a: 46). The K.4 Committee was renamed the Article 36 Committee after the Amsterdam Treaty (see Chapter 10).

115 The transfer of responsibility for preparation and management of meetings to DG H (under the direction of the rotating Presidency) was a significant procedural change brought in by the TEU. In an attempt to maintain a broad representation of its JHA-related interests the Commission set up a small 'task force' working within the Secretariat-General.

116 The UK had in fact proposed the creation of a European drugs intelligence unit during the Spanish Presidency in 1989. This was acknowledged, along with the fact that Trevi had already completed 'considerable detailed and careful work' on this matter, in the Report from Trevi ministers to the Maastricht European Council in December 1991 (original report, reproduced in Bunyan, 1997: 41).

117 Fijnaut (1996: 199) also highlights that this idea had its origins in the 1985 Schengen Agreement, which had included an annex containing the recommendation that a 'central information exchange' be instituted in connection with drug crimes. A subtle process of policy development was thereby commenced. Much of this discussion inevitably continued in parallel, as the Schengen Implementing Convention (SIC) was not signed until June 1990, with full implementation delayed even further (until 1995).

118 A member of the PGE recalled during interview with the author how the group worked in somewhat insalubrious facilities, occupying a temporary building in Strasbourg.

119 A joint action was passed around eighteen months later, adding a veneer of legitimacy to the secret decision-making procedures that had established the EDU. See OJ L 62, 20 March 1995 for details of this joint action. No changes could have been made at this stage had national parliaments wished to question the intergovernmental decisions taken in their name in 1993.

120 Bunyan (1995, esp. Chapter 3) provides a thorough analysis of the organizational powers provided for under the Convention. The case of the UK (the first state to complete ratification) showed how national constitutional arrangements can effectively work against democratic review of even a measure as significant as this. UK constitutional procedure offers limited powers of scrutiny for measures of international law (which third pillar instruments are), requiring only that a measure is 'laid before' Parliament for a prescribed period, based on the arcane Ponsonby Rule of 1924 (see House of Lords, 1997a: 6, fn. 5 for details). Third pillar matters thus fall into a category that may have far-reaching national implications yet on which national parliaments (or the European Parliament) have no powers to amend and (as in the UK case) may not even engage in debate concerning the provisions contained in them. Despite this, little media attention was given to the Europol Convention, and then only after the work of NGO Statewatch raised the issue; see 'MPs denied their say on Europol law,' *Guardian*, 8 December 1995.

121 See 'EDU work programme,' *Statewatch Bulletin*, March–April 1997, pp. 3–4. For details of the Resolution, see OJ C 375, 12 December 1996.

122 Ibid.

123   Europol is envisaged as the eventual fulcrum of a computerized network of databases linking all 15 member states. Europol has its own computer system, TECS (the Europol Computer System) on which it holds an expanding range of 'work files' or databases covering specific crime areas. However, the long-term vision envisions an integration of Europol data with data from the Schengen Information System (SIS) and Customs Information System (CIS) to form a 'European Information System' (EIS). Chapter 10 raises several issues concerning the extension of Europol access to data on criminal suspects.

124   Examples include Storbeck (1994) and three articles in the 1 February 1997 edition of *The European* newspaper: 'Europol warns on trade in migrants', 'Political pedantry's high price', and 'The New Frontier in Europe's battle with big-league crime'. See also 'Europol's team is already on the case', *Financial Times*, 8 February 1997 and 'Chief of Europol appeals for cash', *The European*, 13 February 1997. The term and concept of Europol gained widespread currency in the media even though its legal basis was unresolved and it was operating on a proscribed range of crimes (drugs alone until 1995).

125   A UK participant in the PGE explained how long-standing professional relationships are now relatively common amongst European law-enforcement officials, fostered mostly via attendance at fora sponsored by bodies such as Interpol.

126   The most formally structured example is the European Information Network on Drugs and Drug Addiction (REITOX) set up at the end of 1993 and co-ordinated by the EMCDDA since 1995. This 'human and computer' network links together 16 information 'focal points' within the 15 member states, primarily exchanging epidemiological data.

127   While certain operational intelligence data is understandably restricted, transparency remains poor in relation to Europol. After 1997, Europol produced an annual 'EU Organized Crime Situation Report', but in March 2001 it was announced that in future it would produce two reports: a 'secret' version and a 'sanitized' version. Remarkably, even the European Parliament would receive only the latter thereafter.

128   The two organizations have also begun to cooperate on a number of joint reports, notably an assessment of evaluation criteria for the 2000–2004 EU drugs strategy (EMCDDA-Europol, 2000).

Notes to Chapter 9

129   In the 'Note to the Council' that accompanied the Commission proposal it was stated that 'It is indeed the entry into force of the TEU which provides the principal justification for the Union to look again at the existing [1992] European Plan against drugs' based on the 'new level of political commitment' and the new institutional framework (Commission, 1994). Subsidiarity had emerged as a guiding principle for implementation of the overall TEU at this stage, and was also cited as another factor behind the need to readdress the 1992 action plan.

130   It has been suggested that the 'unclear wording' of Article K.1(4) TEU, which assigned competence on matters concerning drug addiction to the

third pillar, provided a basis for the claims of third pillar competence concerning demand reduction (European Parliament, 1992a: 55).

131 Representatives from the Commission, the European Parliament, the Committee of the Regions, the Economic and Social Committee, EMCDDA and EDU also attended. Individuals from non-EU bodies were also invited, drawn from the Pompidou Group, UNDCP, WHO, WCO, and Interpol. Academic representatives also took part in specialist workshops around the main themes of the Conference.

132 The Police Cooperation Working Party (WG 2 under the new structure, formerly Trevi WG II) considered the Commission's proposals on the action plan but did not take a position 'since the document does not deal with specific matters of technical police cooperation or basic and advanced police training' (Council, 1995a: 2). The first pillar Health Working Party also submitted a report covering its field of competence.

133 In the subsequent report of the Madrid Experts (Council, 1995d: 11) a footnote records that the Group did not reach consensus on this point, although no further details were provided.

134 The report quoted here is the second revision of the draft submitted by the Madrid Experts to Council on 22 November 1995. It is fairly common to find a number of versions of documents, but – given the restricted access to Council documentation – it is not always possible to be sure the document is necessarily the final version. Reasonable judgement has thus to be exercised in the use of such material.

135 Some attempt was made to point out the need for an 'in-depth' analysis of the causes and consequences of the drugs problem at EU level, together with an acknowledgement that supply indicators and direct or indirect demand indicators do not always show a clear relationship (Council, 1995d: 9–10). Nevertheless, the primary basis of the argument in support of anti-trafficking measures within the report was based on seizure statistics alone.

136 Presidency Conclusions, Madrid European Council, *EU Bulletin*, 12-1995: 16.

137 Details of the number of meetings held by the various working parties within the JHA framework were supplied in an answer to a written question from an MEP (OJ C 134, 30 April 1998: 6–7). As an illustration of the general lack of openness surrounding third pillar activities it should be noted that the question was submitted in July 1997, yet the answer was published around nine months later. Even then, details supplied were minimal and did not fully address the MEP's points. The third pillar of the TEU, under Article K.6, provided for an annual debate on third pillar matters in the European Parliament as well as mandating the Presidency to supply information to the Committee on Civil Liberties and Internal Affairs. However, the volume of third pillar business – particularly intense at this time – inevitably meant that some degree of selection had to be made at the scrutiny stage by the Committee (it submitted around five drug-specific reports in the 12 years 1986–98).

138 The WPLAC also submitted a report within its own (highly specific) terms of reference. The report is discussed in Chapter 11 of this book.

139 See Horstink-Von Meyenfeldt (1996) for a view on the background to the 'tightening up' of this policy.

140 See 'Dutch win time in coffee shops war', *Independent*, 30 November 1996.

141   In the United Kingdom, when a man convicted of cocaine smuggling received a prison sentence of 30 years (meaning parole after 20 years, compared to the average term served by a murderer of 15.4 years at this time) drug trafficking became a 'more serious' crime than murder in terms of the prison sentence awarded. See 'Judges "rate drugs worse than murder"', *Guardian*, 20 August 1996. Unquestionably, the UK would have therefore been a strong advocate of the Resolution.

142   Annex I of the report (Council, 1996d: 24) lists three forms of interaction on 'international action' involving the United States. First, it notes that meetings were held between the Presidency, Council Secretariat, the Commission and the US 'on Justice and Home Affairs issues (including drugs)'; second, 'Attendance of US experts at EU seminars' and, third, proposed 'Exchange of information at expert level' between the WPDOC and US experts. The latter is most interesting in that it confirms that third pillar activity unequivocally led drug-related discussions at the international level. This form of dialogue was not accompanied by a clear means of transparency or accountability.

143   A majority of member states were determined to prevent any treaty changes in relation to police cooperation, opposing German and Austrian views within the IGC favouring 'communitarization' of this and other third pillar areas (den Boer and Wallace, 2000: 513).

144   Boekhout van Solinge (2002: 96) suggests that this proposal arose out of internal conflict between the Dutch Ministries of Justice and Health apparent during the EU agreements reached on harmonization. He suggests that the proposal was designed to minimize the chances of such a situation recurring.

145   The transition is shown in the agendas for working group meetings in this period. On 31 January 1997 the group was known as the 'Drugs Experts Group' but by 24 March it was known as the Horizontal Drugs Group. Despite this it was still referred to as the Working Party on Drugs and the Horizontal Working Party on Drugs at other times thereafter, revealing beyond doubt that it was an evolutionary rather than a completely new body.

146   A 1998 Council Resolution typifies how official accounts have consistently presented the connection between drugs and organized crime in a general and non-contextualized way. The Resolution simply made reference to action against illegal drugs 'which account for a significant part of the operations of organized crime' (OJ C 408/2, 29 December 1998).

147   Even more surprisingly, by the end of 1997 the Luxembourg President-in-office had to admit to the European Parliament that member states could not agree a definition of 'organized crime' despite the package of measures set for implementation (Monar, 1998).

Notes to Chapter 10

148   In May 2001 the JHA Council made it a priority to develop an updated SIS (that is, SIS II) by 2006. In September 2001 the Commission decided to take responsibility for funding and developing SIS II. At the end of 2001 a Commission document (Commission, 2001c) recorded that the SIS had around 10 million items of data stored in its computers, including 'alerts'

on around 1 million individual persons. Critics have questioned the safe-guards associated with these data, particularly with regard to how they will be amalgamated with CIS data, and – in future – brought into a *European information system (EIS)*.

149 The Convention on the use of information technology for customs pur-poses (the Customs Information Convention) was signed on 26 July 1995 (OJ C 316, 27 November 1995). By 2002, only Belgium, Denmark and Luxembourg had not completed ratification and, since November 2000, states that had ratified were already applying its provisions.

150 The Europol mandate was extended to include all of 'the serious forms of international crime listed in the Annex to the Europol Convention' (OJ C 362, 18 December 2001: 1). This most recent extension of the Europol mandate – a decision taken solely on the basis of a Council Decision (that is, without requiring debate in national parliaments) – now gives Europol the widest possible interpretation of organized crime. This is despite the aforementioned ambiguity in the definition of organized crime contained in the original Convention.

151 Eurojust is a 'high-level' team of senior lawyers, magistrates, prosecutors, judges and other legal experts seconded from EU member states, established to give immediate legal advice and assistance in cross-border cases to national investigators, prosecutors and judges across the EU. Although Eurojust began operations 'provisionally' in March 2001 – and had handled 180 cases by November 2001 – it was not formally established until a Council decision on 28 February 2002 (OJ L 63, 6 March 2002). The organi-zation was initially based in Brussels, before moving to The Hague in December 2002. Eurojust is able to recommend that national authorities take certain steps and also to initiate investigations, but does not have for-mal authority to launch or carry out investigations itself. With regard to the 'European arrest warrant', Council adopted a binding framework decision to establish this measure on 13 June 2002 (OJ L 190, 18 July 2002), setting a timetable for implementation by 1 January 2004.

152 The 'Convention on Mutual Assistance in Criminal Matters', adopted by Council in May 2000 (OJ C 197, 12 July 2000), made provision for such teams (Article 13), along with arrangements covering interception, con-trolled deliveries and covert investigations. Ratification of the Convention has been slow, with only Portugal completing the process by mid 2002.

153 The MDG submitted a first draft of a new action plan on combating organized crime to Council in June 1999. The Article 36 Committee eventually approved this 'new millennium strategy' on 28–29 February 2000, and a Justice and Home Affairs Council meeting on 27 March 2000 subsequently endorsed it.

154 The Spanish Presidency document noted that it had 'informed the Horizontal Working Party on Drugs of all these issues' (Council, 2002b: 8).

155 OJ C 114, 15 May 2002.

156 Several well-funded programmes exist to promote law enforcement cooper-ation and training, including personnel exchange; notably OISIN (opera-tional since 1996) under which 'a large number of projects...have been related to the fight against drug trafficking' (Commission, 1999a: 48).

157 The new DG, which has responsibility for drug policy coordination within the Commission, was formed out of what was known as the Justice and

Home Affairs Task Force (in existence since 1995 and – since 1998 – home to the Drugs Unit that had previously been part of the Secretariat General).

158   The Commission produced a comprehensive 'follow-up table for the Commission, EMCDDA and Europol' to monitor the implementation of the 2002–2004 Action Plan (Commission, 2001a: Annex 1) detailing each activity and those responsible for implementation actions.

159   None the less, both the Vienna Action Plan on how best to implement the provisions of the Treaty of Amsterdam on an area of freedom, security and justice (agreed at the end of 1998) and the Presidency Conclusions from the special Tampere JHA European Council had already called for consideration of this matter (Commission, 1999b).

160   In a press release (14 September 2002) setting out proposed actions concerned with European action against drugs, the incumbent Danish Presidency stated that 'Political agreement on the draft framework decision ... should be reached at the Justice and Home Affairs Council meeting in October 2002' (Available http: <http://www.eu2002.dk/news_read.asp?iInformationID = 22343> accessed 26 September 2002). This optimism proved unfounded, and agreement on this legislative matter was not reached during this Presidency.

Notes to Chapter 11

161   It should be noted that this decision was taken against a background of other relevant EU initiatives (outlined in Chapter 9). Drug-related cooperation in the Caribbean and Latin America was also discussed around this time in the context of the EU–US Transatlantic Agenda. Also, on 26 September 1995 a meeting had been held between JHA ministers of the EU, the Commission and ministers with drug responsibilities from the Andean Group (Bolivia, Colombia, Ecuador, Peru and Venezuela). A joint communication resulted from this meeting, advocating a coordinated approach to drug addiction and trafficking matters, followed by 'rapid agreement' of measures on drug precursors between the parties (European Commission, 1996: 387).

162   The institutional location of the working party was confirmed in an official written answer (15 January 1998) to a question from an MEP concerning third pillar expert committees. The response (OJ C 134, 30 April 1998: 7), recorded that the working party met 10 times during 1996 but not at all in the first half of 1997. The reason for the lack of meetings in 1997 (not explained in the written answer) appears to have been because the work of the group was transferred to the Horizontal Working Party on Drugs at this time.

163   There are different ways of defining the countries that comprise the Caribbean region. The EU 'consensus' view defines it as all the islands of the region from the Bahamas in the north-west to Trinidad and Tobago in the Southeast (including Cuba, Hispaniola, the British, French and Dutch territories) plus the other CARICOM states of Belize, Guyana and Suriname, making a total of 28 countries.

164   It is important to realize that under the ACP framework Community funding is allocated on the principle that it is the recipient country that must submit specific proposals for funding (based on five-year tranches of aid). The Commission (at least in theory) does not dictate the content of such

proposals, although in practice it is inevitable that Commission officials offer 'guidelines' on priority areas for funding.

165 After the entry into force of the Amsterdam Treaty, DGVIII became known simply as DG Development.

166 The official chosen was a French-Canadian citizen, posing something of a dilemma. However, in an illustration of the political compromise that often marks such cases, it was discovered that he had an Irish grandmother, making him 'politically acceptable' as the Commission's representative, although he was technically employed as a consultant rather than a full-time official.

167 For example, in the UK the overall 'lead' ministry on drugs issues has generally been the Home Office, but matters involving expert selection have also tended to involve the Foreign Office, HM Customs & Excise, and in some cases the Department for International Development. This process invariably leans toward the nomination of individuals who are used to the procedures, protocols, and policy sensitivities and preferences that apply to the bodies that put them forward.

168 Spain, with strong regional interests in Latin America, would have preferred a wider process including Latin America from the outset. The inclusion of a Spaniard almost certainly reflected the political sensitivities of this situation therefore.

169 Pages 60–7 of Annex C of the expert report detail the persons and bodies consulted during its preparation.

170 As an example, a team of ten examined maritime cooperation, drawn from coast guard officials (four), customs officials (three), and defence agencies (two). The tenth member was an official affiliated to the US State Department. Three of the ten experts were officials of EU countries, only one of whom was based in the Caribbean. Six team members were law enforcement or defense officials from Caribbean countries.

171 After the entry into force of the Amsterdam Treaty in May 1999 the Commission restructured the three Directorates General covering external relations (DG 1, DG 1A, and DG 1B) into a single DG for External Relations.

172 This is confirmed by a number of documents. The 1996 'end of year' drugs report to the European Council (Council, 1996d: Annex III, 36–50) proposed the areas that 'should be pursued in European Union relations in the field of combating drug production and trafficking in Latin America' *following examination of the expert report* by the WPLAC. Some fifteen months later, in a note from the Horizontal Drugs Group covering a then forthcoming EU–Latin America/Caribbean meeting, the EU's priorities set out in the note were stated as being 'taken from the 1996 EU experts report' (Council, 1998d: 1).

173 This datum was included in the Commission-produced Terms of Reference for the Central Asia mission (p. 12) without attributing its source.

174 The TACIS Programme was established to provide technical assistance to Russia and states of the former Soviet Union and Mongolia.

175 The Commission covered the cost of the ambassadors, whilst the UK and France covered the cost of the other two experts respectively. See Appendix for details of the expert team.

176 The Annex specified the elements that should be assessed, what the report should describe (including one point on the problems faced in reducing

illicit domestic demand and in preventing drug abuse) and whom the mission should consult.

177   Coincidentally, the UK also held the Presidency of the G8 at the same time.

178   Figure 9.1 shows the decision-making structure that applied under the UK Presidency.

179   A feature of EU institutional machinery since the TREVI days, 'troika' meetings involve officials from the current Presidency state along with those from the preceding and forthcoming Presidency states, designed to ensure continuity.

Notes to Chapter 13

180   The exact legal status of formal and quasi-formal legislative measures agreed on the basis of the third pillar remains surprisingly vague. See Nugent (1999, Ch. 10) for an overview of European law.

181   Council Recommendation of 25 April 2002 'on improving investigation methods in the fight against organized crime linked to organized drug trafficking: simultaneous investigations into drug trafficking by criminal organizations and their finances/assets' (OJ C 114, 15 May 2002).

182   We may regard this as current thinking, but it must also be seen in the context of over three decades of 'collective EEC–EU thinking' on the drugs problem. A press release setting out the plans of the incumbent Danish Presidency programme in the drugs area in September 2002 stated that 'Taking into account the cross-border nature of the drugs problem there is also a need for a certain overall political agreement at the European level on how to address the drugs problem most appropriately' (14 September 2002, http: <www.eu2002.dk/news>). This is a quite remarkable admission, nine years after the entry into force of the Maastricht treaty and three years after the Amsterdam Treaty entered force.

183   With the decision to allow the director of Europol to negotiate directly with third countries and bodies we should also add the citizens of these countries to this list.

184   The most recent extension of the Europol mandate, via a Council Decision of 6 December 2001, added all of 'the serious forms of international crime listed in the Annex to the Europol Convention' (OJ C 362, 18 December 2001: 1). This decision took effect from 1 January 2002. This reveals that the intention to do this was always there, awaiting the right political climate in which to take the decision. There is evidence to suggest that the general mood of public concern after the September 2001 terrorist attacks provided a politically conducive environment for the decision. Terrorism itself had been added to the Europol remit as recently as 1999.

185   The decision to incorporate all provisions of Schengen cooperation directly into the EU was made via the protocol attached to the Amsterdam Treaty. This had direct consequences for operational policing possibilities in dealing with drug trafficking, despite which the European Parliament had no power to give an opinion on the Schengen Acquis, nor on the practical cooperation between the police, customs and judicial authorities that it provides for (European Parliament, 2000a: 59). This is a vivid example of the lack of transparency inherent to political decisions in this area.

186 Mathiesen (1999: 20–5) provides a full account of the concerns raised by the data-related matters associated with Europol, including the exchange of data with third parties outside of the EU.
187 This may include measures with far-reaching implications for civil liberties. JHA ministers routinely pass points without debate (so-called 'A' points on JHA Council agendas), one example being the decision taken on 19 March 1998 to allow Europol to request and accept information from non-EU sources. The data protection safeguards associated with this decision were not examined by elected representatives; they were taken to be satisfactory based solely on expert advice. National parliaments – or the European Parliament – had no basis on which to debate or challenge either the substance or content of this proposal.
188 In May 1998 a list of the JHA *acquis* drafted to provide an overview showed that a total of 130 legal instruments had been adopted by this time, of which nine were conventions and six were protocols (den Boer and Wallace, 2000: 511). Many of these measures were what could be described as multipurpose in that they facilitated the creation of institutions or measures that could be used to address organized criminal activity rather than being drug-specific (this book has highlighted the key measures in this respect).

Bibliography

Part I: Primary sources and official publications

European Commission and Council of the European Union

European Commission (1988) *Communication of the Commission to the Council on the abolition of controls of persons at intra-Community borders* (Brussels: 7 December 1988) COM (88) 640 final.

European Council/European Commission (1992) *Treaty on European Union* (Luxembourg: Office for Official Publications of the European Communities).

European Commission/EMCDDA (1993) *Inventory of EC (Legal) Texts on Drugs* (Luxembourg: Office for Official Publications of the European Communities).

European Commission (1994) *Communication from the Commission to the Council and the European Parliament on a European Union action plan to combat drugs (1995–1999)* (Brussels: 23 June 1994) COM (94) 234 final.

European Commission (1996) *General Report on the Activities of the European Union 1995* (Luxembourg: Office for Official Publications of the European Communities).

European Commission (1997) *The European Union in action against drugs* (Luxembourg: Office for Official Publications of the European Communities).

European Commission (1998a) *Communication from the Commission to the Council and the European Parliament with a view to establishing a common platform for the Special Session of the UN General Assembly on International Cooperation in the fight against drugs* (Brussels: 8 January 1998) COM (97) 670 final.

European Commission (1998b) *General Report on the Activities of the European Union 1997* (Luxembourg: Office for Official Publications of the European Communities).

European Commission (1999a) *Communication from the Commission to the Council and the European Parliament on a European Action Plan to combat drugs (2000–2004)* (Brussels: 26 May 1999) COM (1999) 239 final.

European Commission (1999b) *Tampere European Council: Presidency Conclusions* (Brussels: 16 October 1999) SN 200/99.

European Commission (2001a) *Proposal for a Council Framework Decision laying down minimum provisions on the constituent elements of criminal acts and penalties in the field of illicit drug trafficking* (Brussels: 23 May 2001) COM (2001) 259 final.

European Commission (2001b) *Communication from the Commission to the Council and the European Parliament on the implementation of the EU Action Plan on Drugs (2000–2004)* (Brussels: 8 June 2001) COM (2001) 301 final.

European Commission (2001c) *Communication from the Commission to the Council and the European Parliament. Development of the Schengen Information System II* (Brussels: 18 December 2001) COM (2001) 720 final.

European Commission (2002) *Communication from the Commission to the Council and the European Parliament. Biannual update of the Scoreboard to review progress on the creation of an 'area of freedom, security and justice' in the European Union (First half of 2002)* (Brussels: 30 May 2002) COM (2002) 261 final.

European Communities (1997) *The European Union in action against drugs* (Luxembourg: Office for Official Publications of the European Communities).

European Union, the Council (1995a) *Note 'I/A' from K.4 Committee to Permanent Representatives Committee/Council. Subject: Commission's Communication on a European Union action plan to combat drugs – Opinion of Council of Justice and Home Affairs* (Brussels: 27 February 1995) 9870/5/94, REV 5.

European Union, the Council (1995b) *Note from Steering Group II to K.4 Committee. Subject: Europol Drugs Unit: Working Programme July 1995–December 1995* (Brussels: 6 September 1995) 9633/95.

European Union, the Council (1995c) *Note from the Working Party on Drugs and Organized Crime to Steering Group II. Subject: Draft report on the combating of drug trafficking – Third Pillar contribution* (Brussels: 8 November 1995) 8941/4/95, REV 4.

European Union, the Council (1995d) *Note from the Experts Group on Drugs to the European Council. Subject: Draft report of the Group of Experts on Drugs to the Madrid European Council* (Brussels: 22 November 1995) 10979/2/95, REV 2.

European Union, the Council (1996a) *Note from the Council Secretariat to Delegations. Subject: Joint Meeting of the CFSP Drugs Working Group and 3rd pillar (JAI) Drugs Working Group, Brussels, 11 October 1996* (Brussels: 16 October 1996) 10675/96.

European Union, the Council (1996b) *Note from Drugs and Organised Crime Working Group to K.4 Committee. Subject: Report on Action Proposal No.27; 12247/95 CORDROGUE 69 SAN 115 Combat and Dismantle illicit Domestic Cultivation and Production of Drugs and summary of the law enforcement problems which need to be addressed* (Brussels: 18 October 1996) 10822/96.

European Union, the Council (1996c) *Note from Evaluation mission to Latin America to Ad hoc Group Latin America/Caribbean (Drugs) and Drugs and Organized Crime Working Group. Subject: Report on drugs in Latin America* (Brussels: 4 November 1996) 11256/96.

European Union, the Council (1996d) *Note from COREPER to Council (General Affairs). Subject: Draft report to the European Council on drugs* (Brussels: 4 December 1996) 10884/5/96, REV 5.

European Union, the Council (1997a) *Note from Drugs and Organised Crime Working Group to K.4 Committee. Subject: Revision of doc. 12247/1/94 ENFOPOL 161 REV1 on the basis of doc. 5717/97 ENFOPOL 22 as a result of the expert meeting of 13/14 February 1997 on the mechanism for reporting on organised crime* (Brussels: 6 March 1997) 6204/1/97, REV 1.

European Union, the Council (1997b) *Note from the incoming UK Presidency to the K4 Committee. Subject: K4 Committee Work Programme for the period from 1 January to 30 June 1998* (Brussels: 15 December 1997) 13292/97.

European Union, the Council (General Secretariat) (1997c) *43rd Review of The Council's Work. The Secretary General's Report 1 January to 31 December 1995* (Luxembourg: Office for Official Publications of the European Communities).

European Union, the Council (1998a) *Note from the Presidency to the Horizontal Drugs group. Subject: Consideration of the main elements of a post-1999 EU drugs Strategy* (Brussels: 7 January 1998) 5061/98.

European Union, the Council (1998b) *Note from the UK Presidency to Horizontal Drugs Group. Subject: United Kingdom Presidency Work Programme on Drugs and Drug-Related issues* (Brussels: 12 January 1998) 13457/97.

European Union, the Council (1998c) *Note from Presidency to Customs Cooperation Working Group (Experts). Subject: Report to the Council on customs joint surveillance exercises in 1997* (Brussels: 29 January 1998) 5317/1/98 REV 1.

European Union, the Council (1998d) *Note from Presidency of Horizontal Drugs Group to High Level group meeting drugs – European Union–Latin America/ Caribbean (Brussels, 23/24.03.98). Subject: The European Union's priorities for future drugs cooperation in Latin America* (Brussels: 13 March 1998) 6838/98.

European Union, the Council (1998e) *Note from Council to European Council. Subject: Report, including key elements of a post-1999 EU drugs strategy, to the European Council on activities on Drugs and drugs related issues under the UK Presidency* (Brussels: 2 June 1998) 7930/2/98, REV 2.

European Union, the Council (1998f) *Note from Council to European Council on Action Plan of the Council and Commission on how best to implement the provisions of the Amsterdam Treaty establishing an area of freedom, security and justice* (Brussels: 4 December 1998) 13844/98.

European Union, the Council (1998g) *Conclusions of the first high-level meeting on drugs between the European Union and states of Latin America and the Caribbean* (Brussels, 23/24 March 1998) 7090/98 (Presse 81).

European Union, the Council (1999) *Note from Horizontal Drugs Group to COREPER. Subject: European Union Drug Strategy (2000–2004)* (Brussels: 26 November 1999) 12555/2/99, REV 2.

European Union, the Council (2000) *Note from Portuguese Presidency to COREPER. Subject: Programme in the field of Justice and Home Affairs* (Brussels: 7 January 2000) 5160/00.

European Union, the Council (2002a) *Note from General Secretariat to Coreper. Subject: Council Working Methods (JHA area) – Analysis of Working Parties in the JHA area* (Brussels: 21 January 2002) 5502/02.

European Union, the Council (2002b) *Note from Spanish delegation to Horizontal Working Party on Drugs. Subject: Results of the Spanish Presidency* (Brussels: 9 July 2002) 10734/02.

European Union, the Council (2002c) *Note from Presidency to Horizontal Working Party on Drugs. Subject: Draft Council Resolution on generic classification of new synthetic drugs* (Brussels: 8 July 2002) 10638/02.

Items related to case studies (Chapter 11)

1. Caribbean Drugs Initiative

European Commission 'The Caribbean and The Drugs Problem', Report of the EU Experts Group (March 1996).

UNDCP (1996) *Plan of Action for Drug Control Coordination and Cooperation in the Caribbean* (UNDCP).

UNDCP (1997) *No one is an island. UNDCP activities report 1997* (UNDCP Regional Office for the Caribbean).

UNDCP–European Commission (1997) *Bridging the Gap* (joint publication of the European Commission Drug Control [Caribbean] Office and the UNDCP Regional Office: December 1997).

Foreign and Commonwealth Office (1998) *Drugs, Drugs Trafficking and Money Laundering in the Caribbean*, UK Paper presented to the Caribbean Forum, 12–13 February 1998, Nassau, Bahamas.

2. Latin America Mission

See European Union, the Council (1996c, 1998d, and 1998g).

3. Central Asia Mission

Terms of reference for 'EC/NIS Justice & Home Affairs Study Phase 1' (internal document produced by DG1A of the European Commission: February 1997).

Report of the EU Expert Group on Drugs Mission to Central Asia (internal document submitted to European Commission: July 1997).

Terms of reference for six projects on Central Asia (internal document produced by DG1A of the European Commission: June 1998).

Report of expert team regarding Central Asian Republics Reinforcement of Border Management in the Caucasian Region (internal report submitted to DG1A).

European Parliament

European Parliament Session Documents (1992) *Report of the Committee on Civil Liberties and Internal Affairs on the setting up of Europol. Rapporteur: Mr L. van Outrive* (26 November 1992), A3-0382/92.

European Parliament Directorate General for Research (2000a) 'The Impact of The Amsterdam Treaty on Justice and Home Affairs', *Working Paper*, vol. I (Brussels: The European Parliament).

European Parliament Directorate General for Research (2000b) 'The Impact of The Amsterdam Treaty on Justice and Home Affairs', *Working Paper*, vol. II: Annexes (Brussels: The European Parliament).

European Monitoring Centre for Drugs and Drug Addiction

EMCDDA (1997a) *Annual Report on the State of the Drugs Problem in The European Union 1997* (Luxembourg: Office for Official Publications of the European Communities).

EMCDDA (1997b) 'Estimating the Prevalence of Problem Drug Use in Europe', *EMCDDA Scientific Monograph Series*, no. 1 (Luxembourg: Office for Official Publications of the European Communities).

EMCDDA (1997c) 'New Trends in Synthetic Drugs in the European Union: Epidemiology and Demand Reduction Responses', *EMCDDA Insights Series*, no. 1. (Luxembourg: Office for Official Publications of the European Communities).

EMCDDA and Europol (2000) *Report by the EMCDDA and Europol on the identification of criteria for an evaluation of European Union Strategy on Drugs (2000–2004) by the Commission*. Available http: <www.emcdda.org> (accessed 30 June 2002).

EMCDDA (2002) *Annual Report on the State of the Drugs Problem in The European Union 2001*. Available http: <www.emcdda.org> (accessed 30 June 2002).

United Nations

United Nations, Division of Narcotic Drugs (1988) *Declaration of the International Conference on Drug Abuse and Illicit Trafficking, and Comprehensive*

Multidisciplinary Outline of Future Activities in Drug Abuse Control (New York: United Nations).

United Nations International Drug Control Programme (1996) *Amphetamine-type Stimulants: A Global Review*, UNDCP Technical Series, no. 3.

United Nations International Drug Control Programme (1997a) *World Drug Report* (Oxford: Oxford University Press).

United Nations International Drug Control Programme (1997b) *Economic and Social Consequences of Drug Abuse and Illicit Trafficking*, UNDCP Technical Series, no. 6.

United Nations International Drug Control Programme (2002) *Global Illicit Drug Trends 2002*. Available http <www.undcp.org/odccp/ global_illicit_drug_trends. html> (accessed 1 December 2002).

United Kingdom Government

House of Commons, Home Affairs Committee (1989a) 'Seventh Report on Drug Trafficking and Related Serious Crime', *Report and Committee Proceedings*, vol. I, (London: HMSO).

House of Commons, Home Affairs Committee (1989b) 'Drug Trafficking and Related Serious Crime', *Minutes of Evidence* (London: HMSO).

House of Commons, Home Affairs Committee (1990a) 'Seventh Report on Practical Police Cooperation in the European Community', *Report and Committee Proceedings*, vol. I (London: HMSO).

House of Commons, Home Affairs Committee (1990b) 'Seventh Report on Practical Police Cooperation in the European Community', *Memoranda of Evidence, Minutes of Evidence and Appendices*, vol. II (London: HMSO).

House of Commons, Foreign Affairs Committee (1995a) 'European Council, Madrid 15–16 December 1995, *Minutes of Evidence. Session 1995–96'*, 30 November 1995 (London: HMSO).

House of Lords, Select Committee on the European Communities (1997a) 'Enhancing Parliamentary Scrutiny of The Third Pillar', *Session 1997–98, 6th Report*, 31 July 1997 (HL Paper 25).

House of Lords Select Committee on the European Communities (1997b) 'Europol: Joint Supervisory Body', *Session 1997–98, 13th Report*, 17 February 1998 (HL Paper 71).

Part II: Secondary sources and selected references

Adler, I. and Haas, P. M. (1992) 'Epistemic Communities, World Order, and the Creation of a Reflective Research Program', *International Organization*, no. 46, pp. 367–90.

Albrecht, H.-J. (1995) 'Drug Policies and National Plans to Combat Drug Trafficking and Drug Abuse. A Comparative Analysis of Policies of Co-ordination and Co-operation', in G. Estievenart (ed.) *Policies and Strategies to Combat Drugs in Europe. The Treaty on European Union: Framework for a New European Strategy to Combat Drugs?* (Dordrecht: Martinus Nijhoff).

Albrecht, H.-J. and Kalmthout, A. van (eds) (1995) *Drug Policies in Western Europe*. Criminological Research Reports by the Max Planck Institute for Foreign and International Penal Law, vol. 41. (Freiburg: Max Planck Institute).

Andelmann, D. (1994) 'The Drug Money Maze', *Foreign Affairs*, vol. 73, no. 4, pp. 94–108.

Anderson, M. (1989) *Policing The World. Interpol and the Politics of International Police Co-operation* (Oxford: Clarendon Press).

Anderson, M. (1994) 'The Agenda for Police Cooperation', in M. Anderson and M. den Boer (eds) *Policing across national boundaries* (London: Pinter).

Anderson, M. and den Boer, M. (eds) (1994) *Policing Across National Boundaries* (London: Pinter).

Anderson, M., den Boer, M., Cullen, P. and Gilmore, W. (1995) *Policing the European Union* (Oxford: Clarendon Press).

Arlacchi, P. (1998) 'Dealing with Drugs', *The World Today* (June 1998), pp. 154–5.

Arnao, G. (1990) 'The Semantics of Prohibition', *International Journal on Drug Policy*, vol. 2, no. 1, pp. 31–3.

Association of Chief Police Officers [ACPO] (1996) 'A European Perspective', *Final Report of the 1996 National Drugs Conference* (closed circulation document).

Barnes, B. (1977) *Interests and the growth of knowledge* (London: Routledge and Kegan Paul).

Baum, D. (1997) *Smoke and Mirrors. The War on Drugs and the Politics of Failure* (Boston: Little, Brown and Company).

Bayer, I. and Ghodse. H. (1999) 'Evolution of International Drug Control, 1945–1995', *Bulletin on Narcotics*, vol. LI, nos. 1 and 2 (New York: United Nations), pp. 1–17.

Baylis, J. and Smith, S. (1997) *The Globalization of World Politics. An Introduction to International Relations* (Oxford: Oxford University Press).

Beck, R., Clark Arend, A. and Van der Lugt, R. D. (1996) (eds) *International Rules. Approaches from International Law and International Relations* (Oxford: Oxford University Press).

Beck, U. (1992) *Risk Society. Towards a new modernity* (London: Sage Publications).

Benyon, J., Turnbull, L., Willis, A., Woodward, R. and Beck, A. (1993) *Police Co-operation in Europe: An Investigation* (Leicester: University of Leicester Centre for the Study of Public Order).

Benyon, J., Turnbull, L., Willis, A. and Woodward, R. (1994) 'Understanding Police Cooperation in Europe: Setting a Framework for Analysis', in M. Anderson and M. den Boer (eds) *Policing Across National Boundaries* (London: Pinter).

Berridge, V. and Edwards, G. (1981) *Opium and the People: Opiate use in Nineteenth Century England* (London: Allen Lane).

Boekhout van Solinge, T. (2002) *Drugs and Decision-Making in the European Union* (Amsterdam: Mets & Schilt Publishers). Available http: <http://www.cedro-uva.org> (accessed July 2002).

Boer, M. den (1994) 'The Quest for European Policing: Rhetoric and Justification in a Disorderly Debate', in M. Anderson and M. den Boer (eds) *Policing Across National Boundaries* (London: Pinter).

Boer, M. den (1996) 'Justice and Home Affairs: Cooperation without Integration', in H. Wallace and W. Wallace (eds) *Policy-Making in the European Union*, 3rd edn (Oxford: Oxford University Press).

Boer, M. den (1997) 'Drugs Policy and Police Cooperation', paper presented at conference on Justice and Home Affairs in the European Union: Meeting the Challenge of Reform (Leicester: February 1997).

Boer, M. den and Wallace, W. (2000) 'Justice and Home Affairs. Integration through Incrementalism?', in H. Wallace and W. Wallace (eds) *Policy-Making in the European Union*, 4th edn (Oxford: Oxford University Press).

Bruun, K., Pan, L. and Rexed, I. (1975) *The Gentlemen's Club. International Control of Drugs and Alcohol* (London: University of Chicago Press).

Bunyan, T. (1993a) 'Trevi, Europol and the New European State', in T. Bunyan (ed.) *Statewatching the new Europe. A handbook on the European state* (London: Statewatch).

Bunyan, T. (1993b) 'Secret Europe', in T. Bunyan (ed.) *Statewatching the New Europe. A Handbook on the European State* (London: Statewatch).

Bunyan, T. (ed.) (1993c) *Statewatching the New Europe. A Handbook on the European State* (London: Statewatch).

Bunyan, T. (1995) *The Europol Convention* (London: Statewatch).

Bunyan, T. (1996) *Researching the European State: A Critical Guide* (London: Statewatch).

Bunyan, T. (1997) *Key texts on Justice and Home Affairs in the European Union. Vol. 1 (1976–1993) From Trevi to Maastricht* (London: Statewatch).

Campodónico, H. (1996) 'Drug Trafficking, Laundering and Neo-Liberal Economics: Perverse Effects for a Developing Country', in N. Dorn, J. Jepsen and E. Savona (eds) *European Drug Policies and Enforcement* (Basingstoke: Macmillan – now Palgrave Macmillan).

Césaire, R. (1995) 'The Drug Priority in the Common Foreign and Security Policy', in G. Estievenart (ed.) *Policies and Strategies to Combat Drugs in Europe. The Treaty on European Union: Framework for a new European Strategy to Combat Drugs?* (Dordrecht: Martinus Nijhoff).

Coomber, R. (ed.) (1994) *Drugs and Drug Use in Society. A Critical Reader* (Dartford: Greenwich University Press).

Cram, L., Dinan, D. and Nugent N. (eds) (1999) *Developments in the European Union* (Basingstoke: Macmillan – now Palgrave Macmillan).

Degenhardt, H. W. (1986) *Treaties and Alliances of the World*, 4th edn (Harlow: Longman Group).

Dehousse, R. (1997) 'Regulation by networks in the European Community: the role of European agencies', *Journal of European Public Policy*, vol. 4, no. 2, pp. 246–61.

Derks, J. and Kalmthout, A. van (1995) 'Components of National Drug Policies and the Need for Comparative Evaluative Research', in G. Estievenart (ed.) *Policies and Strategies to Combat Drugs in Europe. The Treaty on European Union: Framework for a New European Strategy to Combat Drugs?* (Dordrecht: Martinus Nijhoff).

Dorn, N. (1993) 'Subsidiarity, Police Co-operation and Drug Enforcement: Some structures of policy-making in the EC', *European Journal of Criminal Policy and Research*, vol. 1, no. 2, pp. 30–47.

Dorn, N. (1995) 'A European Analysis of Drug Enforcement', in G. Estievenart (ed.) *Policies and Strategies to Combat Drugs in Europe. The Treaty on European Union: Framework for a new European Strategy to Combat Drugs?* (Dordrecht: Martinus Nijhoff).

Dorn, N. (1996a) 'The EU, Home Affairs and 1996: Intergovernmental Convergence or Confederal Diversity?', in N. Dorn, J. Jepsen, and E. Savona (eds) *European Drug Policies and Enforcement* (Basingstoke: Macmillan – now Palgrave Macmillan).

Dorn, N. (1996b) 'Borderline Criminology: External Drug Policies of the EU', in N. Dorn, J. Jepsen and E. Savona (eds) *European Drug Policies and Enforcement* (Basingstoke: Macmillan – now Palgrave Macmillan).

Dorn, N., Jepsen, J. and Savona, E. (eds) (1996) *European Drug Policies and Enforcement* (Basingstoke: Macmillan – now Palgrave Macmillan).

Dorn, N. and South, N. (1990) 'Drug Markets and Law Enforcement', *British Journal of Criminology*, vol. 30, no. 2, pp. 171–88.

Dorn, N., Murji, K. and South, N. (1992) *Traffickers. Drug markets and law enforcement* (London: Routledge).

Duyne, P. C. van. (1993) 'Organized Crime Markets in a Turbulent Europe', *European Journal on Criminal Policy and Research*, vol. 1, no. 3, pp. 10–30.

Elsen, C. (1995) 'Drugs as a Priority in Cooperation in the Fields of Justice and Home Affairs', in G. Estievenart (ed.) *Policies and Strategies to Combat Drugs in Europe. The Treaty on European Union: Framework for a new European Strategy to Combat Drugs?* (Dordrecht: Martinus Nijhoff).

Estievenart, G. (1993) 'Fight against Drugs after Maastricht and the Role of the European Monitoring Centre for Drugs and Drug Addiction', in *Inventory of EC (Legal) Texts on Drugs* (Luxembourg: Office for Official Publications of the European Communities).

Estievenart, G. (1995) 'The European Community and the Global Drug Phenomenon', in G. Estievenart (ed.) *Policies and Strategies to Combat Drugs in Europe. The Treaty on European Union: Framework for a new European Strategy to Combat Drugs?* (Dordrecht: Martinus Nijhoff).

Ferguson, M. (1992) 'The Mythology about Globalization', *European Journal of Communication*, vol. 7, pp. 69–93.

Fijnaut, C. (1996) 'Intergovernmental Cooperation on Drug Control: Debates on Europol', in N. Dorn, J. Jepsen and E. Savona (eds) *European Drug Policies and Enforcement* (Basingstoke: Macmillan – now Palgrave Macmillan).

Foucault, M. (1995) [1969] *The Archaeology of Knowledge* (London: Routledge).

Giddens, A. (1990) *The Consequences of Modernity* (Cambridge: Polity Press).

Gill, S. (1995) 'The Global Panopticon? The Neoliberal State, Economic Life, and Democratic Surveillance', *Alternatives*, vol. 2, pp. 1–49.

Gilmore, W. C. (1991) 'International Action Against Drug Trafficking: Trends in United Kingdom Law and Practice through the 1980's', *Commonwealth Law Bulletin*, pp. 287–313.

Haas, E. B. (1990) *When Knowledge is Power: Three Models of Change in International Organizations* (Berkeley: University of California Press).

Haas, P. M. (1989) 'Do regimes matter? Epistemic communities and Mediterranean pollution control', *International Organization*, no. 43, pp. 377–403.

Haas, P. M. (1990) *Saving The Mediterranean. The Politics of International Environmental Cooperation* (New York: Columbia University Press).

Haas, P. M. (1992a) 'Banning Chlorofluorocarbons: Epistemic Community Efforts to Protect Stratospheric Ozone, *International Organization*, no. 46, pp. 187–225.

Haas, P. M. (1992b) 'Introduction: Epistemic Communities and International Policy Coordination', *International Organization*, no. 46, pp. 1–35.

Haas, P. M. (ed.) (1992c) 'Knowledge, Power and International Policy Coordination', *International Organization*, no. 46 (Special Issue).

Haas, P. M. (1998) 'Compliance with EU Directives: Insights from International Relations and Comparative Politics', *Journal of European Public Policy*, vol. 5, no. 1, pp. 17–37.

Haas, P. M. and Haas, E. B. (1995) 'Learning to Learn: Improving International Governance', *Global Governance*, vol. 1, pt 3, pp. 255–84.

Halliday, F. (1987) 'State and Society in International Relations: A Second Agenda', *Millennium*, vol. 16, no. 2, pp. 215–29.

Hasenclever, A., Mayer, P. and Rittberger, V. (1996) 'Interests, Power, Knowledge: The Study of International Regimes', *Mershon International Studies Review*, no. 40, pp. 177–228.

Hayes, B. (2002) *The Activities and Development of Europol – Towards an Unaccountable 'FBI' in Europe* (London: Statewatch).

Hebenton, B. and Thomas, T. (1992) 'Rocky path to Europol', *Druglink* (November/December issue), pp. 8–10.

Hebenton, B. and Thomas, T. (1995) *Policing Europe. Co-operation, Conflict and Control* (Basingstoke: Macmillan – now Palgrave Macmillan).

Heidensohn, F. and Farrell, M. (eds) (1991) *Crime in Europe* (London: Routledge).

Held, D. (1989) *Political Theory and the Modern State. Essays on State, Power and Democracy* (Cambridge: Polity Press).

Held, D. (1995a) 'Democracy and the New International Order', in D. Archibugi and D. Held (eds) *Cosmopolitan Democracy* (Cambridge: Polity Press).

Held, D. (1995b) *Democracy and the Global Order* (Cambridge: Polity Press).

Held, D. and McGrew, A. (1993) 'Globalization and the Liberal Democratic State', *Government and Opposition*, vol. 28, no. 2, pp. 261–88.

Held, D. and McGrew, A. (eds) (2000) *The Global Transformations Reader* (Cambridge: Polity Press).

Hix, S. (1998) 'The Study of the European Union II: the "New Governance" Agenda and its Rival', *Journal of European Public Policy*, vol. 5, no. 1, pp. 38–65.

Hix, S. (1999) *The Political System of the European Union* (Basingstoke: Palgrave).

Holzner, B. and Marx, J. (1979) *Knowledge Application. The Knowledge System in Society* (Boston, MA: Allyn and Bacon).

Horstink-Von Meyenfeldt, L. (1996) 'The Netherlands: Tightening Up of the Cafés Policy', in N. Dorn, J. Jepsen and E. Savona (eds) *European Drug Policies and Enforcement* (Basingstoke: Macmillan – now Palgrave Macmillan).

Hunter, W. J. and Wasbauer, V. (1995) 'Drugs: A Public Health Priority', in G. Estievenart (ed.) *Policies and Strategies to Combat Drugs in Europe. The Treaty on European Union: Framework for a New European Strategy to Combat Drugs?* (Dordrecht: Martinus Nijhoff).

Hurrell, A. and Kingsbury, J. (eds) (1992) *The International Politics of The Environment: Actors, Interests, and Institutions* (Oxford: Clarendon Press).

Jacobson, H. K. (1984) *Networks of Interdependence. International Organizations and the Global Political System*, 2nd edn (New York: Alfred A. Knopf).

Jamieson, A. (1992) 'Drug Trafficking After 1992. A Special Report', *Conflict Studies*, no. 250.

Jasanoff, S. (1990) *The Fifth Branch. Science Advisers as Policymakers* (London: Harvard University Press).

Keat, R. and Urry, J. (1982) *Social Theory as Science*, 2nd edn (London: Routledge & Kegan Paul).

Kendall, R. (1994) 'Drugs are a threat to our democracies' (Raymond Kendall, Secretary-General of Interpol, interviewed by Michel Arnould), *Council of Europe Forum* (June 1994), pp. 22–3.

Kingdon, J. W. (1984) *Agendas, Alternatives and Public Policies* (New York: HarperCollins).

Kleiman, M. A. R. (1997) 'Drug-Free or Unfree: To Get Heavy Users to stay Clean, Link Parole and Probation to Abstinence', *The Washington Post* (2 February 1997).

Keohane, R. O. (1997) 'International Relations and International Law: Two Optics', *Harvard International Law Journal*, vol. 38, no. 2, pp. 487–502.

Keohane, R. O., Haas, P. M. and Levy, M. A. (1993) 'The Effectiveness of International Environmental Institutions', in P. M. Haas, R. O. Keohane and M. A. Levy (eds) *Institutions for the Earth: Sources of Effective International Environmental Protection* (London: The MIT Press).

Krasner, S. D. (1983) 'Structural Causes and Regime Consequences: Regimes as Intervening Variables', in S. Krasner (ed.) *International Regimes* (Ithaca: Cornell University Press).

Kratochwil, F. V. (1989) *Rules, Norms, and Decisions. On the Conditions of Practical and Legal Reasoning in International Relations and Domestic Affairs* (Cambridge: Cambridge University Press).

Kratochwil, F. V. and Mansfield, E. D. (eds) (1994) *International Organization. A Reader* (New York: HarperCollins).

Lacey, N. (1988) *State Punishment. Political Principles and Community Values* (London: Routledge).

Leroy, B. (1995) 'The United Nations Strategy', in G. Estievenart (ed.) *Policies and Strategies to Combat Drugs in Europe. The Treaty on European Union: Framework for a new European Strategy to Combat Drugs?* (Dordrecht: Martinus Nijhoff).

Levitsky, M. (1992) 'Progress in the International War Against Illicit Drugs', Statement before the Subcommittee on Terrorism, Narcotics, and International Operations of the Senate Foreign Relations Committee, Washington DC, February 20 1992, *U.S. Department of State Dispatch*, vol. 3, no. 9, pp. 156–62.

Lewis, F. (1991) 'The "G-7" Directorate', *Foreign Policy*, no. 85, pp. 25–40.

Liberty (The National Council for Civil Liberties) (1995) *Memorandum to the House of Lords Select Committee on the European Communities on the Draft Convention for Europol* (London: Liberty).

Liberty (The National Council for Civil Liberties) (1996) *Briefing on the Security Service Bill 1996* (London: Liberty).

Lindesmith, A. R. (1968) *Addiction and Opiates*, rev. 2nd edn (Chicago: Aldine).

Litfin, K. T. (1994) *Ozone Discourses: Science and Politics in Global Environmental Cooperation* (New York: Columbia University Press).

Litfin, K. T. (1997) 'Sovereignty in World Ecopolitics', *Mershon International Studies Review*, vol. 41, pp. 167–204.

Mabry, D. J. (ed.) (1989) *The Latin American Narcotics Trade and U.S. National Security* (New York: Greenwood Press).

Mathews, J. T. (1997) 'Power Shift', *Foreign Affairs*, vol. 76, no. 1, pp. 50–66.

Mathiesen, T. (1999) *On Globalisation of Control: Towards an Integrated Surveillance System in Europe* (London: Statewatch).

McGowan, F. (2001) 'Competition Policy. The Limits of the European Regulatory State', in J. Richardson (ed.) *European Union. Power and Policy-Making*, 2nd edn (London: Routledge).

McGrew, A. (1992) 'A Global Society?', in S. Hall, D. Held and A. McGrew (eds) *Modernity and its Futures* (Cambridge: Polity Press).

Monar, J. (1998) 'Justice and Home Affairs', *Journal of Common Market Studies*, vol. 36, pp. 131–42.

Mulkay, M. (1976) 'Norms and Ideology', in M. Mulkay *Sociology of Science. A Sociological Pilgrimage* (Milton Keynes: Open University Press, 1991).

Murphy, C. N. (1994) *International Organization and Industrial Change: Global Governance since 1850* (Cambridge: Polity Press).

Musto, D. F. (1987) *The American Disease: Origins of Narcotics Control* (Oxford: Oxford University Press).

Nadelmann, E. (1989) 'Drug Prohibition in the United States: Costs, Consequences, and Alternatives', *Science*, vol. 245, no. 1, pp. 939–47.

Nadelmann, E. (1990) 'Global Prohibition Regimes: the Evolution of Norms in International Society', *International Organization*, vol. 44, no. 4, pp. 479–526.

Nadelmann, E. (1993) *Cops Across Borders. The Internationalization of U.S. Criminal Law Enforcement* (University Park: Pennsylvania State University Press).

Nadelmann, E. (1998) 'Commonsense Drug Policy', *Foreign Affairs*, vol. 77, no. 1, pp. 111–26.

Nadelmann, E. and Wenner, J. (1994) 'Toward a Sane National Drug Policy', *Rolling Stone* (5 May, 1994), pp. 24–6.

Nelkin, D. (1979) 'Science, Technology, and Political Conflict: Analysing the Issues', in D. Nelkin (ed.) *Controversy: Politics of Technical Decisions* (London: Sage Publications).

Nugent, N. (1999) *The Government and Politics of the European Union*, 4th edn (Basingstoke: Palgrave).

Perl, R. F. (1994) 'International Drug Policy and the U.S. Congress', in R. Perl (ed.) *Drugs and Foreign Policy* (Boulder, Co: Westview Press).

Picciotto, S. (1996) 'Networks in International Economic Integration: Fragmented States and the Dilemmas of Neo-Liberalism', *Northwestern Journal of International Law & Business*, vol. 17, nos. 2/3, pp. 1014–56.

Radaelli, C. M. (1999) *Technocracy in the European Union* (London: Longman).

Reuter, P. (1994) 'The Limits and Consequences of U.S. Foreign Drug Control Efforts', in R. Perl (ed.) *Drugs and Foreign Policy* (Boulder: Westview Press).

Richardson, J. (2001) 'Policy-making in the EU: Interests, Ideas and Garbage Cans of Primeval Soup', in J. Richardson (ed.) *European Union. Power and Policy-Making*, 2nd edn (London: Routledge).

Rosenau, J. (1990) *Turbulence in World Politics. A Theory of Change and Continuity* (London: Harvester Wheatsheaf).

Ruggiero, V. and South, N. (1995) *Eurodrugs. Drug Use, Markets and Trafficking in Europe* (London: UCL Press).

Sabatier, P. A. (1998) 'The Advocacy Coalition Framework: Revisions and Relevance for Europe', *Journal of European Public Policy*, vol. 5, no. 1, pp. 98–130.

Savona, E. (1996) 'Money Laundering, the Developed Countries and Drug Control: the New Agenda', in N. Dorn, J. Jepsen and E. Savona (eds) *European Drug Policies and Enforcement* (Basingstoke: Macmillan – now Palgrave Macmillan).

Scott, P. D. and Marshall, J. (1991) *Cocaine Politics. Drugs, Armies, and the CIA in Central America* (Berkeley: University of California Press).

Slaughter, A.-M. (1997) 'The Real New World Order', *Foreign Affairs*, vol. 76, no. 5, pp. 183–97.

Smith, S. and Baylis, J. (eds) (1997) *The Globalization of World Politics. An Introduction to International Relations* (Oxford: Oxford University Press).

South, N. (1997) 'Drugs: Control, Crime and Criminological Studies', in M. Maguire, R. Morgan and R. Reiner (eds) *The Oxford Handbook of Criminology*, 2nd edn (Oxford: Oxford University Press).

South, N. (ed.) (1995a) *Drugs, Crime and Criminal Justice, Vol. 1: Histories and Use, Theories and Debates* (Aldershot: Dartmouth).

South, N. (ed.) (1995b) *Drugs, Crime and Criminal Justice, Vol. 2: Cultures and Markets, Crime and Criminal Justice* (Aldershot: Dartmouth).

Stares, P. (1996) *Global Habit. The Drug Problem in a Borderless World* (Washington DC: The Brookings Institution).

Statewatch. (1999) *European Monitor*, vol. 1, no. 2 (London: Statewatch).

Statewatch. (2000) *European Monitor*, vol. 2, no. 1 (London: Statewatch).

Statewatch. (2001) *European Monitor*, vol. 3, no. 1 (London: Statewatch).

Stevenson, R. (1994) *Winning the War on Drugs: To Legalise or Not?* Hobart Paper no. 124 (London: The Institute of Economic Affairs).

Stimson, G., Adelekan, M. and Rhodes, T. (1996) 'The Diffusion of Drug Injecting In Developing Countries', *The International Journal of Drug Policy*, vol. 7, no. 4, pp. 245–55.

Storbeck, J. (1994) 'Internal Security. A Single Market for the World's Gangsters', *European Brief*, vol. 2, pt 3, pp. 34–7.

Strange, S. (1995) 'The Defective State', *Daedalus* (Spring issue), pp. 55–74.

Taylor, I. (1997) 'The Political Economy of Crime', in M. Maguire, R. Morgan and R. Reiner (eds) *The Oxford Handbook of Criminology*, 2nd edn (Oxford: Oxford University Press).

Thomson, J. E. (1995) 'State Sovereignty in International Relations: Bridging the Gap Between Theory and Empirical Research', *International Studies Quarterly*, no. 39, pp. 213–33.

Thomson, J. E., and Krasner, S. D. (1989) 'Global Transactions and the Consolidation of Sovereignty', in E-O. Czempiel and J. Rosenau (eds) *Global Changes and Theoretical Challenges. Approaches to World Politics for the 1990s* (Lexington, MA: Lexington Books).

Tragen, I. (1994) 'World-Wide and Regional Anti-Drug Programs', in R. Perl (ed.) *Drugs and Foreign Policy* (Boulder: Westview Press).

Vaeren, C. van der (1995) 'The European Community's International Drug Control Cooperation Policy: A Personal View', in G. Estievenart (ed.) *Policies and Strategies to Combat Drugs in Europe. The Treaty on European Union: Framework for a new European Strategy to Combat Drugs?* (Dordrecht: Martinus Nijhoff).

Walker, N. (1994) 'European Integration and European Policing: A Complex Relationship', in M. Anderson and M. den Boer (eds) *Policing Across National Boundaries* (London: Pinter).

Walker, W. O. III. (1993) 'The Foreign Narcotics Policy of the United States since 1980: an End to the War on Drugs?', *International Journal*, vol. XLIX, no. 1, pp. 37–65.

Walker, W. O. III. (1994) 'U.S. Narcotics Foreign Policy in the Twentieth Century: An Analytical Overview', in R. Perl (ed.) *Drugs and Foreign Policy* (Boulder: Westview Press).

Walker, W. O. III. (ed.) (1996) *Drugs in the Western Hemisphere: An Odyssey of Cultures in Conflict* (Wilmington: Scholarly Resources Inc.).

Wallace, H. (1996) 'Politics and Policy in the EU: The Challenge of Governance', in H. Wallace and W. Wallace (eds) *Policy-Making in the European Union*, 3rd edn (Oxford: Oxford University Press).

Wallace, H. (2000a) 'The Institutional Setting. Five Variations on a Theme', in H. Wallace and W. Wallace (eds) *Policy-Making in the European Union*, 4th edn (Oxford: Oxford University Press).

Wallace, H. (2000b) 'The Policy Process. A Moving Pendulum', in H. Wallace and W. Wallace (eds) *Policy-Making in the European Union*, 4th edn (Oxford: Oxford University Press).

H. Wallace and W. Wallace (eds) (2000) *Policy-Making in the European Union*, 4th edn (Oxford: Oxford University Press).

Williams, P. (1994) 'Transnational Criminal Organisations and International Security', *Survival*, vol. 36, no. 1, pp. 96–113.

Woodward, R. (1993) 'Establishing Europol', *European Journal on Criminal Policy and Research*, vol. 1, pt 4, pp. 7–33.

Zagaris, B. (1992) 'Western Europe and the European Community', in S. Macdonald and B. Zagaris *International Handbook on Drug Control* (Westport: Greenwood Press).

Index